Research Series on the Chinese Dream and China's Development Path

Drawing on a large body of empirical studies done over the last two decades, this Series provides its readers with in-depth analyses of the past and present and forecasts for the future course of China's development. It contains the latest research results made by members of the Chinese Academy of Social Sciences. This series is an invaluable companion to every researcher who is trying to gain a deeper understanding of the development model, path and experience unique to China. Thanks to the adoption of Socialism with Chinese characteristics, and the implementation of comprehensive reform and opening-up, China has made tremendous achievements in areas such as political reform, economic development, and social construction, and is making great strides towards the realization of the Chinese dream of national rejuvenation. In addition to presenting a detailed account of many of these achievements, the authors also discuss what lessons other countries can learn from China's experience.

Xianxiang Xu · Qingmiao Bi · Li Zhang
Editors

Report on the Chinese Business Environment Survey 2020

SSAP

Springer

Editors
Xianxiang Xu
Lingnan College
Sun Yat-sen University
Guangzhou, China

Institute of Mezzoeconomics
Sun Yat-sen University
Guangzhou, China

Qingmiao Bi
Lingnan College
Sun Yat-sen University
Guangzhou, China

Institute of Mezzoeconomics
Sun Yat-sen University
Guangzhou, China

Li Zhang
International School of Business & Finance
Sun Yat-sen University
Guangzhou, China

Institute of Mezzoeconomics
Sun Yat-sen University
Guangzhou, China

ISSN 2363-6866 ISSN 2363-6874 (electronic)
Research Series on the Chinese Dream and China's Development Path
ISBN 978-981-99-6111-5 ISBN 978-981-99-6112-2 (eBook)
https://doi.org/10.1007/978-981-99-6112-2

Jointly published with Social Sciences Academic Press
The print edition is not for sale in China Mainland. Customers from China Mainland please order the print book from: Social Sciences Academic Press.

Translation from the Chinese Simplified language edition: "中国营商环境企业调查报告2020" by Xianxiang Xu et al., © Social Science Academic Press 2020. Published by Social Science Academic Press. All Rights Reserved.

This Springer imprint is published by the registered company Springer Nature Singapore Pte Ltd.
The registered company address is: 152 Beach Road, #21-01/04 Gateway East, Singapore 189721, Singapore

Series Preface

Since China's reform and opening began in 1978, the country has come a long way on the path of Socialism with Chinese characteristics, under the leadership of the Communist Party of China. Over 30 years of reform, efforts and sustained spectacular economic growth have turned China into the world's second-largest economy and wrought many profound changes in the Chinese society. These historically significant developments have been garnering increasing attention from scholars, governments, and the general public alike around the world since the 1990s, when the newest wave of China studies began to gather steam. Some of the hottest topics have included the so-called China miracle, Chinese phenomenon, Chinese experience, Chinese path, and the Chinese model. Homegrown researchers have soon followed suit. Already hugely productive, this vibrant field is putting out a large number of books each year, with Social Sciences Academic Press alone having published hundreds of titles on a wide range of subjects.

Because most of these books have been written and published in Chinese, however, readership has been limited outside China—even among many who study China—for whom English is still the lingua franca. This language barrier has been an impediment to efforts by academia, business communities, and policy-makers in other countries to form a thorough understanding of contemporary China, of what is distinct about China's past and present may mean not only for her future but also for the future of the world. The need to remove such an impediment is both real and urgent, and the *Research Series on the Chinese Dream and China's Development Path* is my answer to the call.

This series features some of the most notable achievements from the last 20 years by scholars in China in a variety of research topics related to reform and opening. They include both theoretical explorations and empirical studies and cover economy, society, politics, law, culture, and ecology, the six areas in which reform and opening policies have had the deepest impact and farthest reaching consequences for the country. The authors for the series have also tried to articulate their visions of the "Chinese Dream" and how the country can realize it in these fields and beyond.

All of the editors and authors for the *Research Series on the Chinese Dream and China's Development Path* are both longtime students of reform and opening v vi Series Preface and recognized authorities in their respective academic fields. Their credentials and expertise lend credibility to these books, each of which has been subject to a rigorous peer-review process for inclusion in the series. As part of the Reform and Development Program under the State Administration of Press, Publication, Radio, Film, and Television of the People's Republic of China, the series is published by Springer, a Germany-based academic publisher of international repute, and distributed overseas. I am confident that it will help fill a lacuna in studies of China in the era of reform and opening.

Shanghai, China Shouguang Xie

Introduction to the Report on the China Doing Business Enterprise Survey (2020)

The construction of China's business environment supports the country's overall high-quality development. The CPC Central Committee and State Council attach great importance to China's business environment construction, and in October 2019, they issued the *Regulations on Optimizing the Business Environment*. The *Regulations* provided, for the first time in the form of government legislation, institutional guarantees for various types of market players to invest and develop business. The *Regulations* also emphasized that, by transforming government functions, market vitality and social creativity will in turn be stimulated, thereby enhancing the impetus for economic development. Now that China has entered the era of shifting from rapid development to high-quality development, the construction of the business environment is one of the country's most important tasks and must thus be continuously deepened and built.

The China Doing Business Enterprise Survey was funded by the National Social Science Foundation's special project "Research on Deepening the Business Environment Construction" (18VSJ069) and National Social Science Foundation's major project "Research on Optimizing China's Business Environment Driven by Modern Information Technology" (20&ZD071). Two nationwide field surveys were performed (in 2018 and 2019, respectively), to track and examine the new accomplishments and problems in China's business environment construction. The first round of surveys was held in July and August 2018. Field surveys were conducted, through stratified random sampling, in 84 cities in 16 provinces across the country. The survey results were then compiled into the China Doing Business Report (2019) and China Government Service Environment Report (2019), which were published by Social Sciences Academic Press (China). The survey results received attention from government officials, relevant ministries and agencies, and people from across the country. In addition, newspapers and other media outlets, including the *People's Daily*, Xinhua News Agency, People.cn, and ThePaper.cn, reported on the study results. The second round of surveys was conducted from July to August 2019. Then, based on the first-hand materials collected during the two years of the field study, the China Doing Business Enterprise Survey Report (2020) was compiled.

The China Doing Business Enterprise Survey Report (2020) evaluates the progress, results, and problems in the construction of the national business environment based on responses from market players, detailed as follows:

First, the Report examines the new accomplishments and problems in China's business environment construction. It does this based on a comparative analysis of the two years of data, from the four aspects of market entry, market regulation, Internet+government services, and service efficiency.

Second, the Report assesses the level of construction of government service hall environments in various regions of China, from the three aspects of hardware, software, and services.

Third, the Report examines in detail the progress in the construction of China's "digital government." Focusing on government services channels such as online service halls and mobile service platforms, and based on the responses from market players, an indicator system is then created, which includes the three dimensions of potential usage rate, actual awareness rate, and actual usage rate of the digital government. This indicator system is then used to analyze the progress and problems of the nationwide digital government construction.

Fourth, the Report examines the macro-performance achieved in the business environment construction from the five aspects of entrepreneurship, innovation, employment, economic growth, and economic structure. Finally, the progress of the business environment construction in regard to serving China's high-quality development is summarized.

The China Doing Business Enterprise Survey Report (2020) consists of three parts. Part I is *Nationwide Progress*. This includes four chapters, respectively covering the performance of the business environment construction, government service environment construction, digital government construction, and business environment construction. Part II details the progress of several select provinces. It includes survey reports on the business environments of Zhejiang, Jilin, Gansu, and Guangdong Provinces, which are respectively located in the four regions of eastern, northeastern, northwestern, and southern China. Part III of the report, *Methods and Data*, details the theoretical framework, field survey, and related data.

Contents

Part I
Nationwide Progress

Chapter 1
Construction of the Business Environment

Qingmiao Bi, Yihao Huang, Yun Zhou, and Xianxiang Xu

1.1 Report Overview

The CPC Central Committee and State Council attach great importance to the construction of China's business environment. Since the business system reform in 2014, there have been new goals, initiatives and achievements every year. According to the 2019 Government Work Report, the focuses of that year were as follows: to facilitate investment and development with a simplified approval process and outstanding services; promote fair competition through impartial regulation; promote the reduction of enterprise-related fees through reform; stimulate the vitality of market players; optimize the business environment; and promote high-quality development.

The present report evaluates the business system reform and the construction of the business environment across China, based on responses from market players in various regions. Based on the national field research conducted in 2018, the "Research on Deepening the Business System Reform" research group conducted the second nationwide field study from July 15 to August 10, 2019. Through hierarchical random sampling, the research group visited 281 government service halls in 110 cities across 24 provinces, where they randomly interviewed the business market players regarding market access, credit regulation, "Internet + government services," service efficiency, and so on. The success rate of this survey interview was about 75%, with a total of 8293 valid questionnaires collected. After the survey, the research group

Q. Bi · Y. Huang · X. Xu (✉)
Lingnan College, Sun Yat-sen University, Guangzhou, China
e-mail: lnsxuxx@mail.sysu.edu.cn

Q. Bi · X. Xu
Institute of Mezzoeconomics, Sun Yat-sen University, Guangzhou, China

Y. Zhou
School of Business, Sun Yat-sen University, Guangzhou, China

X. Xu et al. (eds.), *Report on the Chinese Business Environment Survey 2020*, Research Series on the Chinese Dream and China's Development Path,
https://doi.org/10.1007/978-981-99-6112-2_1

compiled first-hand data and public opinion feedback, then systematically analyzed the new achievements, new problems and new directions in the construction of the nationwide business environment as of August 2019 (see Table 1.1).

The report shows that, from the market players' perspective, **the main accomplishments** of the 2019 national business system reform were in the four areas of **reduced number of permits, single-network processing, increased efficiency and improved quality.**

(1) **The number of permits and amount of time required were decreased.** One of the main work tasks of 2019 was reducing the number of permits that businesspeople required to register a company. The responses from market players reveal that the average number of permits they needed dropped from two in 2018 to 1.8 in 2019, with one province requiring only a single permit. In addition, the time required to process all types of permits decreased year-on-year, with the greatest declines in permits involving taxes, opening bank accounts, and environmental protection.
(2) **The "single-network access" rate reached about 40%**. In 2019, China focused on building a nationwide integrated online government service platform to accelerate the realization of single-network access. The market player responses reveal that the single-network access rate has reached 40%.
(3) **The "completion in one visit" rate increased to 42%**. According to the 2019 government work report, when people needed to complete business-related tasks in person, they would only have to make a single trip. The market player responses show that the rate of completing all tasks in one visit increased from 31% in 2018 to 42% in 2019. In addition, about 33% of market players completed each task within 30 min, and 75% within 1 h. As a result, market players' sense of fulfillment has significantly improved.
(4) **High-quality development was strongly supported**. First, promotion of entrepreneurship: the total number of market players doubled. Second, employment guarantee: 34% of market players created new jobs. Third, steady growth: 49% of market players performed better. Fourth, structure adjustment: 70% of market players are in the service industry. Fifth, promotion of innovation: 44% of market players have innovated.

From the perspective of market players, the following major **issues** are present in the 2019 Business System reform:

(1) **Imbalanced progress among regions**. According to the indicator system, using the distance to frontier (DTF) method to calculate the score, the respective proportions of cities with excellent, good, moderate, pass and fail were 1%, 4%, 24%, 63%, and 8%. This shows that progress was imbalanced from region to region. In terms of market access, market regulation, "Internet + government services," and service-oriented government construction, all regions, including the best and worst, made significant progress.
(2) **Inadequate credit regulations**. The business system reform emphasizes the construction of a new market regulation mechanism with credit regulation as

Table 1.1 Business environment indicator system and latest achievements in 2019

Level 1 indicators	Level 2 indicators	Level 3 indicators	2018	2019	2019 maximum	2019 minimum
Main progress	Market entry	Number of days needed to register a company	7.0	6.9	9.3	3.0
		Number of service windows visited	1.9	1.8	3.1	1.4
		Number of permits processed	2.0	1.8	2.7	1.0
	Credit regulation	National enterprise credit information publicity system usage rate (%)	65	66	79	47
	Internet + commerce	Online service hall awareness rate (%)	59	66	84	47
		Online service hall usage rate (%)	43	48	73	27
	Service efficiency	Number of trips taken to complete a task in the past 6 months	2.3	1.9	2.7	1.6
		Number of service windows visited to complete a task in the past 6 months	1.9	1.4	2.2	1.2
Performance	Employment	Ratio of market players who upsized in the past 6 months (%)	–	34	45	22
	Growth	Ratio of market players with increased performance in the past 6 months (%)	–	49	58	34
	Innovation	Ratio of market players who innovated in the past 6 months (%)	–	44	56	32
	Structure	Proportion of market players in the service sector who registered after the business reform (%)	–	70	97	50

Note The 2019 maximum and 2019 minimum are the maximum and minimum values at the provincial level

Source Research Group on "Deepening the Business System Reform"

the core. Judging from the market players' responses, 81% of them underwent on-site inspections in 2019, among which 35% said they thought that the number of inspections had increased compared to 2018, and 24% thought that the number of on-site inspections from government departments had increased compared to 2018.

(3) **"Growing pains" for small and micro enterprises**. In 2019, the three challenges most frequently mentioned by market players nationwide were fierce market competition, recruitment difficulties and high costs, which were respectively mentioned by 27%, 17% and 14% of respondents. All of these had increased by 1–2% points from 2018, making them the most common challenges and pain points for market players at this time. For small and micro enterprises, these three challenges were mentioned even more frequently. Under such pressure, small and micro enterprises face difficulties in growth because they create fewer jobs, and have low rates of performance improvement and innovation.

From the perspective of market players, there are the following feasible directions for further deepening the reform of the Business System. First, promote the standardization of government services and narrow the gap between regions. Second, continue to promote the implementation of credit regulation policies, and build a competitive-neutral business environment. Third, through the combination of "enhancing government services" and "opening the market field," continue to help market players develop.

1.2 Main Progress (2018–2019)

Based on the work in 2018, the 2019 government work report proposed new goals for the business system reform and business environment construction, including specific requirements such as separating permits and licenses, single-network access, single-window processing, commitment to completion time, and completion of all tasks in one visit. Judging from the 2019 research results, remarkable progress was made in the construction of China's business environment in the four areas of permit reduction, single-network access, increased speed and improved quality.

(1) **Permit reduction: 10% reduction in the number of permits and 22% reduction in the time required**

The 2019 government work report clearly proposed that the reform of separating permits and licenses was to be implemented in all business licensing matters involving enterprises. In addition, the "permit reduction for the benefit of the people" reform action was to be continuously carried out, so that enterprises and businesspeople would not need to waste time making numerous trips to acquire business permits. Judging from the research results, in 2019, market players applied for an average of 1.8 permits, and the longest time it took to do so was 21.7 days, respectively down 10 and 22% from 2018. This shows that remarkable results were achieved in the permit reduction work.

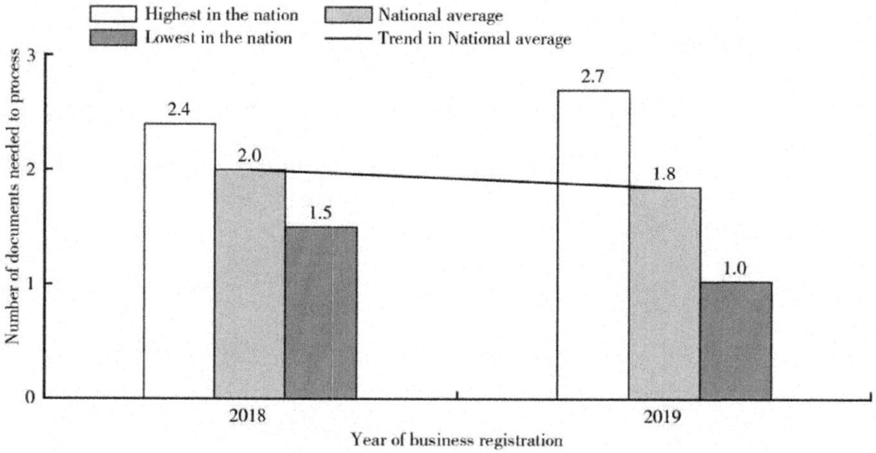

Fig. 1.1 The number of documents required to process decreased from 2.0 in 2018 to 1.8 in 2019. *Source* Sun Yat-sen University Research Group on "Deepening the Reform of the Business System"

1. **Decrease in number of permits obtained from 2 to 1.8**

As shown in the 2018 survey results in Fig. 1.1, market players who registered companies that year needed to apply for an average of two permits, while in 2019 the number dropped to 1.8. From a provincial perspective, the province with the fewest number of permits needed was reduced from an average of 1.5 required in 2018 to one in 2019, thus achieving the goal of single-permit processing. However, the province needing the most permits required 2.4 in 2018 and 2.7 in 2019, for an increase rather than a decrease.

2. **Maximum permit processing time shortened from 27.9 to 21.7 days**

As shown in Fig. 1.2, the time required to process the most time-consuming permit also underwent a clear downward trend, from 27.9 days in 2018 to 21.7 days in 2019. Looking at the situation in each province, in 2018 and 2019, the time it took the fastest province to apply for the most time-consuming permit was 11.5–12.7 days; the slowest province took 60.9 days in 2018, but only 35.3 days in 2019, a reduction of 42%, exhibiting remarkable results.

3. **Permits with greatest reduction in time: taxation, opening bank accounts, environmental protection**

Each type of permits takes a different amount of time to process. As shown in Fig. 1.3, judging from the responses from market players who registered in 2019, the most time-consuming documents were those involving safety, environmental protection, fire protection, venues, food, sanitation, opening bank accounts, taxation, and foreign trade, with the time required ranging from 6 to 55 days.

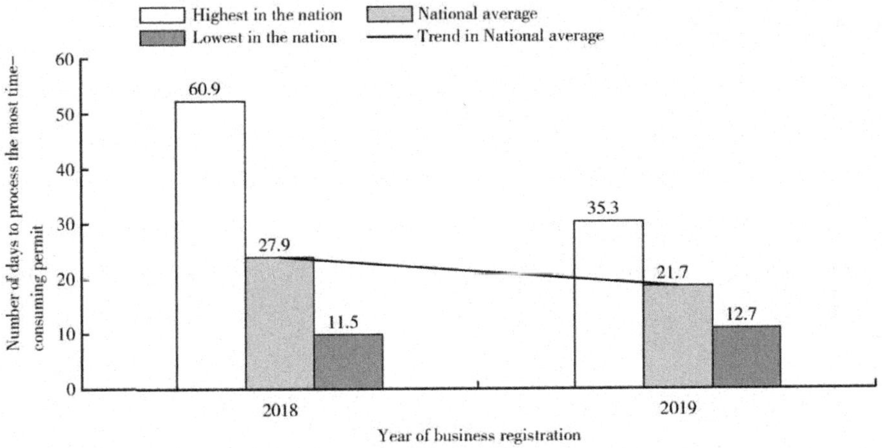

Fig. 1.2 The time required to process the most time-consuming permit was reduced from 27.9 days in 2018 to 21.7 days in 2019. *Source* Research Group on "Deepening the Reform of the Business System"

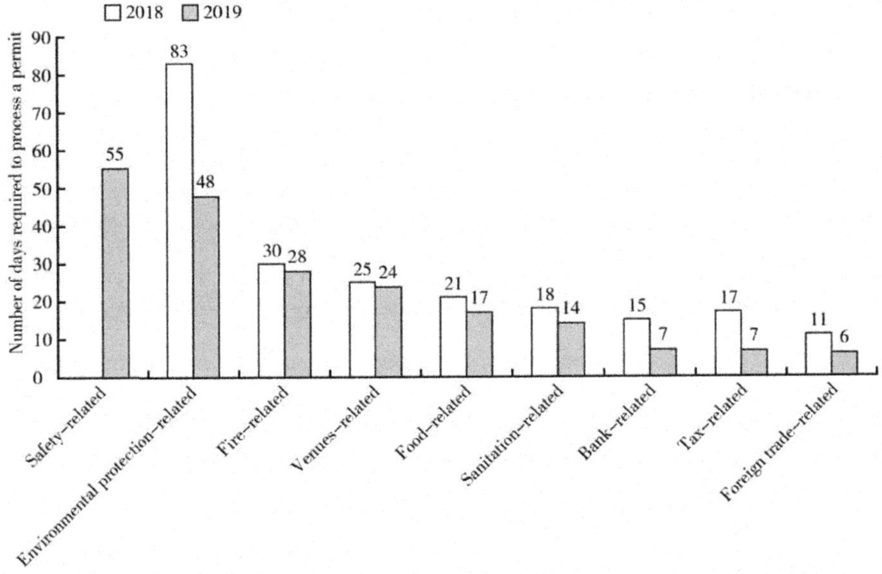

Fig. 1.3 The processing time for all types of permits was reduced. *Notes* No permits related to safety were covered in the 2018 survey. Only market players registered in 2018 and 2019 are included in the calculation. *Source* Sun Yat-sen University Research Group on "Deepening the Reform of the Business System"

Compared with 2018, the processing time for all types of permits was reduced. Among them, tax-related permits underwent the greatest reduction in time consumption, from 17 days in 2018 to 7 days in 2019, a decrease of nearly 59%; this was followed by permits for opening bank accounts, which went from 15 days in 2018 to 7 days in 2019, a decrease of about 53%; finally, permits involving environmental protection dropped from 83 to 48 days, a decrease of about 42%.

4. **Twenty-five percent of market players acknowledged the 2019 permit reduction**

The goal of permit reduction is to make things more convenient for people. Therefore, market players' sense of fulfillment regarding permit reduction is an important indicator for evaluating this work. As shown in Fig. 1.4, in 2019, 25% of market players nationwide said they thought that the number of permits they needed to process had been reduced from 2018, while 53% thought the number had remained unchanged, and 22% thought the number had increased. This shows that, from the perspective of the market players, in 2019 the business environment construction had reduced the number of permits they needed to process, and simplified the procedures.

During the field survey, the research group found observed that the permit reduction work, represented by the "three permits in one," is the business environment construction reform measure that the market players are most familiar with. In the market player interviews, upon mentioning specific reform measures such as the "three permits in one" and "five permits in one," the market players immediately recognized the reference, and made comments such as "It's definitely much more convenient now to obtain permits after implementing the 'three permits in one.'".

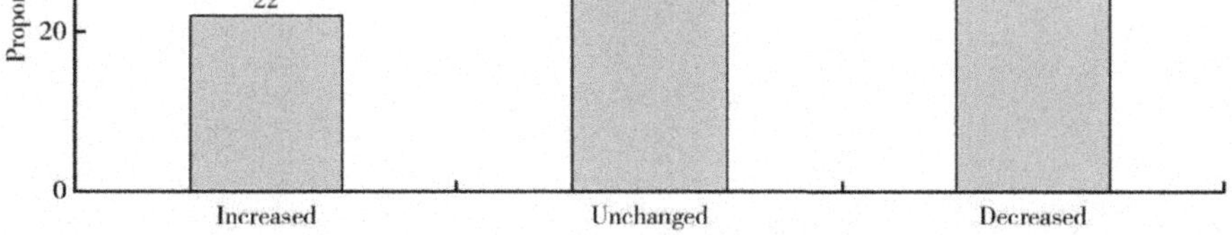

Fig. 1.4 In 2019, about 25% of market players nationwide thought that the number of permits they needed to apply for had decreased. *Source* Sun Yat-sen University Research Group on "Deepening the Reform of the Business System"

(2) **Single-network access reached 40%, and the nationwide government service platform appeal rate reached 57% a month after launch**

The 2019 Government Work Report stated that online approval and services were to be implemented in the Internet + government services work, and that a nationally integrated online administrative service platform was to be built as soon as possible. In addition, single-network access and remote completion were to be achieved, so that more matters could be handled without the need to be physically present. Judging from the research results, the awareness rate and usage rate of the online service halls have all further increased over 2018. About 40% of the market players have achieved single-network access, and the usage rate of the nationwide government service platform has reached 16% 1 month after its launch.

1. **Online service hall awareness rate 66%, usage rate 48%**

In this study, the awareness rate is defined as the proportion of market players who know about the online service halls. As shown in Fig. 1.5, in 2019 the online office hall awareness rate was 66%, 7% points higher than in 2018. Thus the vast majority of market players knew about the online service hall platform.

In this study, the usage rate is defined as the proportion of market players who use the online service halls. In 2019, the online service hall usage rate was 48%, a significant increase compared to 2018's 43%, with nearly half of the market players using the online service halls.

2. **Single-network access reached about 40%**

Single-network access was one of 2019's key tasks. As shown in Fig. 1.6, looking at computer-based online service halls, in 2019, 31% of market players said they often

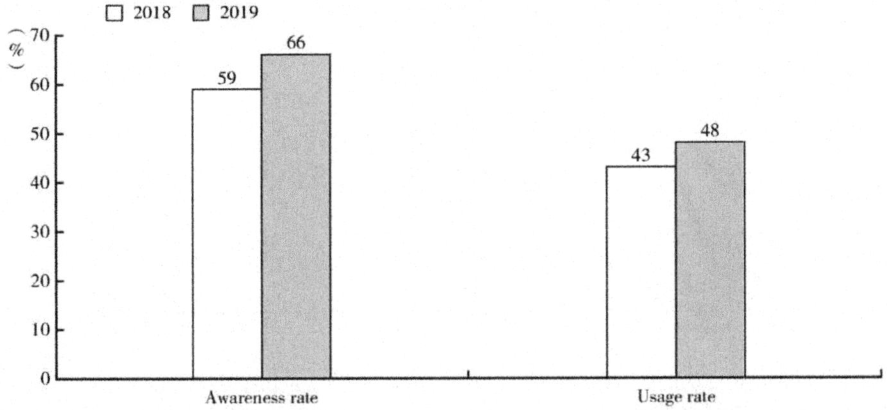

Fig. 1.5 The awareness and usage rates of online office halls both increased in 2019. *Source* Sun Yat-sen University Research Group on "Deepening the Reform of the Business System"

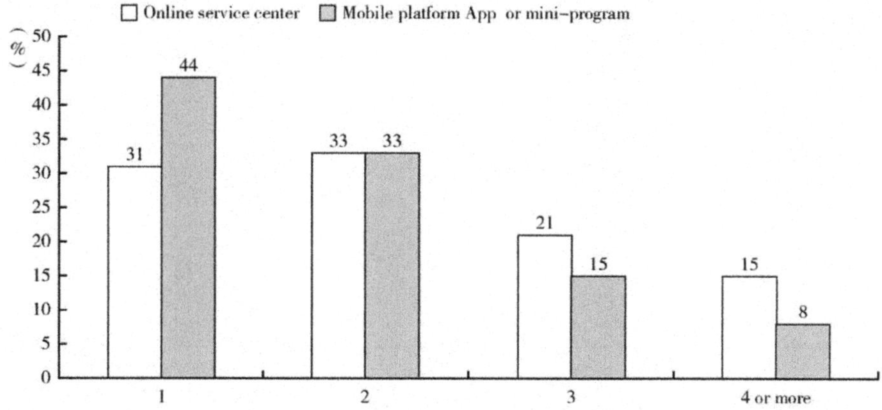

Fig. 1.6 Numbers of online service platforms used in 2019. *Source* Sun Yat-sen University Research Group on "Deepening the Reform of the Business System"

used such a platform. Mobile phone apps or mini-programs are a new type of office platform promoted in recent years, and in 2019 about 44% of market players said they often used one of these mobile service platforms. It can thus be seen from this that the single-network access rate has reached about 40%.

3. **The nationwide administrative service platform's appeal rate reached 57% in 1 month**

To accelerate the nationwide realization of single-network access with remote operation for government services, in June 2019 the General Office of the State Council launched a trial operation of the first nationally integrated government service platform, namely the nationwide administrative service platform.

Judging from the responses of market players, as shown in Fig. 1.7, after 1 month of development (the survey was performed in July to August 2019), the awareness rate of the nationwide administrative service platform reached 28%, and the usage rate reached 16%. This report defines the appeal rate as the proportion of market players who knew about the nationwide administrative service platform and who used it. In other words, it is the ratio of the nationwide administrative service platform's usage rate to its awareness rate. According to this metric, the appeal rate of the nationwide administrative service platform was 57% (16–28%); that is, among the market players who were aware of the nationwide government service platform, 57% chose to use it.

(3) **Efficiency increase: 42% of market players completed all tasks in one visit, and 75% within an hour**

Toward the end of Premier Li Keqiang's 2018 press conference, he proposed six reform goals with the word "one" in the name. One of these goals is to allow market players to complete business-related tasks at government halls in only one

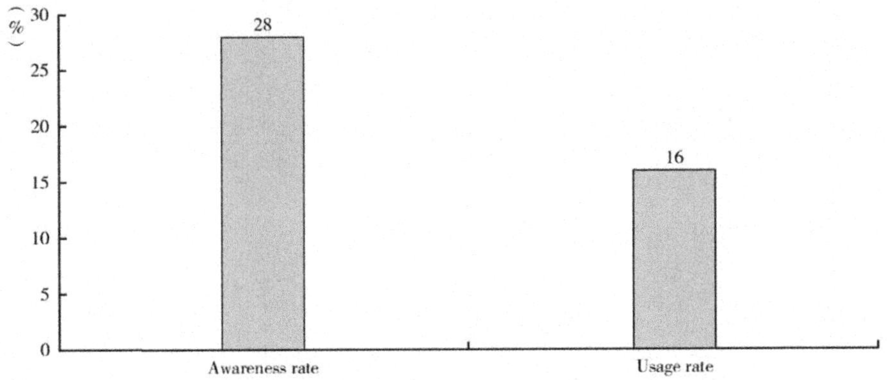

Fig. 1.7 One month after the launch of the nationwide administrative service platform, its awareness rate was 28% and usage rate was 16%. *Source* Sun Yat-sen University Research Group on "Deepening the Reform of the Business System"

trip. The 2019 work report states that tasks that must be completed in person are to be completed at one window and within a certain time, thereby achieving completion of all tasks in one visit. From the implementation situation in 2019, it can be seen that work efficiency has improved significantly.

1. **Forty-two percent of market players completed all tasks in one visit**

As shown in Fig. 1.8, in the 2018 survey, 31% of market players nationwide completed all their tasks in one visit; by 2019, this proportion rose to 42%, an increase of 11% points. The province with the highest completion in one visit rate increased from 56% in 2018 to 61% in 2019; and that with the lowest rate increased from 9% in 2018 to 20% in 2019—more than double the rate of the previous year. This shows that over the past year, the completion in one visit reform has achieved remarkable results nationwide, and the effectiveness of local governments has improved markedly.

As can be seen from the survey results, functional departments in all regions are making great efforts to optimize window services, and striving to achieve the reform goal of completing all tasks in one visit. In Lishui, Zhejiang, the government service center there actively implemented the completion in one visit policy. Many market players specifically stated that the work environment had been greatly improved, making comments such as "You only need one or two trips to the service hall to get things done," revealing that they had truly experienced the service hall's improvement in efficiency. In Hangzhou, Zhejiang, our research team observed that even after work hours had ended, the staff would stay to process all the tasks that visitors were waiting to complete, so that they would not have to return later. This action was well received by the market players there. In Chongzuo, Guangxi, more than 50 departments have been stationed in the government service hall to achieve "one-stop" service. One market player who was visiting to complete tasks said, "From arriving here today to getting my business license, along with all the other processes, I got everything done in a single afternoon. Compared with before, the government's work efficiency

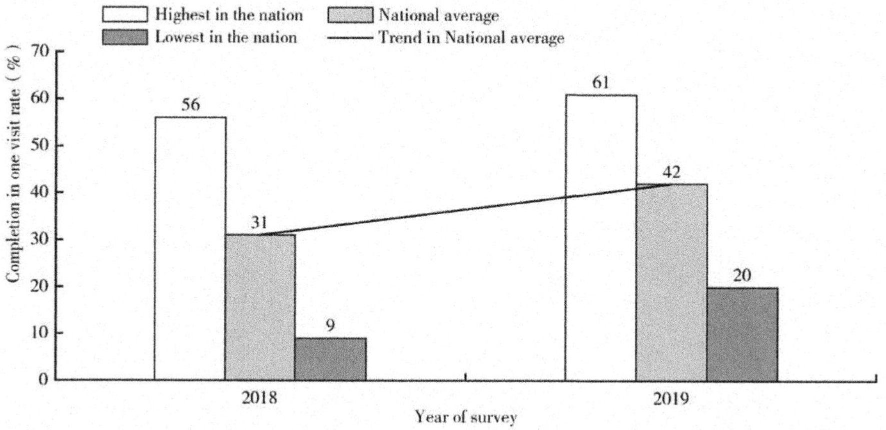

Fig. 1.8 In 2019, 42% of market players completed all their tasks in one visit. *Source* Sun Yat-sen University Research Group on "Deepening the Reform of the Business System."

has really improved, and I'm comfortable handling things myself." In Chaoyang District, Beijing, most market players also reported that they only needed a single visit to complete all their tasks.

2. **Sixty-seven percent of market players completed all tasks at one window**

Single-window processing and consolidated services are specific measures in promoting the goal of completing all tasks in one visit. As shown in Fig. 1.9, in 2018 the nationwide rate of single-window processing was 71%, and in 2019 it was 67%, exhibiting no significant change. This shows that the vast majority of market players in China completed all the tasks they needed at a single window.

One possible reason for 2019's slight decrease in the single-window processing rate from 2018 was the establishment of the new inquiry windows in some regions. In the field survey it was found that, to promote the construction of a service-oriented government, functional departments in various regions needed to focus more on inquiry and instructions, both in advance and during service. In addition to the unified guidance desks in the service halls, special inquiry windows have also been added. For example, in Zhoushan, Zhejiang, our research team discovered that market players who were unfamiliar with the services continued to inquire at the inquiry window, then visited another window to complete their tasks. In Taiyuan, Shanxi, while talking about how convenient it is to get things done now, an interviewee said: "Aside from checking on the computer, there's also a special inquiry window I can go to." This suggests that, when we asked market players how many windows they needed to visit, they may have also included the inquiry window, thereby increasing the number of windows reported in their answers, resulting in a slight decrease in the proportion of single-window processing compared to 2018.

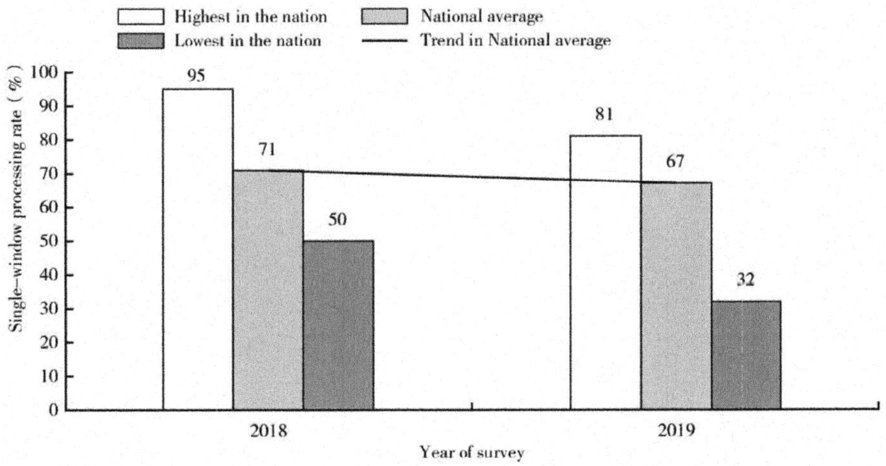

Fig. 1.9 In 2019, 67% of market players completed all tasks at a single window. *Source* Sun Yat-sen University Research Group on "Deepening the Reform of the Business System"

3. **Thirty-three percent of market players completed all their tasks within 30 min**

As shown in Fig. 1.10, in 2018, for market players who visited the government service hall for only one task, 17% of market players completed their tasks within 30 min, and 55% did so in 30–60 min. In the first half of 2019, 33% of people who visited an government service hall to complete a task did so within 30 min, and 42% finished in 30–60 min. Taken together, from 2018 to 2019, the 60-min completion rate increased slightly, from 72 to 75%, while the 30-min completion rate increased from 17 to 33%, nearly doubling.

During the survey, we received positive responses from many market players regarding how the work efficiency had improved. Two market players in Zhanhua District, Binzhou, Shandong said, "Compared to last year, the work efficiency here has really improved. We can get something done in about half an hour, and we almost never have to wait for long." A market player in Haishu District, Ningbo, Zhejiang said, "In recent years, getting things done has gotten a lot faster, and the service attitude is also really good." A market player in Hecheng District, Huaihua, Hunan also said, "Getting things done is really fast now, and very convenient."

4. **Market players' sense of fulfillment has greatly improved**

The reform has saved time: 87% of market players said they think that the time they need to spend has been reduced. As shown in Fig. 1.11, in 2019, 87% of China's market players said they believed that the business environment construction had reduced the time required during visits to the government hall. In the highest-ranking province, 94% of market players thought this way, and even in the lowest-ranking

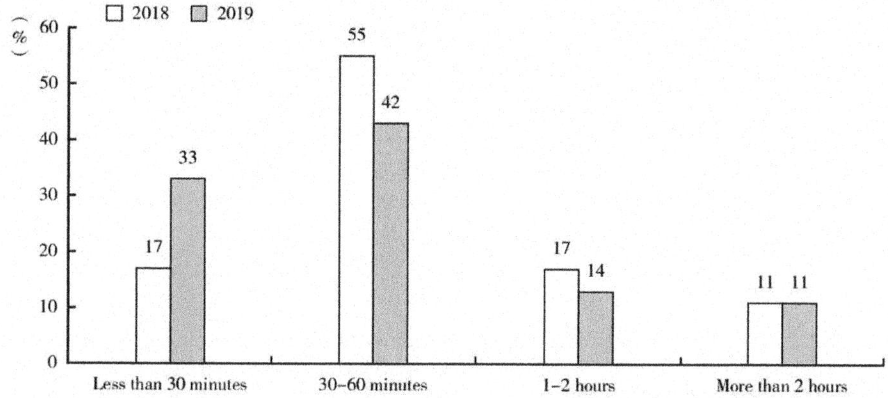

Fig. 1.10 The 30-min completion rate increased from 17% in 2018 to 33% in 2019. *Source* Sun Yat-sen University Research Group on "Deepening the Reform of the Business System"

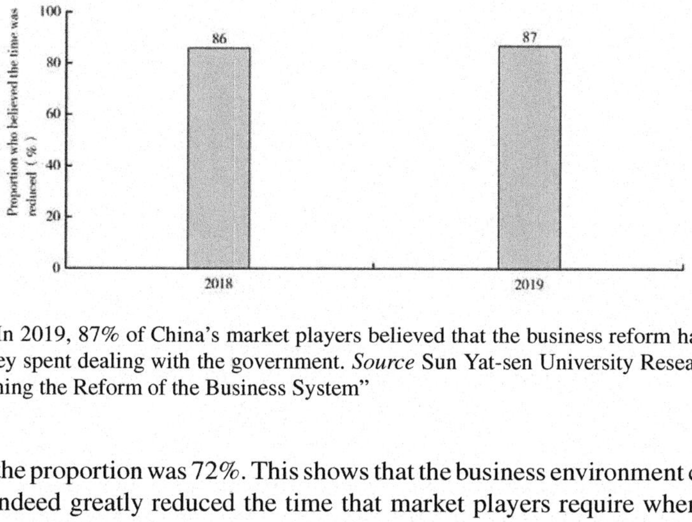

Fig. 1.11 In 2019, 87% of China's market players believed that the business reform had reduced the time they spent dealing with the government. *Source* Sun Yat-sen University Research Group on "Deepening the Reform of the Business System"

province the proportion was 72%. This shows that the business environment construction has indeed greatly reduced the time that market players require when dealing with the government.

The reform also saves costs, with 72% of market players believing that their costs had been reduced, 8% points higher than in 2018. As shown in Fig. 1.12, in 2019 72% of market players nationwide said they thought that the commercial reform had reduced the fees involved in dealing with the government, up from 64% in 2018. In the highest-ranking province, the percentage was 82%, and in the lowest-ranking province it was 61%. Despite certain differences, the business environment construction has greatly reduced the fees for market players when dealing with the government.

The reform has helped business operations, with 66% of market players saying they thought it has had a positive impact on their business, 6% points higher than in 2018. As shown in Fig. 1.13, in 2018, 60% of China's market players believed that the

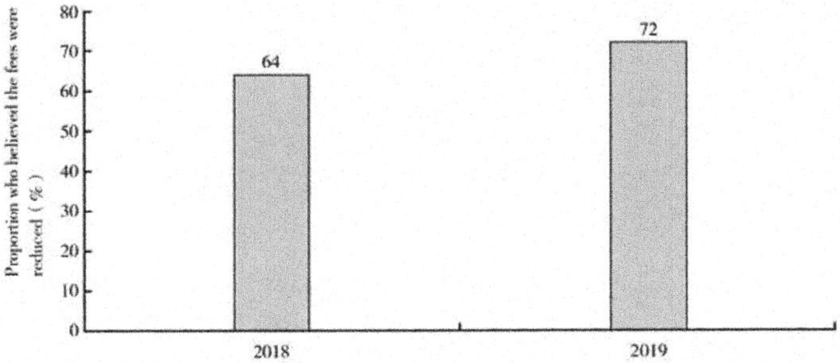

Fig. 1.12 In 2019, 72% of China's market players believed that the business reform had reduced the fees for dealing with the government. *Source* Sun Yat-sen University Research Group on "Deepening the Reform of the Business System"

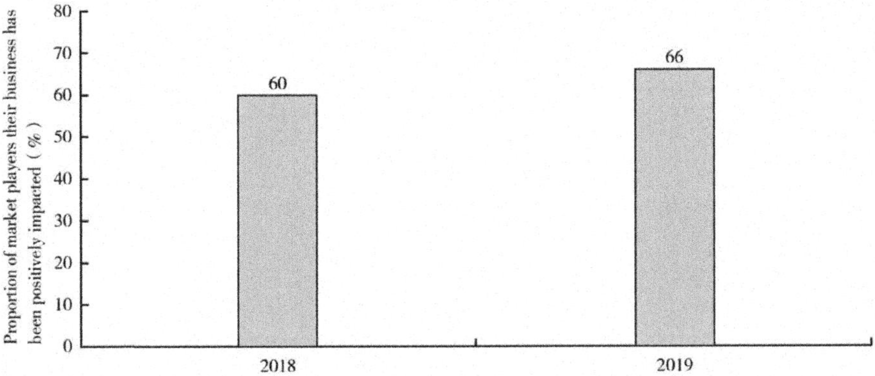

Fig. 1.13 In 2019, 66% of China's market players said they thought that the business reform had a positive impact on them. *Source* Sun Yat-sen University Research Group on "Deepening the Reform of the Business System"

business environment construction had a positive impact on their business, and this percentage increased to 66% in 2019. This shows that increasing numbers of market players have experienced the benefits that the business environment construction has led to, and their sense of fulfillment is constantly increasing.

Based on the survey results, the service efficiency of government personnel is increasing. Consequently, the market players' sense of fulfillment is also on the rise. For example, in Zhongyuan and Huiji Districts of Zhengzhou, Henan, there are special volunteers next to the computers in the self-serve area. When market players need to use these computers to complete tasks, the volunteers greet them warmly, and take the initiative to answer their questions. Some market players have no prior experience with the online government system, in which case the volunteers also guide them step by step. A woman working in Zhongyuan District of Zhengzhou praised the volunteers there, saying, "The volunteers here are great. Just a few days ago, I applied for a permit here, and had to use a computer. There was a young, enthusiastic man, who kept calling me 'Auntie.' He could tell I wasn't very good with computers, and came over and helped me with everything. It didn't take long at all." In Bijie, Guizhou, a supervisor mentioned several times during our conversation that the market players must not be disturbed while carrying tasks. If they were, and other market players waiting missed their queue number, then they would not be pleased to have to take a new one. This gave us a deep understanding of the attitude of service hall staff who care deeply about the market players, and who put their sense of fulfillment above all else.

(4) **Improved quality: quantitative and qualitative support for the high-quality development of enterprises**

The 2019 government work report points out that there are hundreds of millions of market players in China, and the number continues to increase. Therefore, maintaining and increasing the activity of market players is the key to promoting steady economic growth. From the survey results, the business system reform and business environment construction have achieved remarkable results in promoting entrepreneurship, assuring employment, stabilizing growth, restructuring and promoting innovation, thereby laying a solid qualitative and quantitative foundation for the high-quality development of enterprises.

1. **The reform promotes entrepreneurship: the number of market players has doubled**

The high proportion of market players who registered after the reform is a direct manifestation of the fact that the business system reform and business environment construction promote more market players to start businesses. As shown in Fig. 1.14, among the 8293 market players covered by the random sample, the proportion who had registered before 2014 was 47%, while 53% had registered between 2014 and 2019, of which 13% registered in 2019 alone. This shows that, in this sample of the survey, the number of new market players who started businesses and entered the market after the reform has already surpassed the pre-reform number.

2. **The reform assures employment: 34% of market players created new jobs**

Employment is the main livelihood of the people. The number of people employed reflects market players' ability to absorb employment, and is an important foothold for maintaining stability and promoting development. In the field survey, our research team asked the representatives of market players if their companies had upsized, downsized or remained unchanged in the past 6 months. As shown in Fig. 1.15, in the first half of 2019, 34% said their companies had upsized, 55% remained the same, and 11% had downsized. The difference between companies who had upsized and downsized was 23% points. This report defines net increase in employment as the difference between the proportion of enterprises who upsized and those who downsized. In 2019, the nationwide net increase in employment of market players was 23%. This shows that, in the first half of 2019, market players created more jobs and provided more employment opportunities than before.

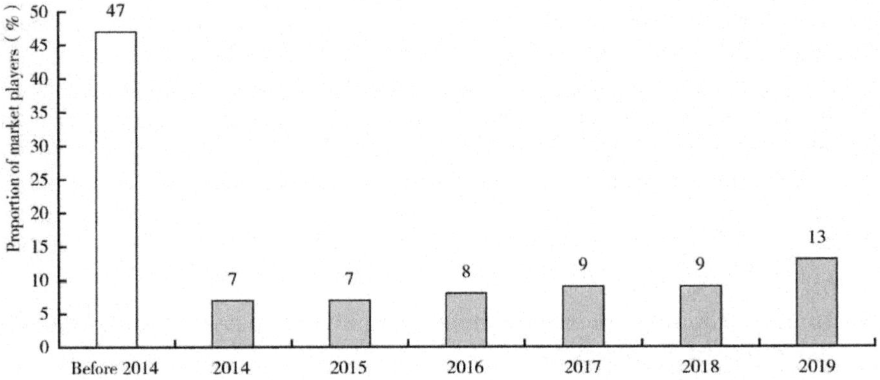

Fig. 1.14 Market players registered between 2014 and 2019 accounted for 53% of the total. *Source* Sun Yat-sen University Research Group on "Deepening the Reform of the Business System"

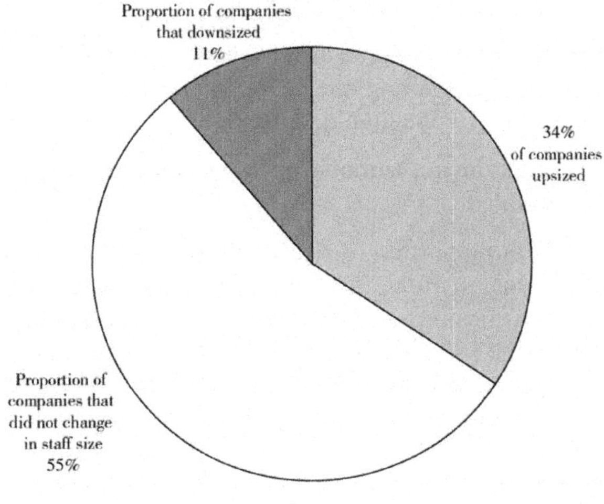

Fig. 1.15 In the first half of 2019, 34% of China's market players upsized. *Source* Sun Yat-sen University Research Group on "Deepening the Reform of the Business System"

3. **The reform stabilizes growth: 49% of market players had increased performance**

At the macro level, economic growth depends not only on the number of market players, but also on their growth. The business system reform promotes the improvement and growth of market players at the micro level, and reflects the achievements of the reform in terms of stabilizing growth. During the field survey, our research team asked the representatives of market players if their companies' sales performance had increased, decreased or stayed the same over the past 6 months. As shown in Fig. 1.16, in the first half of 2019, 49% of market players reported increased performance, 32% did not change, and 19% had decreased performance. This shows that in the first half of 2019, nearly half of the market players performed better than before.

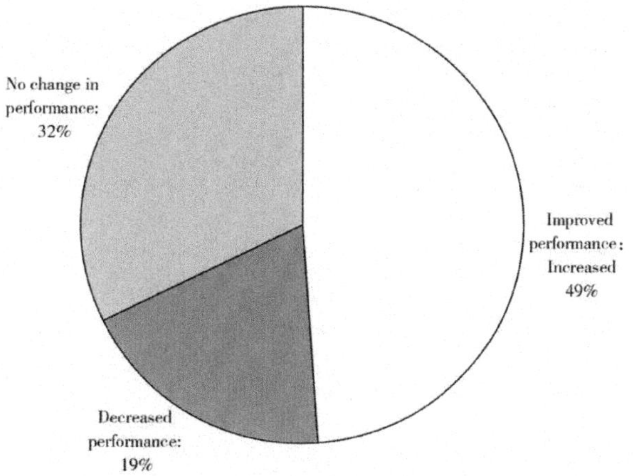

Fig. 1.16 Forty-nine percent of China's market players had increased performed in the first half of 2019. *Source* Sun Yat-sen University Research Group on "Deepening the Reform of the Business System"

4. **The reform restructures the market: 70% of market players were in the service industry**

The business environment construction has engaged the entrepreneurial enthusiasm of market players, with many new market players having registered companies. This has provided an opportunity for industrial transformation, and has laid the quantity-based foundation for market players in the transformation of China's economy to becoming service dominated. According to when market players registered, the respective industry distributions of market players in 2018 and 2019 can be calculated. As shown in Fig. 1.17, the proportion of market players in the service sector increased from 68% in 2018 to 70% in 2019. Emerging industries accounted for 14%, the second largest category of the main industries in the market covered by the survey.

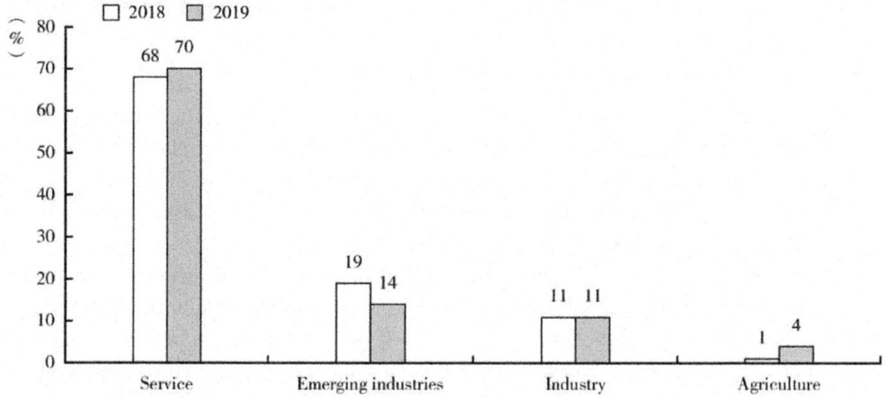

Fig. 1.17 Proportions of market players in various industries in 2018 and 2019. *Source* Sun Yat-sen University Research Group on "Deepening the Reform of the Business System"

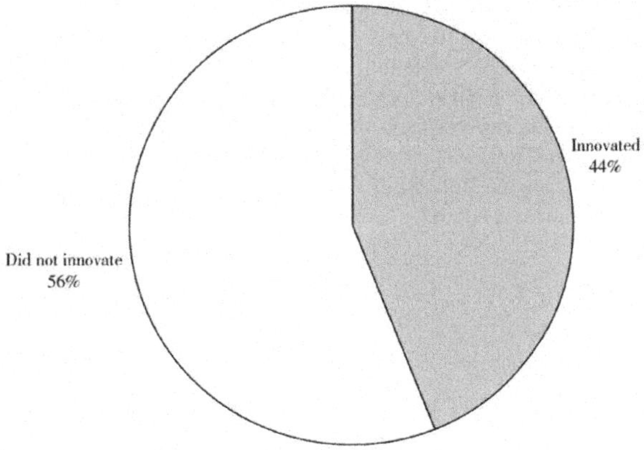

Fig. 1.18 In 2019, 44% of China's market players innovated. *Source* Sun Yat-sen University Research Group on "Deepening the Reform of the Business System"

5. **The reform promotes innovation: 44% of market players innovated**

China attaches importance to enterprises being driven by innovation, and has achieved high-quality development at the macro level through high-quality cultivation of market players. The 2019 government work report points out that we must continue to innovate and promote development, cultivate and strengthen new momentum, enhance scientific and technological support capabilities, and further promote entrepreneurship and innovation among the people. During the field survey, our research team asked representatives of market players whether their companies had launched new products or services in the past 6 months. As shown in Fig. 1.18, 44% of market players had introduced new products or services in the first half of 2019. This shows that over 40% of China's market players innovated in the past 6 months.

(5) **Summary**

From the perspective of market players, the main accomplishments in the construction of the national business environment in 2019 compared with 2018 are as follows.

(1) The permit reduction work has achieved remarkable results. The average number of permits that enterprises needed to apply for dropped from 2.0 in 2018 to 1.8 in 2019, and the time was shortened from 28 to 22 days. The three permits with the greatest reductions in time were those involving taxation, opening bank accounts, and environmental protection.
(2) Forty percent of market players achieved single-network access. The online service hall awareness rate reached nearly 70%, and the usage rate nearly 50%, thus showing that it has entered the stage of large-scale use. The single-network access usage rate has reached about 40%. One month after the launch of the nationwide government service platform, its appeal rate reached 57%.
(3) Work efficiency has been greatly improved. Judging from the responses from market players, the proportion of people who completed a task in a single visit

increased from 31% in 2018 to 42% in 2019. In addition, about 70% of market players were able to complete all their tasks at a single window, and the 30-min completion rate increased from 17% in 2018 to 33% in 2019. Market players' sense of fulfillment has significantly improved.

(4) High-quality development was strongly promoted. First, promotion of entrepreneurship: the total number of market players doubled. Second, employment protection: 34% of market players upsized. Third, steady growth: 49% of market players performed better. Fourth, restructuring: 70% of market players were in the service industry. Fifth and finally, promotion of innovation: 44% of market players innovated.

1.3 Progress in Each Region (2018–2019)

In this report, an index system is created to evaluate the business environment construction across China based on the four dimensions of market entry, market regulation, "Internet + government services" and service efficiency. The distance to frontier method is used to measure local scores. This section analyzes the scores of 110 cities across China.

(1) **One percent of cities reached the "excellent" level and 92% passed**

As shown in Table 1.3 and Fig. 1.19, Shenzhen ranked first among all the cities surveyed, and in 2019 it was the only city with an "excellent" business environment score (85 points or higher). Four cities reached the "good" level (80–84 points), accounting for 4%; 22 had "moderate scores" (70–79 points), accounting for 24%; 59 cities were at the "pass" level (60–69 points), accounting for 63%; and seven cities were at the "fail" level (below 60 points), accounting for 8%. Among the valid samples from 110 cities, the highest score was 85, and the lowest was 51. The top six cities, in order, were Shenzhen, Guangdong; Hangzhou, Zhejiang; Huzhou, Zhejiang; Guangzhou, Guangdong; Ningbo, Zhejiang; and Jiangmen, Guangdong.

(2) **Seven percent more cities passed, and 58% improved**

Nationwide, compared with 2018, the scores for the reform of the nationwide business system and business environment construction has improved significantly. This is shown in that the pass rate increased by 7% points, from 85% in 2018 to 92% in 2019, while the failure rate decreased by 7% points, from 15% in 2018 to 8% in 2019. In 2018, no cities reached the excellent level, but in 2019, 1% of cities did so, a major breakthrough. The proportion of cities at the good level also increased by 1% point over 2018, to 4%. Overall, in 2019 great progress was made in the business system reform and business environment construction.

Looking at individual cities, as shown in Fig. 1.20, among the cities covered by both the 2018 and 2019 surveys, 35 had higher business environment construction progress scores than the previous year, accounting for 57%, while the scores of the remaining 43% of cities either did not change, or declined. As shown in Table 1.3, the

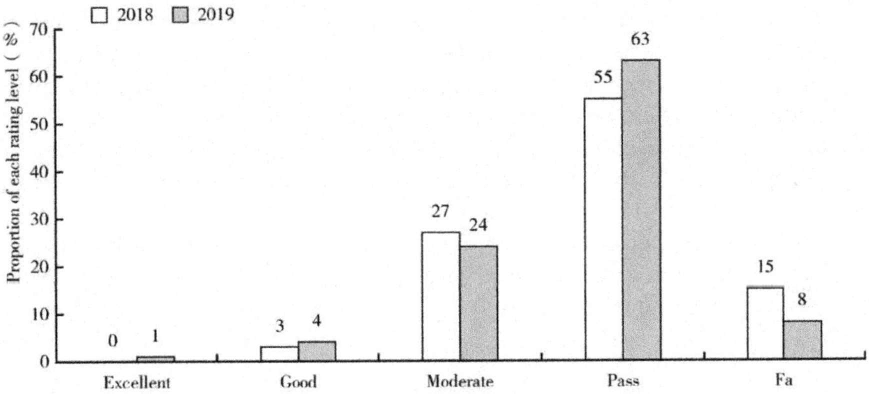

Fig. 1.19 Distribution of urban business environment construction scores for the nationwide survey in 2018 and 2019. *Note* The rating criteria are as follows: excellent (85–100 points), good (80–84 points), moderate (70–79 points), pass (60–69 points), and fail (59 points or lower). The cities of Sanming, Jiayuguan, Longnan, Pingliang, Chaozhou, Jieyang, Zhanjiang, Chongzuo, Xuchang, Binzhou, Zaozhuang, Fangchenggang, Datong, Lüliang, Taiyuan, Yuncheng and Changzhi had fewer than 30 valid sample sizes in 2019, thus their scores for that year are absent. Survey cities newly added in 2019 have no scores for 2018. *Source* Sun Yat-sen University Research Group on "Deepening the Reform of the Business System"

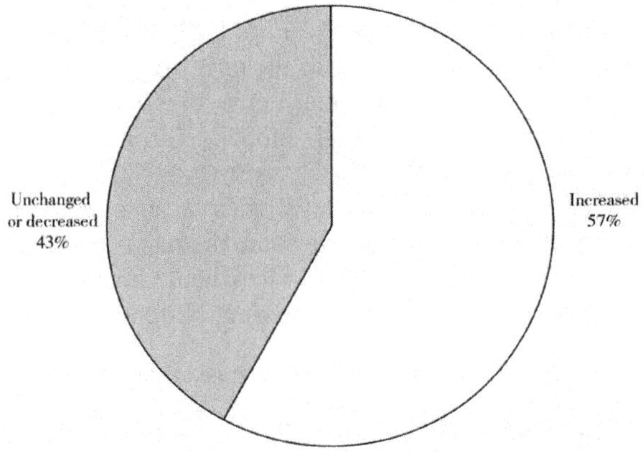

Fig. 1.20 In 2019, 57% of cities made progress in their business environment construction. *Source* Sun Yat-sen University Research Group on "Deepening the Reform of the Business System"

cities with the greatest increases in their scores were Zhaotong, Yunnan (22 points); Quzhou, Zhejiang, Zhoushan, Zhejiang and Yuxi, Yunnan (14 points); and Qinzhou, Guangxi and Lishui, Zhejiang (13 points).

(3) **Shanghai, Guangdong and Zhejiang were voted the top three business environments**

The recognition of market players is the greatest affirmation of the business system reform work. In 110 cities across 24 provinces, respondents gave a list of what they believed were the three provinces with the best business environments. Figure 1.21

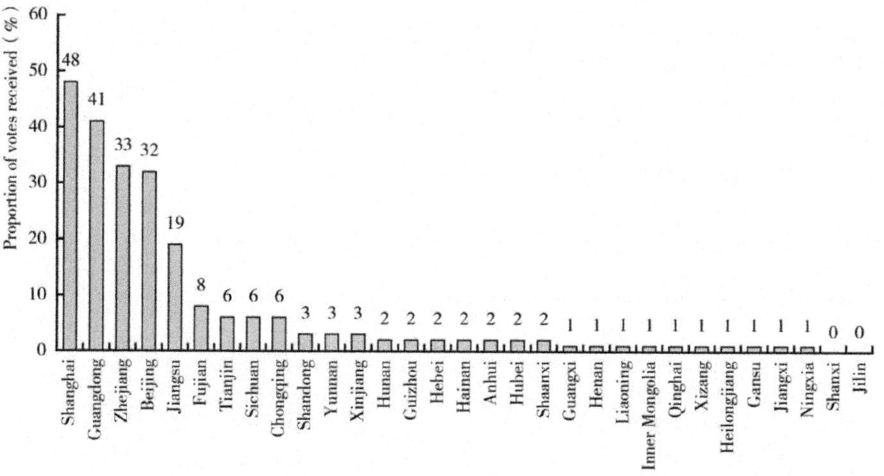

Fig. 1.21 Proportion of votes for business environment in various Chinese provinces in 2019. *Source* Sun Yat-sen University Research Group on "Deepening the Reform of the Business System"

lists the vote results for all provinces in 2019. Shanghai ranked first, followed in order by Guangdong, Zhejiang, Beijing, Jiangsu and Fujian. Looking at the specific vote results, 48% of non-Shanghai market players believed that Shanghai's business environment was quite good, putting it in the top spot; 41% of non-Guangdong market players believed so of Guangdong's business environment, making it second place; and 33% of non-Zhejiang market players believed so of Zhejiang's business environment, ranking it third.

(4) **Zhejiang, Chongqing and Yunnan made the greatest progress**

1. **Zhejiang ranked third nationwide in terms of votes, and made great progress in the three areas of streamlining government services, delegating power and strengthening regulation**

Judging from the votes of out-of-province market players, as shown in Table 1.2, in 2018, 19% of non-Zhejiang market players recognized Zhejiang's business environment construction, ranking it fourth nationwide. By 2019, this vote rate increased to 33%, ranking third.

Judging from the responses from the market players in Zhejiang, it has made remarkable progress in terms of market entry, credit regulation and service efficiency. As shown in Fig. 1.22, in 2018, market players in Zhejiang needed 2.3 permits to register a company, and in 2019 they only needed 1.0, a decrease of 1.3. Thus, Zhejiang has achieved particularly strong results in permit reduction. In 2019, the proportion of market players who viewed the enterprise credit information publicity system reached 58%, 9% points higher than the previous year. The proportion of market players who completed all their tasks in one visit increased sharply from 44% in 2018 to 57% in 2019, showing a marked improvement in service efficiency.

Table 1.2 Comparison of the top ten provinces based on the 2018 and 2019 vote results

2019			2018		
Ranking	Region	Vote rate (%)	Ranking	Region	Vote rate (%)
1	Shanghai	48	1	Shanghai	34
2	Guangdong	41	2	Guangdong	31
3	**Zhejiang**	**33**	3	Beijing	25
4	Beijing	32	**4**	**Zhejiang**	**19**
5	Jiangsu	19	5	Jiangsu	12
6	Fujian	8	6	Fujian	6
7	Tianjin	6	7	Tianjin	3
7	Sichuan	6	7	Sichuan	3
7	**Chongqing**	**6**	7	Hainan	3
10	Shandong	3	**10**	**Chongqing**	**2**
10	**Yunnan**	**3**	10	Shandong	2
10	Xinjiang	3	10	Xinjiang	2
			10	Hunan	2

Source Sun Yat-sen University Research Group on "Deepening the Reform of the Business System"

2. **Yunnan joined the top ten, with a large jump in its awareness rate**

Looking at the votes of out-of-province market players, in 2018, only 1% of non-Yunnan market players recognized its business environment construction, thus it did not rank among the top ten nationwide. By 2019, this vote rate had increased to 3%, thus putting it tenth nationwide, breaking into the top ten for the first time (see Table 1.2).

From responses from market players within the province, Yunnan's progress is mainly reflected in terms of market access, credit regulation, and "Internet + government services." As shown in Fig. 1.23, in 2019, Yunnan's time required to register a company dropped from 6.4 to 5.7 days, and the number of permits needed dropped from 2.4 to 2.2. This shows a drastic improvement in convenience of market entry there. The proportion of market players who viewed the enterprise credit information publicity system in Yunnan reached 78% in 2019, 19% points higher than the previous year. The online service hall awareness rate increased from 43% in 2018 to 76% in 2019, reflecting the remarkable results achieved in Yunnan's construction of "Internet + government services."

3. **Chongqing climbed from tenth to seventh place, with convenient market entry**

As shown in Table 1.2, in 2018, 2% of non-Chongqing market players recognized its business environment construction, ranking it tenth nationwide. By 2019, this vote rate had increased to 6%, pushing it up three places to seventh.

Table 1.3 Scores and rankings of various cities in the progress of their business environment construction

City	2019		2018		City	2019		2018	
	Score	Level	Score	Level		Score	Level	Score	Level
Shenzhen	85	Excellent	–	–	Chongqing	66	Pass	–	–
Hangzhou	83	Good	71	Moderate	Qujing	66	Pass	–	–
Huzhou	83	Good	71	Moderate	Yinchuan	66	Pass	60	Pass
Guangdong	83	Good	82	Good	Bijie	66	Pass	75	Moderate
Ningbo	82	Good	–	–	Hanzhong	66	Pass	72	Moderate
Jiangmen	79	Moderate	76	Moderate	Changde	66	Pass	68	Pass
Jinhua	78	Moderate	69	Pass	Shijiazhuang	66	Pass	–	–
Quzhou	78	Moderate	64	Pass	Zhoukou	66	Pass	58	Fail
Beijing	77	Moderate	78	Moderate	Changchun	66	Pass	54	Fail
Zhaotong	77	Moderate	55	Fail	Jinan	66	Pass	–	–
Zhoushan	77	Moderate	63	Pass	Bengbu	65	Pass	59	Fail
Lishui	76	Moderate	63	Pass	Suizhou	65	Pass	–	–
Shanghai	76	Moderate	–	–	Liuzhou	65	Pass	–	–
Suqian	76	Moderate	–	–	Nanning	65	Pass	53	Fail
Shaoguan	76	Moderate	–	–	Kunming	65	Pass	65	Pass
Yangjiang	75	Moderate	67	Pass	Jiuquan	65	Pass	68	Pass
Xuzhou	74	Moderate	–	–	Huaihua	64	Pass	60	Pass
Qingdao	73	Moderate	–	–	Yueyang	64	Pass	68	Pass
Fuzhou	72	Moderate	61	Pass	Jingmen	64	Pass	–	–
Nanjing	72	Moderate	–	–	Huanggang	64	Pass	–	–
Suzhou	72	Moderate	–	–	Guigang	64	Pass	63	Pass
Taizhou	72	Moderate	–	–	Ankang	64	Pass	67	Pass
Changsha	71	Moderate	72	Moderate	Quanzhou	63	Pass	62	Pass
Xi'an	71	Moderate	72	Moderate	Zhangye	63	Pass	70	Moderate
Fuyang	70	Moderate	72	Moderate	Yulin	63	Pass	77	Moderate
Hefei	70	Moderate	72	Moderate	Tongling	62	Pass	54	Fail
Zhengzhou	70	Moderate	65	Pass	Lanzhou	62	Pass	67	Pass
Haikou	69	Pass	–	–	Tangshan	61	Pass	–	–
Xinyang	69	Pass	62	Pass	Tongchuan	61	Pass	64	Pass
Yancheng	69	Pass	–	–	Hengshui	61	Pass	–	–
Xianning	69	Pass	–	–	Siping	60	Pass	60	Pass
Wuhu	69	Pass	81	Good	Songyuan	59	Fail	53	Fail
Qinzhou	69	Pass	56	Fail	Guyuan	58	Fail	53	Fail
Zibo	69	Pass	66	Pass	Langfang	58	Fail	–	–
Putian	69	Pass	60	Pass	Zhangjiakou	58	Fail	–	–

(continued)

Table 1.3 (continued)

City	2019		2018		City	2019		2018	
	Score	Level	Score	Level		Score	Level	Score	Level
Wuhan	69	Pass	–	–	Chengde	58	Fail	–	–
Luoyang	69	Pass	–	–	Wuzhong	57	Fail	63	Pass
Shaoyang	68	Pass	67	Pass	Xining	51	Fail	–	–
Changzhou	68	Pass	–	–	Sanming	–	–	63	Pass
Baishan	68	Pass	61	Pass	Jiayuguan	–	–	72	Moderate
Jilin	68	Pass	–	–	Longnan	–	–	65	Pass
Yichang	68	Pass	–	–	Pingliang	–	–	69	Pass
Tianjin	68	Pass	63	Pass	Chaozhou	–	–	72	Moderate
Hengyang	68	Pass	69	Pass	Jieyang	–	–	73	Moderate
Huaibei	68	Pass	74	Moderate	Zhanjiang	–	–	62	Pass
Dongying	67	Pass	70	Moderate	Chongzuo	–	–	63	Pass
Yulin	67	Pass	56	Fail	Xuchang	–	–	71	Moderate
Yuxi	67	Pass	53	Fail	Binzhou	–	–	61	Pass
Ezhou	67	Pass	–	–	Zaozhuang	–	–	67	Pass
Anyang	67	Pass	61	Pass	Fangchenggang	–	–	–	–
Guiyang	67	Pass	63	Pass	Datong	–	–	–	–
Luohe	67	Pass	67	Pass	Lüliang	–	–	–	–
Pu'er	67	Pass	65	Pass	Taiyuan	–	–	–	–
Ningde	66	Pass	67	Pass	Yuncheng	–	–	–	–
Zunyi	66	Pass	67	Pass	Changzhi	–	–	–	–

Note The data are from the China Doing Business Enterprise Survey. The rating criteria are as follows: excellent (85–100 points), good (80–84 points), moderate (70–79 points), pass (60–69 points), and fail (59 points or lower). When calculating the market access indexes, only samples of market players registered between 2014 and 2019 were included. The following cities had fewer than 30 registered samples in 2014–2019, and thus their scores for 2019 are absent: Sanming, Jiayuguan, Longnan, Pingliang, Chaozhou, Jieyang, Zhanjiang, Chongzuo, Xuchang, Binzhou, Zaozhuang, Fangchenggang, Datong, Lüliang, Taiyuan, Yuncheng and Changzhi. Survey cities newly added in 2019 have no scores for 2018

The responses from market players within Chongqing showed that its performances in permit reduction and credit regulation both exceeded the national averages. As shown in Fig. 1.24, in 2019 Chongqing market players needed 1.4 permits to register a company, 0.6 lower than the 2014–2018 average, thus it progressed faster than the national average. In addition, 70% of Chongqing's market players checked the corporate credit information publicity system, 4% points higher than the national average (Table 1.3).

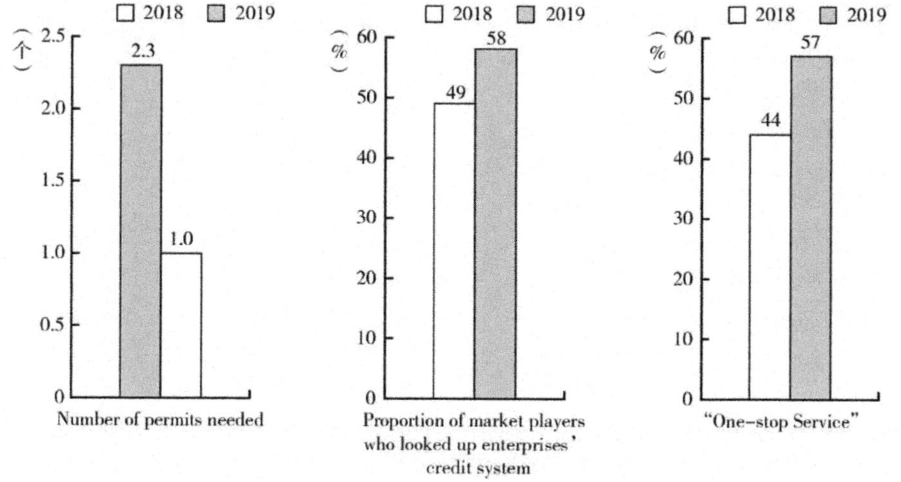

Fig. 1.22 Zhejiang Province's main accomplishments in 2019. *Source* Sun Yat-sen University Research Group on "Deepening the Reform of the Business System"

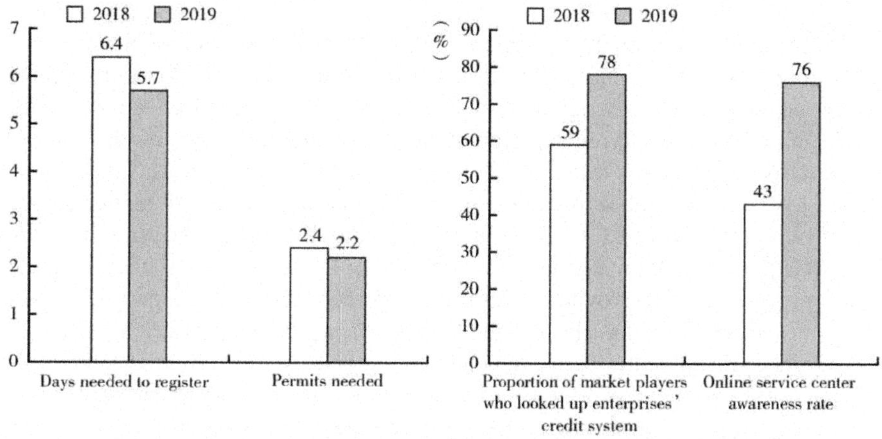

Fig. 1.23 Yunnan Province's main accomplishments in 2019. *Source* Sun Yat-sen University Research Group on "Deepening the Reform of the Business System"

1.4 Core Problems of the Business Environment Construction

At present, the main problem China's business system reform faces is the imbalanced reform progress from region to region. Despite the reform's remarkable achievement of doubling the number of enterprises in a short period of time, enterprises are facing many new problems, such as fierce competition, difficulty in recruitment, and high costs, while small and micro enterprises face difficulties in growth.

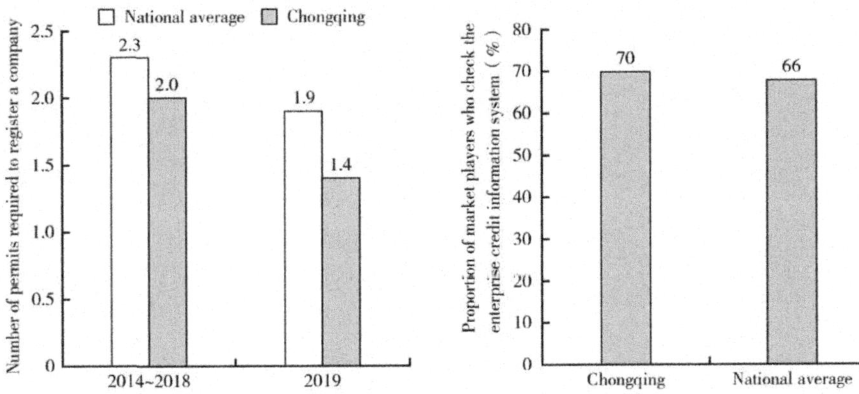

Fig. 1.24 Chongqing's main accomplishments in 2019. *Source* Sun Yat-sen University Research Group on "Deepening the Reform of the Business System"

(1) In terms of market entry, the level of convenience of access varies greatly from region to region

Easing market entry is the first step in the reform of streamlining government services, delegating power and strengthening regulation. Although the national average of facilitating market entry has greatly improved, the degree of market entry convenience varies widely from region to region. As shown in Fig. 1.25, in the fastest province it took 3 days to register a company, while in the slowest province it took 9.3 days, more than three times the former. As for the number of service windows needed to visit, the number in the highest-ranking province was 1.4, and that in the lowest-ranking one was 3.1, the latter being 2.2 times the former. The province with the fewest permits had an average of 1.0, successfully achieving the goal of single-permit processing. The province with the worst score required 2.7 permits, nearly three times the number of the best province. This shows that there is a clear difference in the level of market entry convenience from region to region, with the score of the lowest-ranking province being roughly one-third that of the highest-ranking one.

Even within a given province, market players in various regions hold different perceptions toward the convenience of market entry. Taking a province in eastern China as an example, in a city there, one market player interviewed said that registering a company there only took about a day and a half. Meanwhile, in another city of the same province, some market players said it would take several months to do so, and had to visit service offices in several districts. Market players in other districts of this city also held different views. At the government service hall of a new district in eastern China, some market players said they could acquire a general industry license in a day and a half, while in another district of the same city, some market players said they had already made three or four trips to supplement materials, yet still had not completed the process.

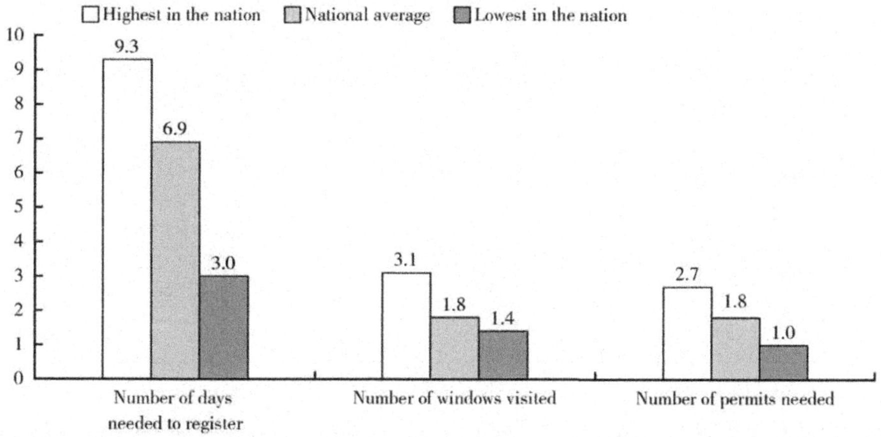

Fig. 1.25 In terms of market entry, there is a large difference in the level of convenience between regions. *Source* Sun Yat-sen University Research Group on "Deepening the Reform of the Business System"

The responses of market players show that the "multiple permits in one" system has not been fully completed, with delays in applying for permits, thus making market entry inconvenient. For example, in a province in the eastern region, many market players said that applying for a permit was one of the challenges in doing business: "The services we need for applying for a business license are pretty simple, but it's still hard for companies to get some of the permits they need." In a city in the eastern region, some market players reported on the changes brought about by the commercial reform by saying, "The three-in-one and five-in-one permits don't really mean anything. Theoretically, you just need one permit, but they just gave something a new name without fixing the problem. It still takes just as much time and trouble as before."

(2) Credit regulations are lacking, and market players are often inspected

The business system reform emphasizes strengthening regulation both during and after the fact. With so many new market players, the workload of regulation both during and after work has doubled, and credit regulation has become a new regulation model. Consequently, the state has created a new regulation system with unified credit as the core. At the same time, with credit regulation as the core, the state has established random spot checks and joint regulation models, with the goal of reducing physical inspections and departments. Judging from the responses from market players, there remain problems at this stage, such as on-site inspection and the large number of departments.

First, market players have undergone many on-site inspections. As shown in Fig. 1.26, judging from the market players' responses, 81% were inspected on site by government departments in 2019. Among them, 35% believed that the number

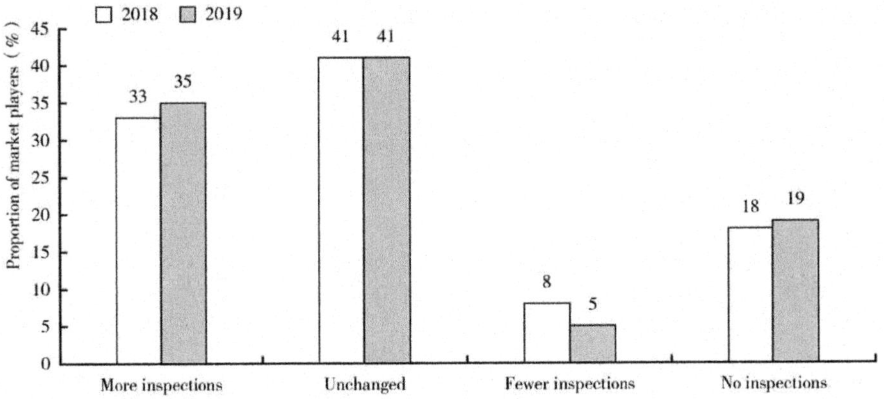

Fig. 1.26 Number of times market players were inspected on site. *Source* Sun Yat-sen University Research Group on "Deepening the Reform of the Business System"

of inspections had increased, 2% points higher than the previous year, and 5% said they underwent fewer on-site inspections, a decrease of 3% points.

Second, there are many government departments performing on-site inspections. As shown in Fig. 1.27, the market players' responses reveal that in 2019 about 24% of them believed that more government departments had conducted on-site inspections than the previous year, an increase of 4% points. Meanwhile, 6% of market players believed that fewer government departments had made on-site inspections, no different from 2018.

The progress of various regions shows that the degree of credit regulation varied from place to place. As shown in Fig. 1.28, an average of 19% of enterprises were not inspected on site. The province with the highest proportion of enterprises not

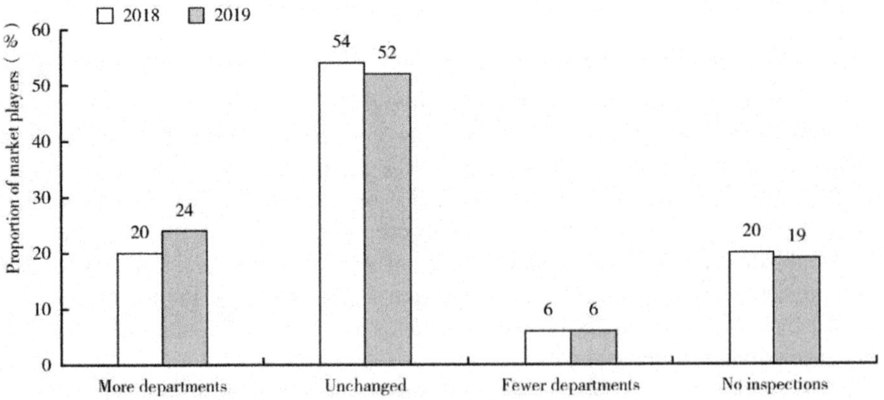

Fig. 1.27 Number of departments that inspected market players on site. *Source* Sun Yat-sen University Research Group on "Deepening the Reform of the Business System"

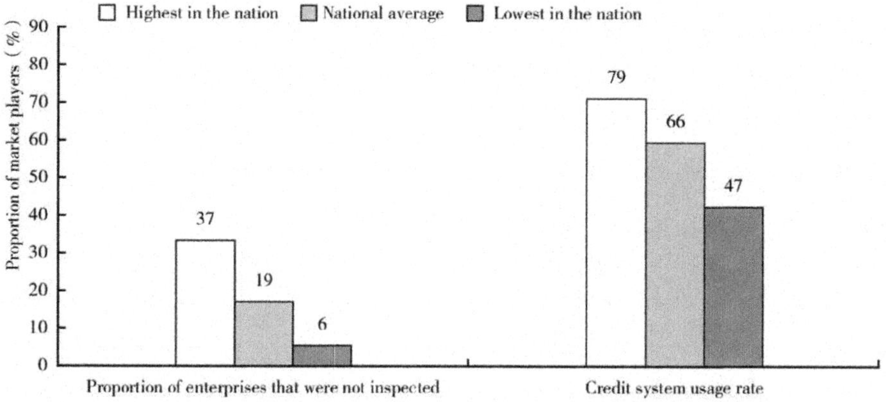

Fig. 1.28 There is a significant gap in credit regulation among regions. *Source* Sun Yat-sen University Research Group on "Deepening the Reform of the Business System"

inspected on site had a rate of 37%, and the worst-performing province had a rate of only 6%. In 2019, 66% of market players said that, before trading with other market players, they would check their credit information through the National Enterprise Credit Information Publicity System. The province with the highest usage rate of the system scored 79%, and the lowest scored 47%, a difference of 32% points. This shows that there is a significant gap in credit regulation from place to place.

Market players believe that, although the increase in inspections shows the government's increased responsibility and market operation standardization, it has greatly impeded their business operations. For example, in cities in the eastern and western regions, most market players reported that market regulation had increased in recent years, with more frequent on-site inspections by government departments. One man in a city in the central region, after having made several trips up- and downstairs to complete tasks related to commerce and tax, approached one of our researchers to complain as follows: "The main problem now is that there are so many market inspections. It's like they're a 'one-size-fits-all' solution, and they've become a formality we just have to go through." Some market players in an eastern province also remarked that market inspections had increased, making it more difficult for them to do business there. Finally, several interviewees from an eastern city said that in recent years the permit requirements for their industry had increased, and government inspections had become quite a bit more frequent. Compared with the past, setting up the same kind of enterprise now requires more work to meet the market access requirements.

(3) **In terms of "internet + government services," awareness and usage rates vary widely**

The construction of "Internet + government services" is an important decision and action on behalf of the CPC Central Committee and State Council. As shown in Fig. 1.29, in the first half of 2019, the nationwide online service awareness rate reached 66%, while the usage rate reached 48%. The construction of a nationwide

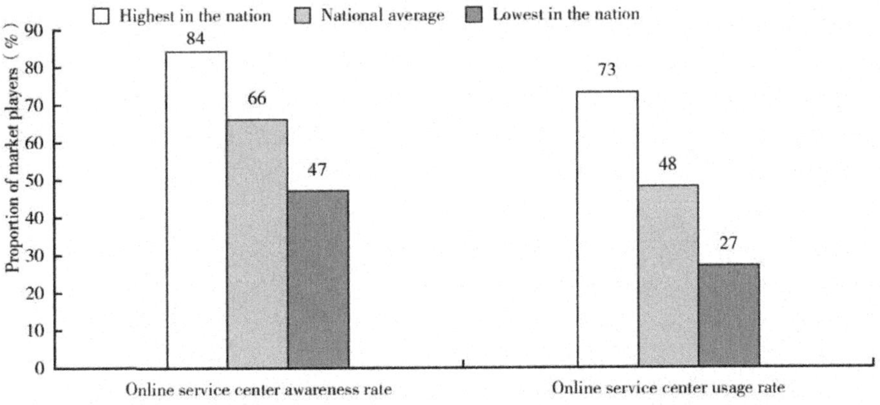

Fig. 1.29 There is a large gap in the progress made among regions in the construction of online service halls. *Source* Sun Yat-sen University Research Group on "Deepening the Reform of the Business System"

digital government has thus entered the large-scale awareness stage, and is now progressing toward the large-scale use stage. However, there is an undeniable large gap from region to region. The online service awareness rate in the highest-ranking province was 84%, while that of the lowest-ranking province was only 47%. The usage rate of the highest-ranking province was 73%, putting it in the stage of large-scale use stage, but that of the lowest-ranking province was only 27%, about one-third of the former.

The different degrees of importance attached to "digital government" is one of the important factors in the unbalanced development of digital government among regions. In prefecture-level cities where digital government is the focus of work and publicity, a "full-process/semi-process electronic" service was launched for the online service hall. These cities have made great efforts in the publicity, promotion and construction of the online service platform, increasing the awareness and usage rate of market players there. For example, in Zibo, Shandong, when asked how they knew to complete tasks online, one market player said, "When I came here before, the person at the service window told me I could do it on my computer. There was also a lot of information posted at the service hall, and the process was pretty easy to follow." In Jilin City, Jilin Province, our research team learned through their interviews that most market players there were aware they could complete tasks online, and most had learned this from the service hall staff. However, some cities have not yet paid attention to the digital government construction, nor used it as a supplement to offline processing. In these cities, although their service halls are equipped with computers and they have posted promotional materials, the staff there have not actively promoted the use of digital government. Consequently, these cities have low digital government awareness and usage rates, and still need to give it more attention.

(4) In terms of service efficiency, there is a large gap from in completing all tasks in one visit

At the 2018 annual sessions of the NPC & CPPCC National Committee (also known simply as the "Two Sessions"), Premier Li Keqiang clearly proposed the reform goals of streamlining government services, delegating power and strengthening regulation" and the "Six Ones." At the halfway mark of 2019, after 1 year had passed, the proportion of market players in China who only needed one visit to complete a task was 42%. Compared with 31% in 2018, it is clear that progress had been made in this phase. However, looking at individual provinces, as shown in Fig. 1.30, the best-performing province in terms of completing all tasks in one visit had a rate of 61%, while the rate of the worst-performing province was 20%, about one-third of the former. As for single-window processing, the best-performing province had a rate of 81%, and that of the worst province was 32%, a difference of 49% points. Finally, for 30-min completion, the best province had a rate of 57%, while that of the worst province was 6%, the latter being less than one-ninth that of the former. All of these show large gap between regions.

Even in different cities in the province and different districts of the same city, there are differences in the efficiency of government services. For example, in three districts of a city in the eastern region, staff in the first district will begin serving the next market player while the previous one makes photocopies, thus reducing the waiting time. In the second district, the staff very patiently answer questions from market players, so that each can quickly get the help they need, even when in the self-serve area. The third and final district has a very large number of market players, yet there are only six business windows. Although the staff there are very efficient,

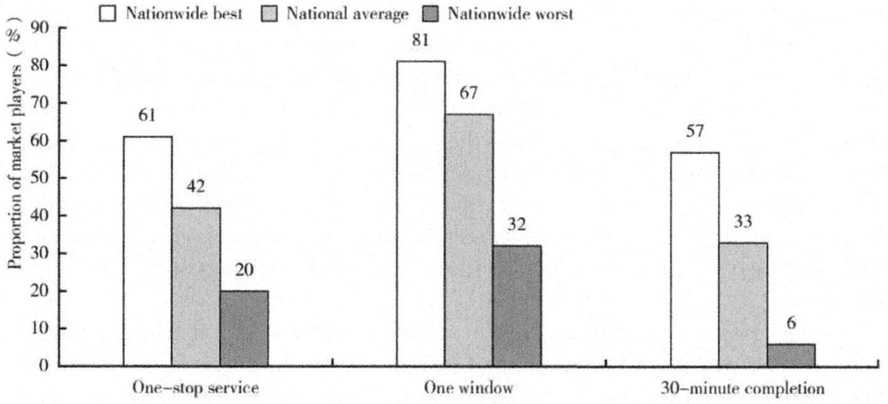

Fig. 1.30 There is a large gap in progress between regions in building a service-oriented government. *Source* Sun Yat-sen University Research Group on "Deepening the Reform of the Business System"

market players generally need to wait about 40 min before being served. Another example is that in the government service halls of Huichuan and Bozhou Districts of Zunyi, Guizhou, market players often praise the service hall staff's attitude and efficiency. One market player said, "In Zunyi City, Honghuagang District is the best place to go to get things done. The other districts aren't quite as good."

Based on the market players' responses, the lack of clear instructions from the service hall staff is the primary reason for the inefficiency of government services. In a city in the central region, one interviewee said, "It really only takes 10 min to gather the required materials to get something processed, but the staff often don't explain it in detail. They just give us the materials, and send us go to the form filling area where we're supposed to fill it out according to the template." In addition, one market player said, "I'm older, and not highly educated. When looking at those templates and documents, it's hard to tell what exactly I'm supposed to do. If I misunderstand something, I'll have to wait in line again, and it often takes 3 or 4 h to finish what I went there to do." This shows that the staff here did not clearly explain the instructions and points of note, thus inconveniencing the market players. The lack of standardization between windows is another major main reason for the inefficiency of government services. In a city in the western region, many interviewees said that the number of visits it takes to complete a task depends on how well they have prepared their materials. Some businesses must make three or four trips, because each time they are informed of different problems with their materials, thus they have to prepare the materials once again according to different "amendments," then return and wait in line once again. One woman complained, "There's always some problem or other with the material. If you go to another window with a different person, they'll find some new problem with the materials. Can't they just solve all the problems at once?" In a city in the eastern region, a market player who could not complete all their tasks in one visit complained, "They said I could get everything done in one trip, so that's what I had expected to do, but I ended up making several trips, which kind of bothered me.... I read online what materials I had to prepare, but when I got there, the information they asked me for was different from what it said online." Another market player said she was told that her materials were incomplete. She made a total of three visits, each time speaking with different staff members, and each told her different things, so she had to keep coming back. The lack of standardization between staff and between windows greatly impedes market players in completing tasks, and also reduces the service windows' efficiency and market players' level of satisfaction.

Another problem is that, due to the service window staff's inefficiency, market players must wait for a long time, and end up not being satisfied with the service. For example, in an eastern city, many market players reported that the wait time at the government service hall was excessively long, often taking an entire afternoon to complete tasks. In a city in the eastern region, many market players interviewed reported that the wait time at the service hall was extremely long. We observed that many market players spend an entire morning in the waiting area, then even might have to continue waiting in the afternoon. During an interview with one man, he told us, "I got here at 8 o'clock to get a number, but after waiting for over an hour they still haven't called me. My experience is that I need to wait a whole morning, and if I don't get here until the afternoon, I probably won't get called at all." In an eastern city, the service hall staff begin work at 9:00, but market players typically start lining up to take numbers at 7:30. If they wait until after 8:00 to line up, they will likely have to wait until the afternoon to be served. When we arrived at the service hall at 8:30, before the staff had begun work, we spoke to the financial director of a company. She said in exasperation, "The staff here are really inefficient, and their attitude is terrible. It's impossible to get everything done in a single morning, and sometimes you even have to wait until the afternoon." During our investigation there, this woman continued to wait, and at noon she was still waiting.

(5) **Most market players face the "new three challenges," while small and micro enterprises have "troubles on top of troubles"**

The "new three challenges" faced by market players are fierce market competition, recruitment difficulties, and high costs. The business system reform involves resolving challenges and pain points such as acquiring permits and licenses, and exiting the market. However, the feedback from market players in 2019 shows that these are no longer the main challenges they face. The respective proportions of market players who mentioned difficulties in starting a business, applying for permits and exiting the market were only 3%, 7% and 3%, showing little change compared to 2018. These have thus become the "old three challenges." In 2019, the three challenges most frequently mentioned by market players nationwide were fierce market competition, high labor costs, and recruitment difficulties. The respective proportions of these three challenges mentioned were 27, 17 and 14%, with increases of 1–2% points over 2018, thus making these the most widespread challenges and pain points for market players today, known as the "new three challenges" (see Fig. 1.31).

For small and micro enterprises, increasingly fierce market competition and labor costs are greater challenges than for medium- and large-sized enterprises. In Fig. 1.32, the main challenges are divided according to the size of the market players, and the differences in the degree of difficulty faced by small and micro enterprises and large ones are examined. It is shown that 28% of small and micro enterprises said that that market competition was fierce, while 21% of medium- and large-sized enterprises said so, 7% points lower than the former. In terms of labor costs, 17% of small and micro enterprises said labor costs were high, while 16% of large- and medium-sized enterprises said so, a difference of 1% point. In terms of recruitment, small and micro enterprises and medium- and large-sized enterprises faced the same pressure in recruiting employees, with 14% of both categories indicating so. Therefore, although the business environment construction has facilitated market entry for small and micro enterprises, as the total number of enterprises continues to increase, small and micro enterprises face great difficulties in terms of growth, and need further support.

Under competitive pressure, small and micro enterprises faced the challenges of having fewer opportunities to create jobs, and showed low rates of performance improvement and innovation. As shown in Fig. 1.33, the proportion of small and

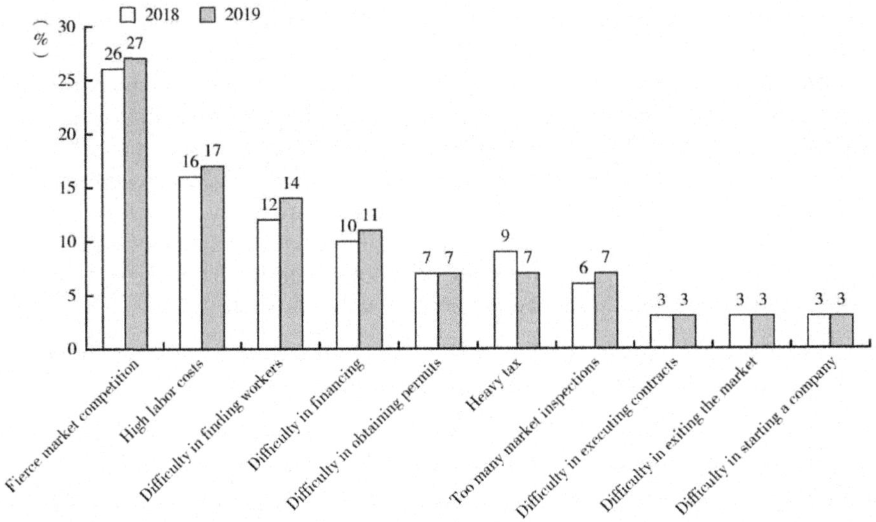

Fig. 1.31 In 2019, fierce market competition, high labor costs, and difficulties in recruitment were the "three new challenges". *Source* Sun Yat-sen University Research Group on "Deepening the Reform of the Business System"

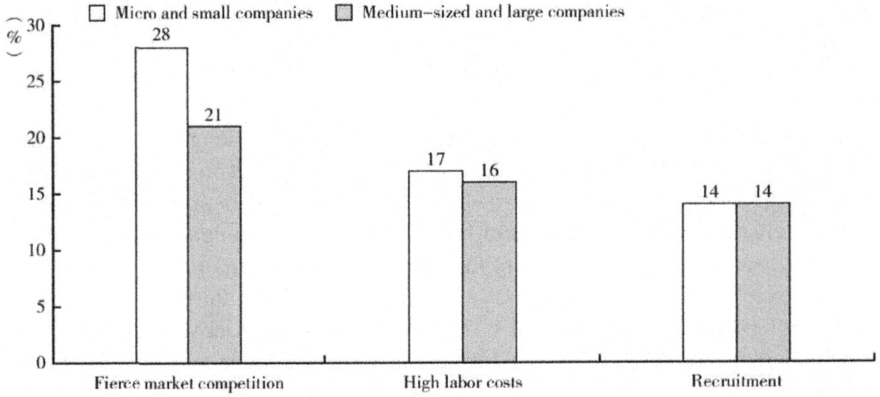

Fig. 1.32 In 2019, small and micro enterprises faced fiercer competition than medium- and large-sized ones. *Source* Sun Yat-sen University Research Group on "Deepening the Reform of the Business System"

micro enterprises who upsized was about 32%, while 47% of medium- and large-sized enterprises did so; in addition, 40% of small and micro enterprises innovated, while 60% of medium- and large-sized enterprises did so; finally, 47% of small and micro enterprises had increased performance in the past 6 months, while 60% of medium- and large-sized enterprises reported as such.

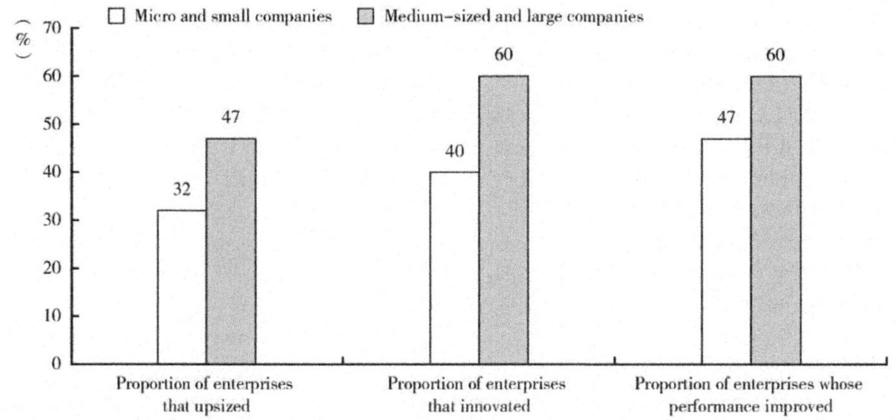

Fig. 1.33 Small and micro enterprises faced challenges in growth. *Source* Sun Yat-sen University Research Group on "Deepening the Reform of the Business System"

During our field survey, market players nationwide complained about difficulties in recruitment, expansion and doing business. For example, in Langfang, Hebei, our research team spoke to many people who were at the service office to dissolve their businesses. Based on their feedback, the main cause of this was the loss of workers, and some factories that needed many workers faced bankruptcy. In an eastern city, one business owner explained, "It's pretty hard to hire workers here. It's not a great place for hiring people. There aren't many young people left, since most of them go somewhere else to make a living." In a city in the central region, when talking about the "general business environment," many interviewees said it was "getting harder and harder." During the field survey, our research team spoke to several market players whose companies were undergoing restructuring. When business became challenging, they faced the difficulties head-on, and immediately adjusted. One interviewee mentioned, "To improve our outlook, we hope to receive more support and assistance from the government."

1.5 Potential Directions for Optimizing the Business Environment Construction

The business system reform adheres to the people-centered idea of development, and enhances market players' sense of fulfillment. The reform seeks to focus on and promote achieving the hopes and desires of the people. As always, reform is a long—and uphill—battle. Based on the current progress, results and problems faced in the nationwide business environment construction, and considering China's new economic development situation, we propose three potential directions for further deepening the construction of the business environment.

In the short term, we must promote the construction of standardized government services, and narrow the development gap between regions. The respective proportions of cities across the country at the excellent, good, moderate, pass and fail rates were 1%, 4%, 24%, 63% and 8%, exhibiting imbalanced progress between regions. In terms of market access, the worst-performing province took almost threefold the time, number of windows and number of permits as the best-performing one did. For market regulation, the province with the highest credit information publicity system usage rate scored about twice that of the worst-performing one. In the construction of "Internet + government services," the online awareness rate of the highest-scoring province nationwide was nearly twice that of the lowest-scoring province. Finally, for the rate of completing all tasks in one visit, the best-performing province had a score more than three times that of the lowest-scoring one. For these reasons, to narrow the gap in the business environment construction between regions, it is necessary to promote the standardization of government services, refine and quantify the service standards and work processes, improve nationwide service efficiency, and achieve the consolidation and equalization of market access, credit regulation, "Internet + government services" and service efficiency of all regions.

In the mid-term, we must continue to strengthen credit regulation, and build a competition-neutral business environment. Compared with 2018, in 2019 there were increases in both the number of times market players were inspected by the government and the number of departments. This required much human and material resources from the functional departments, and seriously disrupted market players' operations. Market players face increased pressure for inspections, indicating that credit regulation has not been fully implemented, and the construction of a new type of regulation system centered on market players' credit has yet to be completed. Therefore, to further strengthen the implementation of credit regulation, we must give full play to the advantages of "Internet + regulation" based on credit information and big data, and continue to promote the implementation of credit regulation and "oversight through inspections by randomly selected inspectors of randomly selected players and the public release of inspection results." In addition, we must also regulate the market in accordance with the rules of equal treatment, and build a competitive-neutral market environment.

In the long term, we must strengthen the construction of a service-oriented government, deepen the opening of the domestic market, and support the growth of small and micro enterprises. The construction of a service-oriented government remains insufficient. For example, even though the rate of completing tasks in a single visit has now reached 42%, there remains much distance from the goal of 100%. In addition, the main challenges faced by market players have changed from the "old three challenges," related to government services, to the "new three challenges," rooted in the market's supply and demand level, thus making it difficult for small and micro enterprises to grow. Therefore, to deepen the reform of the Business System, we must continuously promote the transformation of government functions and improve the efficiency and level of government services. We must also continuously open up and build more areas of the market, so as to fundamentally resolve the issues of fierce competition, high costs, and difficulties in recruitment. Through the combination of enhancing government services and opening up new areas of the market, we aid the growth and transformation of market players, especially small and micro enterprises, and thus continue to unlock market vitality and promote high-quality economic development.

Chapter 2
Construction of the Government Service Environment

Qingmiao Bi and Xianxiang Xu

2.1 Report Overview

With market players as the main perspective, this report systematically evaluates China's business environment construction using the services provided by government service halls. Government service environment refers to the environment in which functional government departments provide public services to market players. Generally speaking, these services are provided at local government service halls. Market players' sense of fulfillment stems from the environment provided by their local government service hall. The government's work in optimizing these services depends on the pain points, obstacles and challenges that the market players experience within this government service environment. Comparing these two perspectives horizontally, the differences in the government service environment across the country reflects to a certain extent the differences in the business environment construction from region to region; as for vertical comparison, the improvement of the local government service environment reflects the progress of the business environment construction in these places.

China began gradually establishing government service halls in 2001, and by 2014 more than 90% of prefecture-level municipalities had set up such halls. The goal of these government service halls is to centralize the various approval departments that were previously independent and decentralized within the same office hall, thereby coordinating their work to reduce the time enterprises spend at various functional departments, shortening the lengthy approval cycle, and improving the transparency and efficiency of the approval process. Beginning in 2001, prefecture-level government service halls were gradually established, and by the start of the

Q. Bi · X. Xu (✉)
Lingnan College, Sun Yat-sen University, Guangzhou, China
e-mail: lnsxuxx@mail.sysu.edu.cn

Institute of Mezzoeconomics, Sun Yat-sen University, Guangzhou, China

X. Xu et al. (eds.), *Report on the Chinese Business Environment Survey 2020*, Research Series on the Chinese Dream and China's Development Path,
https://doi.org/10.1007/978-981-99-6112-2_2

nationwide business environment construction in 2014, a total of 310 prefecture-level cities had set up such halls, accounting for 93% of all prefecture-level municipalities. In addition, the respective average numbers of departments, projects and service windows set up in each prefecture-level city were 45, 335 and 90.

The China Doing Business Enterprise Survey analyzes and evaluates the local government service environment based on field research conducted in 2018 on government service halls in 182 districts nationwide in 84 cities across 16 provinces. Through hierarchical random sampling, the project team selected 16 provincial government services division units, with the details as follows: two municipalities directly under the Central Government: Beijing and Tianjin; 12 provinces: Jilin, Zhejiang, Anhui, Fujian, Shandong, Henan, Hunan, Guangdong, Guizhou, Yunnan, Shaanxi and Gansu; and two autonomous regions: Guangxi Zhuang Autonomous Region and Ningxia Hui Autonomous Region. Next, from among the 16 provincial government services divisions the following were selected: 84 prefecture-level government services division units (including 72 prefecture-level cities and 12 municipalities directly under the Central Government), and 182 districts and counties. After the investigation, the project team compiled the first-hand data and public opinion responses collected during the survey. Based on this, the project team then examined the new accomplishments, challenges and developmental directions in the construction of the nationwide government service and business environments.

The report showed that the two main problems in the construction of the national government service environment are that some elements are lacking, while others are imbalanced. The first problem refers to the fact that, while hardware and software facilities are widely available, the service field is generally lacking. The second problem is the imbalance in the construction of the government service environment from region to region. The respective rates for excellent, good, moderate and pass levels were 0%, 5%, 47% and 43%, while those below 5% were considered to have failed. By summarizing the typical practices of various regions in terms of government service environment construction and listing outstanding issues, we propose three directions for further deepening the government service environment construction throughout China: eliminating shortcomings in hardware, upgrading in terms of software, and making breakthroughs in the service field (Table 2.1).

2.2 Current Status of China's Government Service Environment Development

The current state of development of China's government service environment has a total score is 70 points, a moderate level. Among the three areas, the levels of hardware and software both have ratings of "good," but the service level has a "fail" rating. Thus the development of the government service environment varies widely from region to region.

Table 2.1 Nationwide government service environment construction indicator system and latest progress

Metric	Score	Rating	Maximum	Minimum
Level 1 indicator				
Overall government service environment score	70	Moderate	87	55
Level 2 indicators				
Hardware level score	81	Good	100	45
Software level score	84	Good	100	63
Service level score	44	Fail	75	20

Source The rating criteria of Sun Yat-sen University Research Group on "Deepening the Reform of the Business System" are as follows: 90–100: excellent; 80–89: good; 70–79: moderate; 60–69: pass; under 60: fail

(1) **China's government service environment scored 70 points (moderate)**

As shown in Fig. 2.1, calculated based on the data collected from field research in 182 districts of 84 cities across 16 provinces of China, the overall nationwide government service environment score was 70 points, a moderate level.

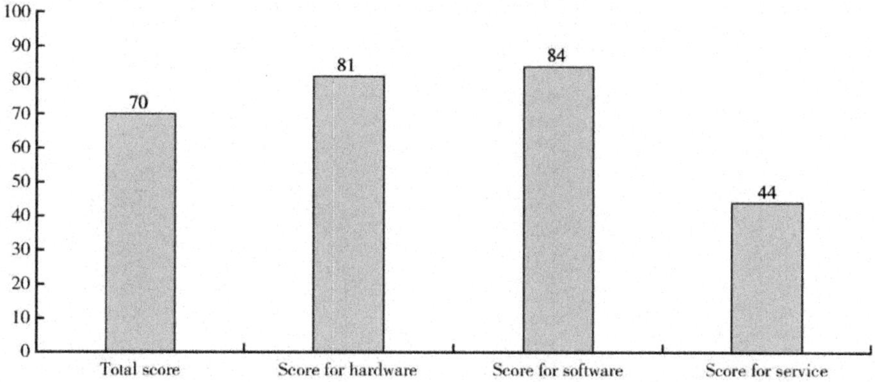

Fig. 2.1 China's overall government service environment score is at a moderate level. *Note* The data source is the China Doing Business Enterprise Survey. The score is calculated based on the distance to frontier (DTF) method that was used in the World Bank's Doing Business Report to evaluate each country's score. Then the average is weighted according to population. See the Appendix for details on the calculation process. The scoring levels are divided as follows: 90–100 points: excellent; 80–89: good; 70–79: moderate; 60–69, pass; less than 60, fail

1. **Good level of hardware**

The hardware score covers four dimensions: convenience of public transportation, and availability of performance facilities, convenience facilities and feedback facilities. In more detail, as shown in Fig. 2.2, the highest score was that of the availability of feedback facilities, at 93 points, that is, 93% of China's government service halls had comment boxes. This was followed by the convenience facility availability score, at 90 points, of which the waiting area, seats, washrooms, heating and air conditioning ratings almost all reached 100%, while the rating of sufficient and comfortable seats was 74%, and the café rating was also 74%. The efficiency facility availability score was 74 points, of which the equipment rate of printers and photocopiers reached 90%, the ratings of waiting number machines, LED number call display, and self-serve computers all reached around 80%, and about 50% of the halls provided photo services. The lowest score was that of the convenience of public transportation, at 69 points: on average, it took 4 min to walk to a given government service hall from the nearest bus stop.

2. **Good level of software**

The software score consists of two dimensions: the clarity of the procedure instructions and the service window open rate. Specifically, as shown in Fig. 2.3, the service window open rate scored 92 points, that is, the national average of open business

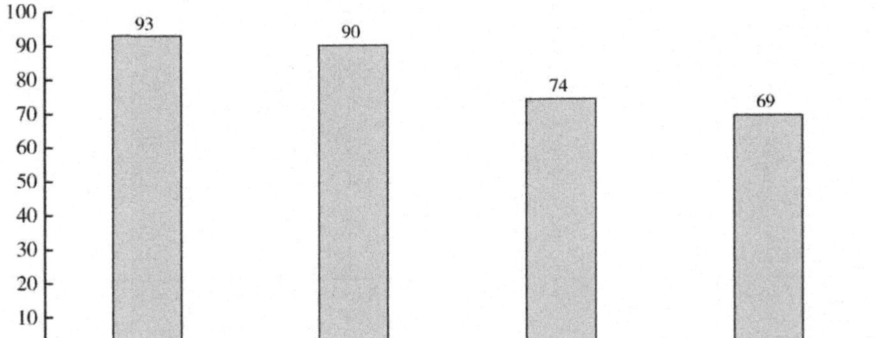

Fig. 2.2 China's government service environment hardware level scored 81 points. *Note* The data source is the China Doing Business Enterprise Survey. The score is calculated based on the distance to frontier (DTF) method that was used in the World Bank's Doing Business Report to evaluate each country's score. Then the average was weighted according to population. See the Appendix for details on the calculation process. The scoring levels are as follows: 90–100 points: excellent; 80–89: good; 70–79: moderate; 60–69: pass; less than 60: fail

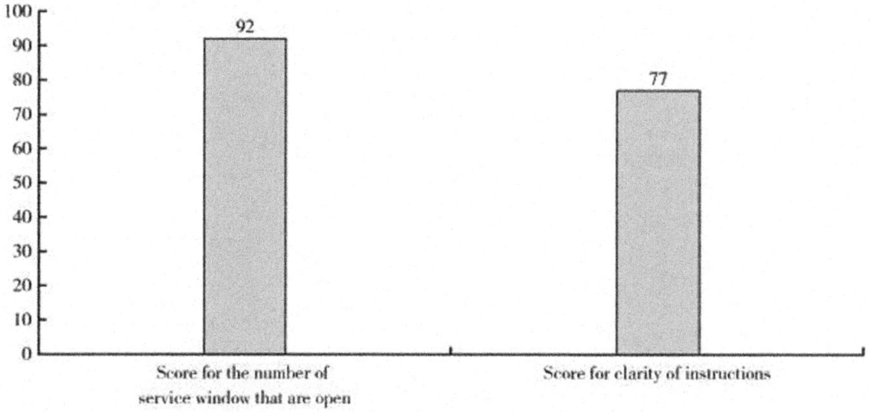

Fig. 2.3 China's government service environment software scored 84 points. *Note* The data source is the China Doing Business Enterprise Survey. The score is calculated based on the distance to frontier (DTF) method that was used in the World Bank's Doing Business Report to evaluate each country's score. Then the average was weighted according to population. See the Appendix for details on the calculation process. The scoring levels are divided as follows: 90–100 points: excellent; 80–89: good; 70–79: moderate; 60–69, pass; less than 60, fail

service windows in the government service halls was 92%. Meanwhile, the clarity of procedure instructions scored 77 points. A total of 92% of government service halls provided basic procedure instructions, 89% had inquiry staff, 72% provided form filling templates, and 54% made public commitments to completion time.

3. **Service was not up to par**

The service score is composed of two dimensions: the quality and quantity of services provided. As shown in Fig. 2.4, the score of service quality was 57, a failing rate. Specifically, 30% of market players completed all tasks in one visit, and 68% completed all tasks at one window. On average, it took 1.4 h to complete a task during each visit. Therefore, China is far from achieving its reform target goals of 100% of all tasks being completed in one visit and at one window. The service quantity score was 32 points, well below the pass line. On average, at a given window within a time span of 20 min, fewer than two people were served.

Overall, China's hardware and software construction is at a good level, but the service level has failed. Taking the three together, the national government service environment scored a total of 70 points, for a moderate performance.

(2) **China's government service environment construction is imbalanced**

1. **Imbalanced the development of hardware, software and service**

The horizontal solid line in Fig. 2.5 is a reproduction of Fig. 2.1. The software level is the best, the hardware level is second, and the service level lags behind. The score of the software level was 84 points, while the service level scored 44 points, a difference of 40 points. In other words, the service level score is only about half that of the software level.

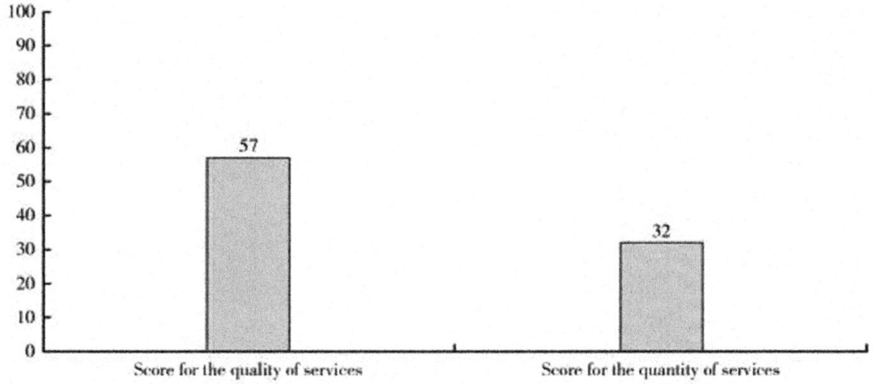

Fig. 2.4 China's government service environment services scored 44 points. Note: The data source is the China Doing Business Enterprise Survey. The score is calculated based on the distance to frontier (DTF) method that was used in the World Bank's Doing Business Report to evaluate each country's score. Then the average was weighted according to population. See the Appendix for details on the calculation process. The scoring levels are divided as follows: 90–100 points: excellent; 80–89: good; 70–79: moderate; 60–69, pass; less than 60, fail

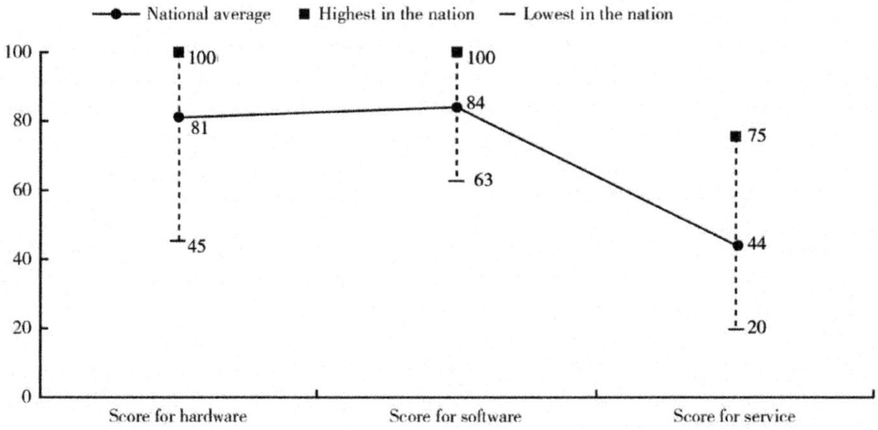

Fig. 2.5 China's government service environment construction is imbalanced. *Note* The data source is the China Doing Business Enterprise Survey. The score is calculated based on the distance to frontier (DTF) method that was used in the World Bank's Doing Business Report to evaluate each country's score. Then the average was weighted according to population. See the Appendix for details on the calculation process

2. **Imbalanced government service environment construction**

In Fig. 2.5, the vertical dotted line shows the differences among the regions (including prefecture-level cities and municipal districts of a municipality directly under the Central Government, hereafter collectively referred to as "regions") with the highest and lowest scores nationwide in terms of hardware, software and service levels. The longer the vertical line, the greater the difference, that is, the more imbalanced the regions. As shown in Fig. 2.5, the difference in the hardware and service levels from region to region is 55 points, while the difference in the software level is 37 points, for an average difference of 32 points. It can thus be seen that the development of the government service environment among regions varies widely.

2.3 Current Progress of Governmental Environment Development in Various Regions

(1) **Total scores: excellent 0%, good 5%, moderate 47%, pass 43%, fail 5%**

The establishment of government service halls is the basis for providing centralized approval services, and for evaluating the government service environment. Of the 84 prefecture-level government services division units surveyed and sampled, five regions had not set up government service halls, thus their scores are absent.[1] Of the other 79 regions, none scored more than the 90 points required to reach the "excellent" level, the highest score being 87 points, with four regions exceeding 80 points to reach the "good" level, accounting for 5% of the total. The regions scoring 70–79 points were the most numerous, at 37, accounting for 47% of the total. Meanwhile, 34 had a "moderate" score of 60–69, accounting for 43%, and four prefecture-level cities had a "fail" score, accounting for about 5% (see Table 2.2).

(2) **Hardware scores: excellent 22%, good 39%, moderate 18%, pass 14%, fail 8%**

The region with the highest hardware score was Sanming City, Fujian Province, with a full 100 points. All efficiency, convenience and feedback facilities there were fully equipped, and public transportation was also the most convenient, with only a 1-min walk from the nearest bus stop to the government service hall. Next, there were 17 regions with excellent hardware scores of over 90 points, 31 with 80–89 points (good), 14 with 70–79 points (moderate), 11 with 60–69 points (pass), and six that failed, respectively accounting for 22%, 39%, 18%, 14% and 8% of the total (see Fig. 2.6). Among the regions that failed, the one with the lowest score was a city in the eastern region. The scores for the waiting number machine, LED ticket number display, self-serve computers and photo equipment there were all zero, for a total hardware score of 45.

[1] The five regions were Shunyi District of Beijing, Daxing District of Beijing, Zhanjiang City in Guangdong Province, Jiayuguan City in Gansu Province, and Pingliang City in Gansu Province. Since the surveys in these five regions were conducted by the local Bureaus of Industry and Commerce, their administration service hall operating environment scores are not included here. The establishment rate of administrative service halls in the eight-four sample regions is about 94%. This is roughly consistent with the 93% establishment rate under the nationwide samples, thus confirming that the survey samples are representative.

Table 2.2 Overall government service environment scores

Region	Score	Level	Ranking	Region	Score	Level	Ranking
Xicheng District, Beijing	87	Good	1	Zaozhuang, Shandong	69	Pass	42
Hongqiao District, Tianjin	82	Good	2	Hangzhou, Zhejiang	69	Pass	42
Yinchuan, Ningxia	81	Good	3	Jinan, Shandong	69	Pass	42
Changsha, Hunan	80	Good	4	Lishui, Zhejiang	69	Pass	42
Hengyang, Hunan	79	Moderate	5	Zhengzhou, Henan	69	Pass	42
Sanming, Fujian	79	Moderate	5	Qinzhou, Guangxi	69	Pass	42
Huaihua, Hunan	79	Moderate	5	Chaozhou, Guangdong	69	Pass	42
Tongzhou District, Beijing	79	Moderate	5	Fuyang, Anhui	68	Pass	50
Yangjiang, Guangdong	78	Moderate	9	Guiyang, Guizhou	67	Pass	51
Haidian District, Beijing	78	Moderate	9	Jinnan District, Tianjin	67	Pass	51
Fuzhou, Fujian	77	Moderate	11	Yulin, Shaanxi	67	Pass	51
Guangzhou, Guangdong	77	Moderate	11	Zhaotong, Yunnan	67	Pass	51
Pu'er, Yunnan	77	Moderate	11	Wuqing District, Tianjin	67	Pass	51
Wuzhong City, Ningxia	77	Moderate	11	Zhangye, Gansu	66	Pass	56
Huaibei, Anhui	76	Moderate	15	Shaoyang, Hunan	66	Pass	56
Changde, Hunan	76	Moderate	15	Tongchuan, Shaanxi	66	Pass	56
Xuchang, Henan	76	Moderate	15	Yueyang, Hunan	66	Pass	56
Zibo, Shandong	76	Moderate	15	Heping District, Tianjin	66	Pass	56
Kunming, Yunnan	75	Moderate	19	Binzhou, Shandong	65	Pass	61
Dongying, Shandong	75	Moderate	19	Siping, Jilin	65	Pass	61
Longnan, Gansu	75	Moderate	19	Jinhua City, Zhejiang	64	Pass	63
Hexi District, Tianjin	75	Moderate	19	Guigang, Guangxi	63	Pass	64

(continued)

Table 2.2 (continued)

Region	Score	Level	Ranking	Region	Score	Level	Ranking
Putian, Fujian	74	Moderate	23	Nanning, Guangxi	63	Pass	64
Bijie, Guizhou	74	Moderate	23	Baishan, Jilin	63	Pass	64
Ankang, Shaanxi	74	Moderate	23	Yulin, Guangxi	62	Pass	67
Chongzuo, Guangxi	74	Moderate	23	Anyang, Henan	62	Pass	67
Jiuquan, Gansu	73	Moderate	27	Huzhou, Zhejiang	62	Pass	67
Yuxi, Yunnan	72	Moderate	28	Hanzhong, Shaanxi	61	Pass	70
Jiangmen, Guangdong	72	Moderate	28	Fangchenggang, Guangxi	60	Pass	71
Xi'an, Shaanxi	72	Moderate	28	Bengbu, Anhui	60	Pass	71
Fengtai District, Beijing	72	Moderate	28	Tongling, Anhui	60	Pass	71
Wuhu, Anhui	72	Moderate	28	Jieyang, Guangdong	60	Pass	71
Ningde, Fujian	72	Moderate	28	Songyuan, Jilin	60	Pass	71
Zunyi, Guizhou	72	Moderate	28	Changchun, Jilin	58	Fail	76
Hebei District, Tianjin	71	Moderate	35	Luohe, Henan	56	Fail	77
Quzhou, Zhejiang	70	Moderate	36	Zhoukou, Henan	55	Fail	78
Guyuan, Ningxia	70	Moderate	36	Xinyang, Henan	55	Fail	78
Quanzhou, Fujian	70	Moderate	36	Shunyi District, Beijing	–	–	–
Lanzhou, Gansu	70	Moderate	36	Daxing District, Beijing	–	–	–
Zhoushan, Zhejiang	70	Moderate	36	Zhanjiang, Guangdong	–	–	–
Hefei, Anhui	70	Moderate	36	Jiayuguan, Gansu	–	–	–
Laiwu, Shandong	69	Pass	42	Pingliang, Gansu	–	–	–

Note The source of the data is the China Doing Business Enterprise Survey. The ranking includes 79 prefecture-level government services divisions, of which 69 are prefecture-level municipalities and 10 are municipalities directly under the Central Government. Another five prefecture-level government services divisions do not have government service halls: the surveys there were conducted by the local Bureaus of Industry and Commerce, thus these are not included in the government service environment ranking. The scoring levels are divided as follows: 90–100 points: excellent; 80–89: good; 70–79: moderate; 60–69, pass; less than 60, fail

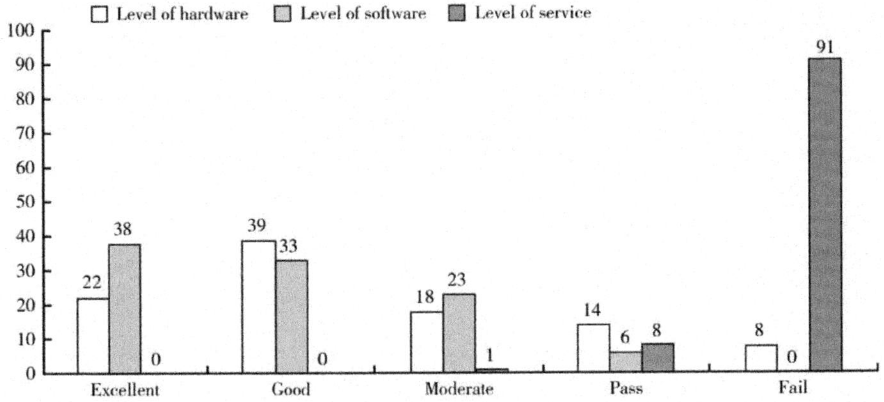

Fig. 2.6 Distribution of hardware, software and service level scores. *Note* The source of the data is the China Doing Business Enterprise Survey. The scoring levels are divided as follows: 90–100 points: excellent; 80–89: good; 70–79: moderate; 60–69, pass; less than 60, fail

(3) **Software scores: excellent 38%, good 33%, moderate 23%, pass 6%, fail 0%**

The highest software score of 100 signifies that the instructions for completing tasks are completely clear (fully equipped with inquiry staff, instructions and templates, and with a full commitment to completion time), and all of the service windows are open. Twelve regions received perfect scores in this regard, namely Beijing's Xicheng, Haidian, Tongzhou and Fengtai Districts; Tianjin's Hexi, Hebei, Heping and Jinnan Districts; Hengyang and Changde Cities of Hunan; and Longnan and Jiuquan Cities of Gansu Province. There were 30 regions with software scores exceeding 90, along with 26 that scored 80–89 (good), 18 that scored 70–79 (moderate), five that scored 60–69 (pass), and six that failed, respectively accounting for 38%, 33%, 23%, 6% and 0% of the total (see Fig. 2.6). Among them, the lowest score was a city in the central region, with 63 points. The unclear procedure instructions there were mainly reflected in the lack of service staff in the hall, along with no form filling templates, and no commitment to completion time.

(4) **Service scores: excellent 0%, good 0%, moderate 1%, pass 8%, fail 90%**

The service score was generally low, with the highest score in Xicheng District of Beijing, at 75 points. In terms of quantity of services provided, Xicheng's average of serving six people in 20 min was the fastest nationwide. As for service quality, 19% of market players completed all their tasks in a single visit, while 64% completed all tasks at one window, and each visit to the service hall took about 1.5 h. Only Beijing's Xicheng District scored more than 70 points (moderate), six regions scored 60–69 points (pass), while the remaining 72 regions all had failing service scores. The lowest score was that of a city in the eastern region, at 20 points: it provided services to an average of one person every 20 min, 9% of market players completed all tasks in one visit, 60% at one window, and visits there took an average of about 3.5 h.

Table 2.3 Comparison of the four highest- and lowest-ranking regions

Region	Score				Ranking			
	Total score	Hardware	Software	Service	Overall ranking	Hardware	Software	Service
Top four ("good" level)								
Xicheng District, Beijing	87	89	100	75	1	19	1	1
Hongqiao District, Tianjin	82	86	95	65	2	27	19	4
Yinchuan, Ningxia	81	91	85	68	3	15	36	2
Changsha, Hunan	80	88	99	54	4	22	14	15
Average of the four regions		89	95	66		21	18	6

(5) **The high-scoring regions benefited from high service levels**

The four regions with overall scores of "good" (80 points or more), along with their respective hardware, software and service scores and rankings, are shown in the top half of Table 2.3. The hardware rankings of these four regions ranged between 15 and 27, 8 points higher than the national hardware average; their software rankings were between 1 and 36, 11 points higher than the national average; and their service rankings were between 1 and 15, 22 points higher than the national average. It can thus be seen that the four regions with the highest total scores surpassed the national averages in all respects, with their levels of service surpassing it by the greatest margin.

2.4 Typical Practices in Each Region

Based on the first-hand experience of the research team and responses collected from market players throughout the month-long field survey, the report lists the following six typical practices that stand out in the government service environment construction.

(1) **Hangzhou's "one-stop" residents' homes provide comfort and convenience**

Image of a residents' lounge in Yuhang District, Hangzhou City, Zhejiang Province

Hangzhou, Zhejiang's "one-stop" government service center offers outstanding convenience. All types of office windows in Hangzhou are concentrated in special "residents' homes." A variety of tasks including social security, marriage registration, tax payment and business registration can all be handled at this one place. One interviewee said, "It's much more convenient now. I used to have to run around to a bunch of different places. Now I just go up and down the stairs. Even if I have to wait a long time, at least I'm still waiting in the same building."

Aside from the wide range of business tasks, the hardware facilities at the Hangzhou residents' homes are also very comprehensive. The residents' homes have a special twenty-four-hour self-serve area, equipped with self-serve kiosks that can be used around the clock to process various asks. During business hours, volunteers assist people in using these stations. In addition to this, there is a full range of services such as photocopying, printing and stamping. At the residents' home in Hangzhou's Jianggan District, there is even a foreign currency exchange window.

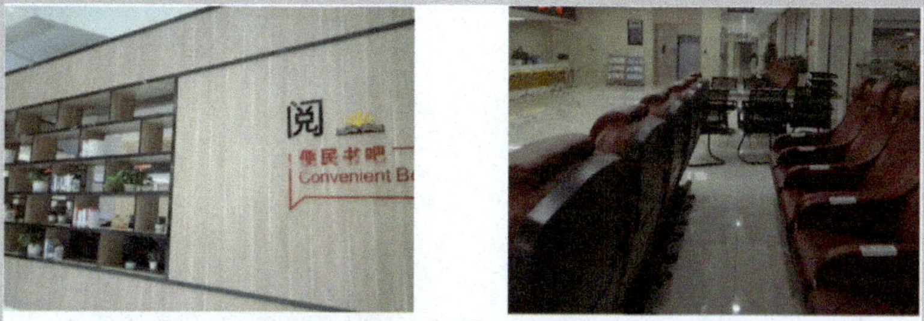

Images of a convenient book bar and self-serve massage chairs in Huzhou

Aside from Hangzhou, government service halls in Huzhou, Zhejiang and Yinchuan Cities of Ningxia, and Ningde, Fujian have also made innovations in their work of "making things easier for people." For example, the service hall in Nanxun District, Huzhou, Zhejiang replaced the seats in the general waiting area with self-serve massage chairs, and they also added a "convenient book bar," providing various types of books for people to read. Another example is the seven-story residents' hall in Yinchuan, where, in addition to providing more than 700 service windows and over 400 types of approval and services, there are also convenient areas such as "reading islands," children's play areas, and food vendors.

(2) Tianjin's distinctive "helper" service provides a smooth experience

Image of the government service hall of Hebei District, Tianjin

One of the outstanding features of the Tianjin government service hall is that it provides "helper" services. In Hebei District of Tianjin City, in addition to the regular window and guide desk staff, there is also a team of Party members clad in white shirts affixed with a CPC emblem, whose duty is to help people visitors complete tasks. When the hall is not particularly busy, they can even walk people through the entire process. Compared to the more common practice of having inquiry staff, these helpers are more like one-on-one consultants, who undoubtedly make the task completion process clearer and the experience smoother. Although several other districts in Tianjin are not quite as formal, they also have helper windows that provide such services. The interviewees highly praised this service.

(3) Wuzhong's public processing time limits clarify procedures

Image of a bulletin board with processing time in Litong District, Wuzhong, Ningxia

There is one aspect of the service hall in Litong District, Wuzhong City, Ningxia that is highly commendable: the details of each task are publicly posted, along with the number of days it usually takes to complete each. Publicly announcing the time that each task will take to complete is no simple undertaking. As a public commitment by the government, it makes them accountable to market players. The public list makes the business process clearer for market players, and gives them a greater degree of control.

(4) Jinan's clear instructions facilitate completing all tasks in one visit

From left to right: The government service center in Shizhong, District, Jinan City; screenshot of its WeChat public account, a screenshot the WeChat public account for Hongta District, Yuxi, Yunnan)

In Shizhong District of Jinan City, although there are many people completing tasks there, the government service hall is highly efficient. During the survey period, our research team found that in addition to the high open window rate and online pre-approval, there is one other important factor here: the businesspeople there have a firm understanding of the procedures and materials they need, thus they can get everything done in little time.

This high efficiency is a result of effective instructions. Compared to the dilemmas faced by other regions, such as having to visit several times or not having the proper materials, what makes Shizhong District so successful in informing the people there of the proper procedures and what materials to prepare? Our observations showed two reasons for their success. First, in the Shizhong District's physical service hall, the staff are kind and patient, and they give fully detailed answers and guidance regarding the steps and materials required. Second, the online government service center's WeChat public account provides guidelines on all the required processes and materials, so that all people need to do is prepare the materials according to these requirements, and they can complete all their tasks in a single trip.

Aside from Jinan in eastern China, in the southwest there is another place where the instructions provided through online platforms have been highly praised: Hongta District of Yuxi, Yunnan. By logging in to the government services network, people can submit their materials, and complete their pre-examination. In addition, through the Yuxi government service WeChat public account (called Yuxi Government Services), people can also do things such as reserve and pick up wait numbers, check the progress of their application, and inquire about the procedures. This helps people better understand the process and materials needed to complete tasks, so that they can do so in fewer trips. As a result, during the survey in Hongta District, our research team found that many people had "come prepared": they had made an appointment and arrived with all their materials ready, and were simply waiting to submit them. A woman who had been in business for many years lamented during her interview as follows: "Before, when I came here to get something done, I mostly prepared materials based on my past experience and questions I asked the staff here. Sometimes I had to run back and forth a few times because I was one thing short. Now it's much better. You can go online and see what materials you need to submit, and can prepare in advance. It saves so much effort, and makes getting things done much easier."

(5) Huaihua's smart government services and single-window processing

Single-window processing is currently the main working model promoted in the business environment construction. Previously, processing and delivery of documents were both done at the same window. Each window had various responsibilities, and people who were completing tasks and picking up items needed to wait their turn. The goal of the current reform is for the front desk window to be a comprehensive reception station, where all materials are submitted. Then the window uses a unified data sharing and exchange platform and government services information system for back-end approval. For market players, this means that they only need to go from one window to the next, with their data being passed on automatically, thus greatly shortening the waiting time.

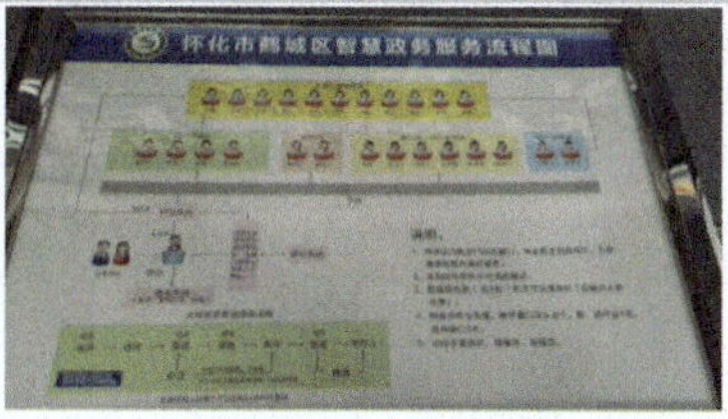

From left to right: instruction billboard for single-window processing in Huaihua, Hunan; a news report on Huaihua's single-window processing

As one of the pilot locations, Huaihua, Hunan has done much exploration and publicity work. While visiting the government service hall in Hecheng District, Huaihua, one clear discovery our research team made was that the window layout here differed from that of the other government service halls. There was no clear separation for each resident department, such as the business window and environmental protection window; instead, the hall was divided into a comprehensive reception area, acceptance area and document delivery area. After speaking to the service hall staff and reading the Smart Government Services Flow Chart, our researchers learned that this hall was one of the pilot locations of the single-window processing halls project. Designed based on "Internet + government services," a single-window comprehensive acceptance and approval model was implemented there. This included front desk comprehensive acceptance, back-office classification approval, and unified window document delivery. After market players submit their materials, the receiving window staff scan them, and while the data are sent to the back office, the relevant functional departments follow the approval procedure. At this time, market players need only use their phone to scan the QR code on the acceptance form to inquire about the progress of the task, resulting in a process that is clear and transparent.

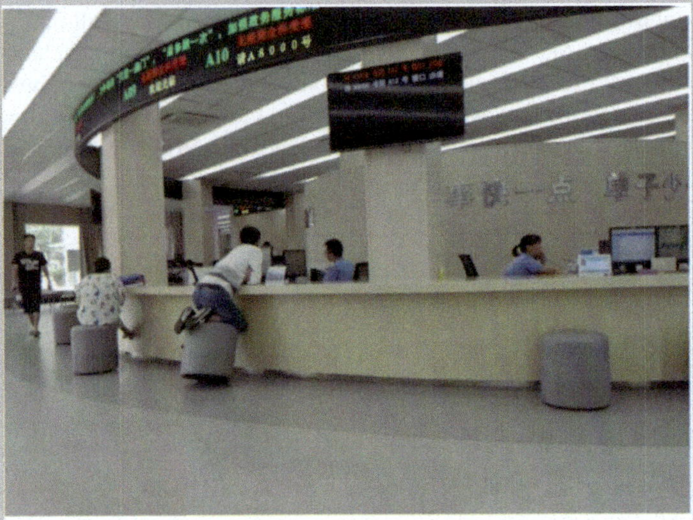

Image of the "all-in-one counter" in Quzhou, Zhejiang

There are numerous regions that implement single-window processing. For example, in Kecheng District of Quzhou, Zhejiang, each the windows had a sign with the words "All types of tasks may be completed here." In Hongta District of Yuxi, Yunnan, we saw that single-window processing was done too. Most of the interviewees there said things such as "You can get everything done in one visit, and it takes less than an hour." This change has made it more convenient for people to complete tasks.

2.5 Purpose of Constructing the Government Service Environment

Government service environment construction is a common practice worldwide, and most countries' performance in this regard has improved. Government service approval and government regulation are by no means unique to China. Djankovet et al. listed the number of steps that market players in 85 countries needed to process through the government when starting a company, along with the time it took, and the fees incurred. By 2018, a total of 190 economies had been covered by the survey.[2] From 2002 to 2018, the performance of all government services provided by governments worldwide had improved. Canada, which ranked number one in 2002, shortened the time it took to deal with the government in starting a business from 2 to 1.5 days. Meanwhile, the Dominican Republic, which ranked the lowest in 2002, shortened its time from 8 to 16.5 days, and China from 92 to 23 days. Therefore, the overall situation in the economies of the world is that government functions provide government services, while market players spend much time and money going through the process of registering a business. The present report defines the government service environment as the environment in which market players deal with functional government departments. Judging from the reduction in time and money, governments around the world have made progress in their government service environment construction, and the construction of government service environments is a universal trend.

Studies performed in both China and other countries have verified the positive role of an improved working environment in government service halls in terms of promoting market entry for enterprises, increasing employment, and accelerating economic growth. For example, in 2002, Mexico introduced the rapid business opening system (SARE) to promote the market entry of potential businesses and output growth, and in 2005 Portugal introduced one-stop "On the Spot Firm" registration to facilitate market entry and job creation. In China, the government service environment is constantly being optimized, as reflected in reforms such as government service examination and approval, and business environment construction, along with the continued deepening the business environment construction, while numerous studies are also being performed. By examining government service halls that provide government service environments in China, studies have identified the process of extending the government service examination and approval reform and the factors involved in the establishment of these centers. Such studies have also empirically tested the hypothesis that establishing government service halls promotes market entry and innovation at the micro level, while promoting economic growth at the macro level.

On the basis of existing research, this study further elucidates the government-provided government service environment, so as to facilitate examining its impact on market players. As the main channel through which market

[2] The "Starting a Business" Index in the *Doing Business Report* published by the World Bank.

players deal with government departments, the government service environment provided by the government service halls greatly affects the institutional costs and sense of fulfillment of market players (such as enterprises and individual businesses) in the approval process, while also influencing their decisions. This in turn influences the effectiveness of "the people becoming innovators and entrepreneurs," and even economic growth. This study delved deep into the government service halls throughout China, and through on-site observations of the hardware, software and service levels there, the government service environment was given a total score, so as to examine the role of government service environment construction.

Regions with higher-ranking government service environments tended to have many market players. The business environment construction aims to reduce the institutional cost of the people being innovators and entrepreneurs. More comprehensive hardware and software facilities and higher work efficiency will reduce the time that potential market players need to register their businesses. Potential market players then respond to this and enter the market, thus promoting the formation of widespread entrepreneurship and stimulating the market. In Fig. 2.7, the horizontal axis is the government service environment score of the survey region, and the vertical axis shows the numbers of market players and enterprises. As can be clearly seen from the figure, the advantages and disadvantages of the government service environment are positively correlated with the number of market players, that is, regions with better government service environments have more market players.

Regions with better government service environments have many employment opportunities and high income levels. More market players lead to more jobs, while increased demand in the job market leads to higher wages. In Fig. 2.8, the horizontal axis is the government service environment score of the region studied, and the vertical axis shows the urban employment rate and average wage. It can be clearly seen from the figure that regions with better government service environments have higher employment rates and higher employee incomes.

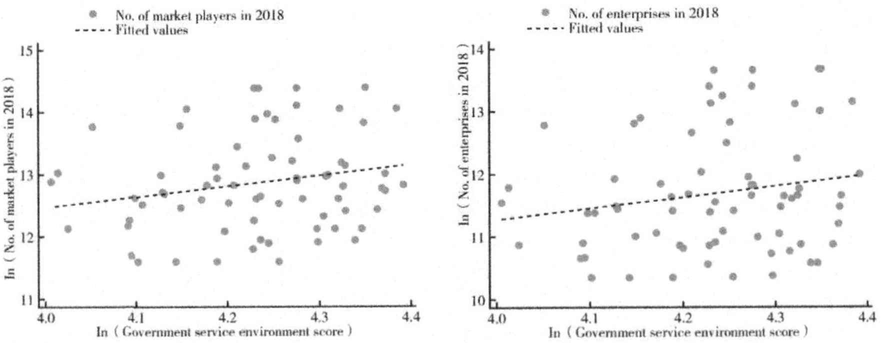

Fig. 2.7 A good government service environment means many market players. *Note* The government service environment score data are taken from the China Doing Business Survey, performed in the first half of 2018, and the market player data are from the business information collected by Qixin.com in 2018

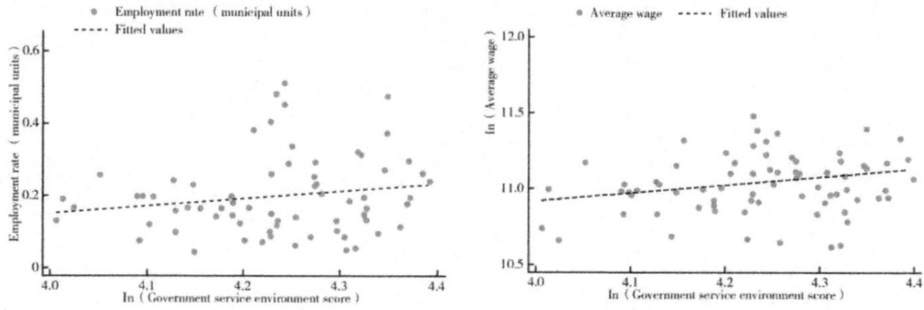

Fig. 2.8 A good government service environment means a high employment rate and high average wage. *Note* The government service environment score data are from the China Doing Business Survey for the first half of 2018, and the average wage data of employed and working employees are from the *China Urban Statistics Yearbook 2017*. The *China Urban Statistics Yearbook 2017* does not include data at the municipal level for municipalities directly under the Central Government, thus Beijing and Tianjin are not included in the figure

Regions with better government service environments have higher government fiscal revenues. An increase in the number of market players means an increase in the tax base, and thus an increase in government fiscal revenue. Figure 2.9 confirms the hypothesis that regions with better government service environments have higher fiscal revenues.

Promoting the market entry of enterprises at the micro level is bound to be conducive to economic growth at the macro level. Therefore, a better government service environment is related to a higher rate of economic growth. In Fig. 2.10,

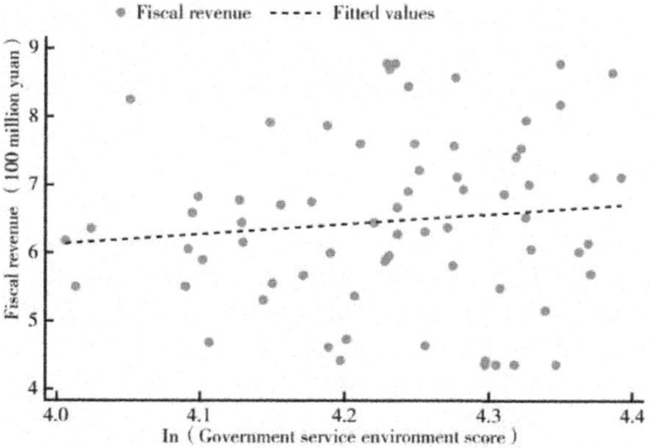

Fig. 2.9 A good government service environment yields higher fiscal revenue. *Note* The government service environment score data are from the China Doing Business Survey for the first half of 2018, and the fiscal revenue and GDP data are from the *China Regional Statistics Yearbook 2017*. The *China Urban Statistics Yearbook 2017* does not include data at the municipal level for municipalities directly under the Central Government, thus Beijing and Tianjin are not included in the figures

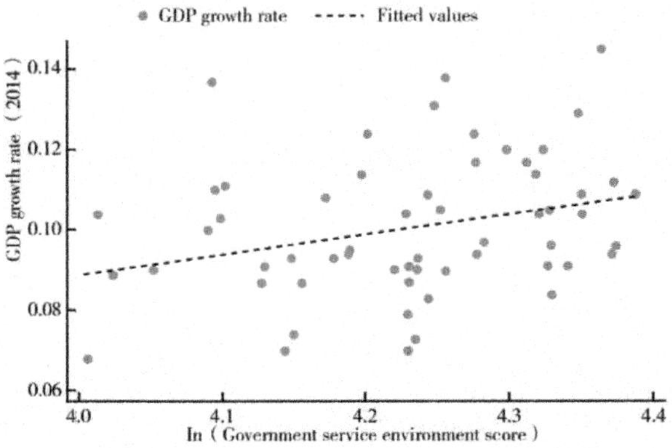

Fig. 2.10 A good government service environment leads to fast economic growth. *Note* The government service environment score data are from the China Doing Business Survey for the first half of 2018, and the fiscal revenue and GDP data are from the *China Regional Statistics Yearbook 2017*. The *China Urban Statistics Yearbook 2017* does not include data at the municipal level for municipalities directly under the Central Government, thus Beijing and Tianjin are not included in the figures

the horizontal axis is the survey region's government service environment score, and the vertical axis is the GDP growth rate. Regions with better government service environments have faster economic growth.

The positive responses we received from market players regarding entrepreneurship during our field survey provided us with further evidence. For example, a young woman in Hangzhou showed interest in our survey. At first, she was not aware of the business reform system, but when we explained what "five permits in one" was, she was pleasantly surprised: "Oh, it's that easy to apply for a business license now? In that case, I think I'll try opening my own store later this year." In Dongying, Shandong, an interviewee said, "It's now much easier to start a business on your own with a few like-minded friends and colleagues. You can do everything yourself. There are more opportunities for young people, and it's a world where you can show what you're capable of." Administration services staff in Jiaocheng District of Ningde, Fujian came up with creative ways to support entrepreneurship and innovation. They set up an government service hall next to the University Student Entrepreneurship Park, and opened a fast track channel to help university students start businesses. The results of the field survey show that the promotion of the business and government service environment construction has to a certain extent driven potential businesspeople to engage in entrepreneurship and innovation.

2.6 Main Problems in Constructing the Government Service Environment

(1) **Poor hardware facilities**

Hardware facilities are the first point of contact at government service halls. As the head of one government service hall told us during our survey, "The government service hall is the face of the city, so it must be done properly." However, judging from the results of the nationwide survey, problems such as incomplete hardware facilities, inconvenience in use and lack of comfort remain in some regions.

A government service hall in a district in the eastern region where there are no seats.

Not enough seats in a district in the central region.

Government service halls in some regions lack some hardware facilities. This is evidenced by the fact that nationwide, 20% of government service halls are not equipped with waiting number machines, 22% do not have operable computers, 25% do not have LED displays, and 52% do not provide standardized photo services. For example, in a government service hall in the eastern region, the lighting throughout the hall was very poor, and even if the lights were on during the day, the hall was very dark. There were also no waiting number machines, no air conditioning, and no seats by the service windows, and staff brought their own fans. As for the visitors there, they had to bear the high temperature as they stood—hunched over uncomfortably—at the service window and talked to the staff.

In some regions, the hardware facilities in government service halls are not sufficiently convenient and comfortable: 18% of government service halls did not have enough waiting seats for everyone, 26% provided seats that were not comfortable enough, and 26% did not have drinking water facilities. In a district in the eastern region, although the government service hall had drinking water facilities and washrooms, they were in the office area on the second floor, not near the service windows on the first floor. In a district in the central region, the government service space was small, and people had to line up at the door. There were also not enough waiting seats, and the seats in front of the service windows were quite low, further adding to the overall poor level of comfort.

(2) **Unclear procedure instructions**

In some regions, the instructions for completing tasks are unclear, there are no forms or templates, and the service window staff are poorly trained. Specifically, 8% of government service halls did not detail the basic procedures for completing tasks, 11% did not have inquiry staff, 28% did not provide templates for filling forms, and 46% did not publicly commit to completion times. A common sentiment among people who went there to complete tasks was "Just tell me all at once what materials I need to bring, and how to fill in the form and revise it."

At one district in the eastern region, templates for filling in the forms were completely absent.

At another district in the same region, there were no guidelines for how to use the self-serve stations.

First, some government service halls did not detail the processes or provide templates for filling in forms. For example, in one district in the eastern region, the form filling templates were not provided. In another district in the same region, one person, believing that there were no instructions for the self-serve station or form filling templates, complained it was difficult to get things done, saying, "Why doesn't it say where to write our full names and where to write our initials? I did it wrong, and now I have to start over again." However, it must be clarified that in some regions, the lack of instructions and templates may be a drawback of the new "paperless office" policy. In a province in the central region, through our on-site interviews with staff and visitors, our researchers learned that the province had implemented a new paperless office policy. At paperless government service halls, it is no longer necessary to complete paper forms or submit paper materials, thus they no longer provide form filling templates. This to a certain extent gave our researchers a first-hand observation of unclear task completion instructions.

In addition to the lack of clarity caused by the absence of detailed instructions and templates, a more prominent and widespread problem nationwide is that inquiry and service window staff could not provide clear instructions and answers to questions. Specifically, there were three manifestations of this: First, the window staff themselves were not highly skilled, and lacked familiarity with the procedures. For example, in a district in the eastern region, visitors said that the new staff were not familiar with the registration process: "There are four windows open, but only the section chief at this one really knows what they're doing. The rest of the staff are new, and it's tough for them to get things done. They don't really know what they're doing, and they all tell you to prepare different things, so now I only go to the section chief's window." Researchers in a city in the eastern region observed that "reform is fast, but learning is slow." In June 2018, some authority had just been delegated there to facilitate people completing tasks. However, the window staff at the government service hall were not very familiar with this area of work, which ended up only making matters worse. **Second, the window clerks did not inform the visitors of all the required steps and materials at one time**. For example, in a city in the eastern region, an interviewee said, "The staff only tell you what materials you need for the current step, and don't tell you about the whole process all at once, so you end up having to make multiple trips." In a city in the eastern region, two men who had traveled there from Guangzhou to open a company were on their fifth or sixth visit, and still were not done. When we asked them the reason for this, they said, "First, we didn't call in advance to ask about the procedures, and second, the clerk here only told us half of what we needed to know. One clerk said we were missing one thing, and had to go get it and come back, then another clerk said we were missing something else. If they just told us what we needed at the beginning, we wouldn't have had to come here so many times." **Third, some government service hall staff were unfriendly**. For example, one person in a city in the eastern region said that the staff were "kind of mean." In a district in the western region, a woman with poor hearing had to ask the clerk to repeat what they had said several times, upon which the clerk grew impatient. And one person in a district in the western region even told the researchers that the work efficiency there was closely tied to the clerk's mood on a given day, and was uncontrollable.

(3) **Mismatch between service window supply and demand**

There are two situations where supply and demand do not correspond: one is that supply exceeds demand, that is, there are too many open windows, and too few market players, resulting in many windows being idle; and the other is that supply does not reach demand, namely there are not enough windows, making it difficult for market players to obtain wait numbers, and there are long wait and processing times.

Idle service hall windows in a district in the eastern

A crowded waiting room in a district in the eastern

The number of windows in some regions exceeds demand. During the field survey, our researchers observed that many office halls were completely empty, with no visitors at any of the windows, such as at the government service hall of a district in the eastern region. This particular hall had been transformed from a real estate office. The rectangular lobby was very spacious, and among the 28 service windows arranged in a row on either side of the lobby, 16 of them processed business-related tasks. At the other was a waiting area composed of four rows of five white leather seats. However, as can be seen from the above photo, there were only one or two service windows at the entrance where people could inquire and process tasks. Therefore, the supply of service windows far exceeded demand, thus exhibiting inefficient resource allocation.

In some places there were not enough service windows. For example, in a district in the eastern region, where the wait times were long, an interviewee reluctantly showed our researchers all the wait numbers she had taken: over 60 in total. She had collected all these because both service windows and waiting seats were so short in supply. As another example, in a different district of the same region, only five of the more than 20 service windows in the hall were for processing industrial and commercial tasks. Among them, the license issue and exchange window had been temporarily suspended during our visit. Even if all the business windows had been open, some people would still have had to wait 2 or 3 h, and one woman we interviewed said she had been waiting from the morning till the afternoon. Several interviewees in this district reflected as follows: "It doesn't take long to get things done once you're at the window, but it takes forever for them to call your number. It's mainly because there aren't enough windows, but also they only give out 15 wait numbers at a time, and only start to give out the next batch once those 15 are gone, so you have no idea how long you'll have to wait."

(4) Only 30% of market players completed all tasks in one visit

The logical starting point of the "streamlining, delegating and strengthening" reform is the people-centered concept of development. It aims to promote a shift from facilitating government management to facilitating people in completing the tasks they need, and building a service-oriented government. The specific goals of the 2018 reform are that enterprise representatives can complete all the tasks they need at one place, and in a single visit. The responses from our interviewees show that, in the first half of 2018, an average of 30% of market players completed all their business tasks in one visit, while 68% completed everything at one window. During each visit, it took an average of 1.4 h to complete a single task. This clearly signifies that the reform goals have not been met, and that visitors there are not satisfied.

Zhejiang's catchphrase: "Get everything done in one visit," and Huzhou, Zhejiang's: "No visit necessary."

Zhejiang, which pioneered the goal of completing all tasks in one visit, is now on its way to not requiring its market players to make even a single visit. Our study data show that, in the first half of 2018, 44% of market players in Zhejiang completed all the business tasks they needed in a single visit. While this is higher than the national average of 30%, it is still quite a way behind the goal of 100%. In a city in the eastern region, businesspeople generally reported that in most cases they needed to make "multiple trips." Some also said that some cities had a prerequisite for businesspeople completing all tasks in one visit, namely that they must arrive with all their required materials, otherwise they would have to make multiple trips.

2.7 Potential Directions of Deepening the Government Service Environment Construction

Our study results show that, nationwide, the hardware facilities and software facilities required for the government service environment construction are basically complete overall, yet the service field is generally inadequate. The business environment construction has confronted prominent issues and key problems that have plagued the management and service reform for many years, thus the reform has grasped and promoted the necessary matters to fulfill the hopes and expectations of the people. After assessing the prominent problems faced in the government service environment construction pointed out above, and China's new economic and social development situation, the reforms require deepening in the following three aspects.

(1) **Hardware must be improved**

Insufficient hardware directly affects both the first impression of businesspeople visiting to complete tasks and work efficiency. In some parts of China there are significant shortcomings in terms of hardware construction, along with incomplete performance facilities, and equipment being either lacking or difficult to use. For example, a district in the eastern region urgently needed basic seating and air conditioning to provide a comfortable environment for visitors. Another district in the central region needed to add seats to meet the number of the businesspeople there, and to improve the comfort level of the seats. In addition, nearly half of the of the government service halls nationwide did not provide standardized photo services. Overcoming these drawbacks is clearly one of the directions for deepening the construction of the government service environment nationwide.

(2) **Software must be upgraded**

Some of the common problems faced nationwide are the lack of clarity in the steps required to complete tasks, too many or too few service windows, and the difficulty in improving businesspeople's sense of fulfillment. Judging from the current situation, improvements in the following three areas must be made: **First, clarify all required steps, and provide paper-based or electronic guidelines of them, along with form filling templates**. For example, at a government service hall in the central region that was "going paperless," during its transition from offline to online approval, paper-based process lists and templates were still provided. **Second, increase the training of service window staff to ensure that they provide businesspeople with the information they need**. Our survey study results show that the service window staff were not highly knowledgeable, which directly affected the rates of only needing to inquire once and completing all tasks in one visit. Therefore, it is urgent to strengthen the training of window staff regarding business tasks. Each service window staff member must be familiar with the entire procedure, and able to immediately answer any questions market players may have. **Third, supply service windows in proportion to demand**. The excessive number of service windows in a district in the eastern region wastes government services resources, while the shortage thereof in another district in the same region leads to difficulty in obtaining wait numbers, and long wait times. Therefore, in terms of software elements, setting the number of service windows according to the actual situation and adjusting the number of clerks based on appointments and other means is one direction of further improvement.

(3) **Breakthroughs must be made in service**

The main reasons for poor service are that businesspeople must make many trips and visit numerous windows. In this regard, some breakthroughs have already been made since the 2018 reform. On March 20, 2018, at the NPC & CPPCC National Committee annual sessions (the "Two Sessions"), Premier Keqiang proposed the "Six Ones" goals of the "streamlining, delegating and strengthening" reform. In terms of "completing all tasks in one visit," the best-performing region (Baishan, Jilin) scored 75%, yet the national average was only 30%. This means that many regions throughout the country have yet to achieve this goal, and no new breakthroughs have been made in this regard. As for "single-window processing," the best-performing regions (Pu'er, Yunnan and Guyuan, Ningxia) achieved 100%, yet the national average was 60%, which means that 97% of regions have yet to reach the target. Therefore, only by confronting the difficulties and pain points that businesspeople encounter in completing tasks and effectively implementing the Central Government's regulation and service reform measures can we hope to make new breakthroughs in deepening the construction of the government service environment.

Chapter 3
Construction of the "Digital Government"

Qingmiao Bi, Yun Zhou, and Xianxiang Xu

The construction of a digital government is an important decision and deployment of the CPC Central Committee and State Council. The report of the 19th National Congress of the Party proposed to strengthen the construction of a "digital China." Later, the 2018 government work report once again emphasized the promotion of "Internet + government services." Throughout this time, China's construction of a digital government has continued to advance, taking digital government as a starting point from which to improve the business environment, enhance market players' sense of fulfillment, and develop a high-quality service economy.

Based on the responses from the questionnaires completed by 8,293 market players, whom we interviewed in 110 cities across twenty-four provinces, this report evaluates the construction of China's digital government. In this report, the term digital government collectively refers to online service halls, mobile service platforms, and other business service channels. We constructed an indicator system from the three dimensions of digital government potential usage rate, actual awareness rate, and actual usage rate. We then systematically analyzed the accomplishments made and issues faced by the nationwide digital government as of August 2019. Finally, we proposed several potential directions in which to further deepen the demand-side construction of digital government (see Table 3.1).

The report shows that China's digital government construction has enormous potential demand. It has already entered the stage of large-scale awareness, and is progressing toward the that of large-scale use. As shown in Table 3.1, China's digital government construction had an average score of seventy-one points (level

Q. Bi · X. Xu (✉)
Lingnan College, Sun Yat-sen University, Guangzhou, China
e-mail: lnsxuxx@mail.sysu.edu.cn

Institute of Mezzoeconomics, Sun Yat-sen University, Guangzhou, China

Y. Zhou
School of Business, Sun Yat-sen University, Guangzhou, China

X. Xu et al. (eds.), *Report on the Chinese Business Environment Survey 2020*, Research Series on the Chinese Dream and China's Development Path,
https://doi.org/10.1007/978-981-99-6112-2_3

Table 3.1 Indicator system for demand-side construction of China's digital government and latest progress as of 2019

Metric	Score	Rating	Maximum	Minimum
Level 1 indicator				
Total digital government construction score	71	B	95	35
Level 2 indicators				
(1) Digital government potential usage score	92	A	100	74
(2) Digital government actual awareness score	69	C	95	18
(3) Digital government actual usage score	53	D	90	13

Note Maximum and Minimum refer to the maximum and minimum values among the 110 cities covered by the survey. The rating criteria are as follows: A: eighty-five to 100 points, B: seventy to eighty-four points, C: sixty to sixty-nine, and D: sixty points or fewer. The total score is the average of the three secondary indicators
Source Sun Yat-sen University Research Group on "Deepening the Reform of the Business System."

B). Among the scores, the digital government potential usage rate had a score of ninety-two (level A). This shows that market players are strongly willing to use digital government, and it has a solid foundation for development. The digital government actual awareness rate had a score of sixty-nine (level C), showing that digital government has entered the large-scale awareness stage. The digital government actual usage rate had a score of fifty-three points (level D), thus it is currently progressing toward the stage of large-scale use.

At present, the main issue in the demand-side of digital government construction is that it is inadequate and imbalanced. First, thirty-nine percent of potential demand has not been met, and the demand-side of the digital government construction remains insufficient. Among all market players, thirty-one percent said they were unaware of digital government, thus publicity work is insufficient; thirty-four percent said that digital government services were incomplete, thus service construction is insufficient; and twenty-six percent said that digital government could not handle all the steps in the procedure, showing that process construction is insufficient. Second, there is an imbalance in the demand-side of the digital government construction. Looking at the progress in various regions, six percent of local and municipal digital governments were at level A, fifty-six percent were at level B, twenty-two percent were at level C, and seventeen percent were at level D.

We recommend four directions for further deepening the demand-side of the digital government construction. First, pay attention to the demand-side construction of the digital government, further increase efforts to actively promote the digital government, and raise the digital government awareness rate. Second, accelerate the supply-side construction of the digital government, increase the supply of digital government services, promote whole-process digital government services, and continue to raise the digital government usage rate. Third, promote balanced development between regions through the standardization of digital government. Fourth, promote the integrated development of online and offline government services.

3.1 Nationwide Progress of the "Digital Government" Construction

This section examines the demand-side construction of China's digital government from the four dimensions of desire to use, awareness, use, and ease of use. Judging from the market players' responses, the demand-side construction of China's digital government has already entered the stage of large-scale awareness, and is progressing toward the stage of large-scale use.

(1) **Ninety-three percent of market players believe that digital government is the general trend**

As shown in Fig. 3.1, when asked if they thought digital government was a general trend in government services, ninety-three percent of market players nationwide responded that they believed so, five percent said they were unsure, and only two percent did not think so. This shows that market players nationwide generally agree that the construction of a digital government is the general trend.

Market players believe that the development of digital government can make things more convenient, and thus acknowledge that digital government is the general trend. In Xinyang, Henan, a representative of a market player preparing to open an agricultural products trading company and applying for an industrial and commercial business license expressed surprise and joy regarding the changes that digital government had brought about: "You used to have to make lots of trips to start a business, but now it's done online, so it hardly takes any time at all." In Hongshan District of Wuhan, Hubei, one market player said, "I applied for a business license, and everything was all done online. It took very little time, and I've never had to visit the service hall. From the online application on the computer to receiving the package via courier, I got everything done in one go." In Tongnan District of Chongqing, many

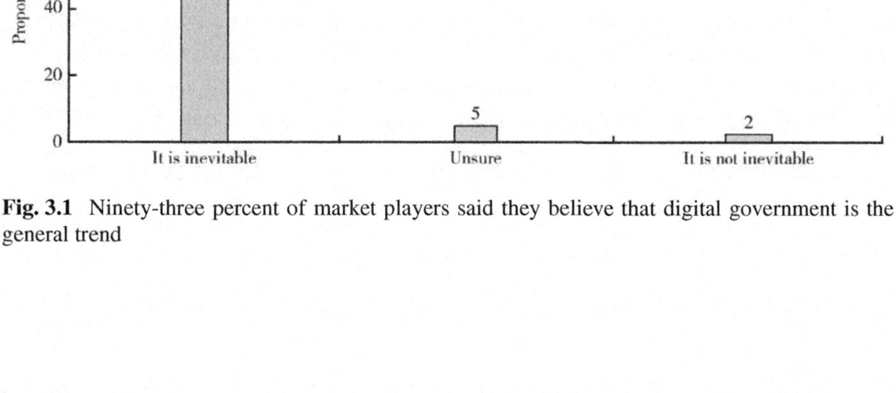

Fig. 3.1 Ninety-three percent of market players said they believe that digital government is the general trend

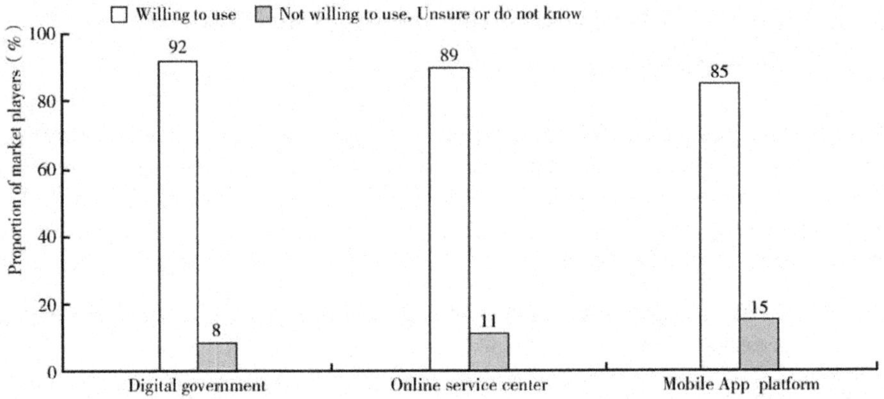

Fig. 3.2 Ninety-two percent of market players said they are willing to use digital government

market players also said, "It's much more convenient than before. Now lots of things can be done online, it's really convenient."

(2) **Ninety-two percent of market players expressed their willingness to use digital government**

As shown in Fig. 3.2, if business-related tasks can be done through digital government, then on average ninety-two percent of market players nationwide said they were willing to use it. Among them, eighty-nine percent said they would use the online service halls, while eighty-five percent would use the mobile apps. This shows that there is great potential market demand for digital government construction, and most market players nationwide are willing to use digital government.

Market players are willing to use digital government because it saves them time and money. In Zaozhuang, Shandong, when asked why there were so few staff in the lobby, one market player responded as follows: "It's becoming easier to do business tasks online. Lots of people can do everything online, so they don't need to come to the service hall." When the researchers asked if they believed completing business tasks by computer or mobile phone was a general trend, most of them said yes: "Definitely! It's so convenient, who would want to have to come here?" In Jieyang, Guangdong, market players said that if the government could accelerate the promotion of online government services, then it would make things more convenient, because having to make numerous trips takes up much of their time, and they are very willing to give online government services a try. The interviewees' responses show that, if it is indeed convenient to do business-related tasks through digital government, then the vast majority of market players would be strongly willing to use it.

(3) **Sixty-nine percent of market players are aware of digital government**

In this report, the digital government the awareness rate is defined as the Proportion of market players who know about it. As shown in Fig. 3.3, the national average digital

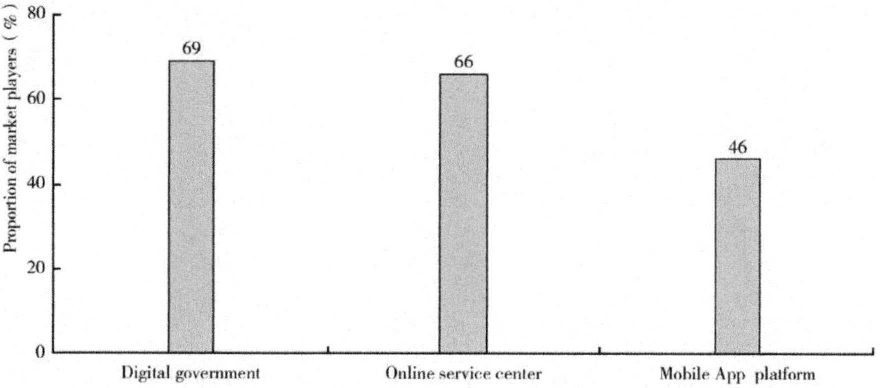

Fig. 3.3 Sixty-nine percent of market players said they are aware of digital government

government awareness rate was sixty-nine percent, among which the awareness rate of online office halls was sixty-six percent, and that of mobile apps was forty-six percent.

(4) **About sixty percent of market players learned of digital government from government departments**

The active promotion of government departments is currently the main way that market players learn about digital government. As shown in Fig. 3.4, forty-six percent of market players said they had learned about online service halls through the staff there, while fifteen percent said they had learned about them from advertisements. Thus a total of sixty-one percent of market players had learned about the online service halls through active promotion by functional departments. In addition, forty-four percent of market players who had learned about the mobile apps through the service hall staff, and sixteen percent through advertisements, for a total of sixty percent. This shows that active promotion by government departments has played a major role in increasing the digital government awareness rate.

In Zibo, Shandong, when asked how they had learned that the entire process could be done digitally, one market player responded as such: "The clerk told me. I had come here before, and the window clerk told me I could do it on my computer. There was also a lot of information to read in the service hall, and it wasn't that hard to follow the process." In Jilin, our researchers discovered during the interviews that most market players were aware they could complete business-related tasks online, and most had learned so through service hall staff.

Nearly twenty percent of market players had learned about digital government from friends. This shows that digital government has a good reputation: market players who have experience with it find it easy to use, then they recommend it to other market players, thus boosting the awareness rate.

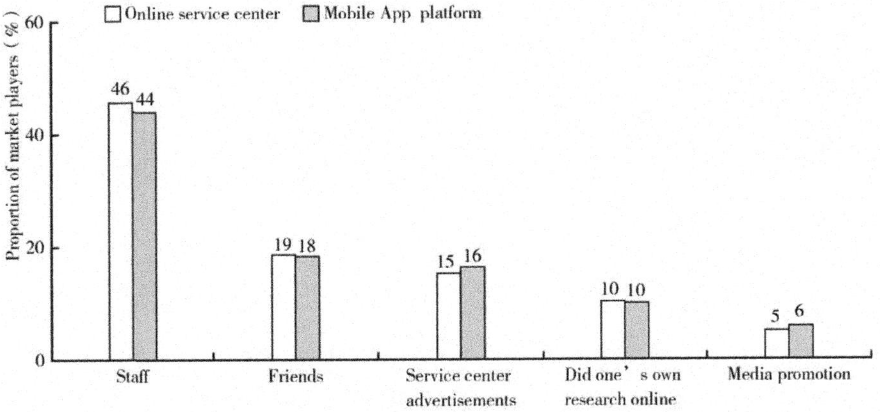

Fig. 3.4 Sixty percent of market players had heard about digital government through active promotion by government departments. *Note* Another six percent of market players had learned about digital government through other channels

(5) Fifty-three percent of market players use digital government

This study defines usage rate as the proportion of market players who use digital government. As Fig. 3.5 shows, the national average digital government usage rate was fifty-three percent. Among all market players, forty-eight percent said they used online offices to complete business-related tasks, while twenty-six percent said they used the mobile apps. This shows that, among the market players using digital government platforms, the online service hall, which was developed earlier, has now become the method by which nearly half of the market players complete business tasks. The mobile service platform—the channel most promoted in recent years—has also achieved remarkable results, with nearly thirty percent of market players having already chosen to use it.

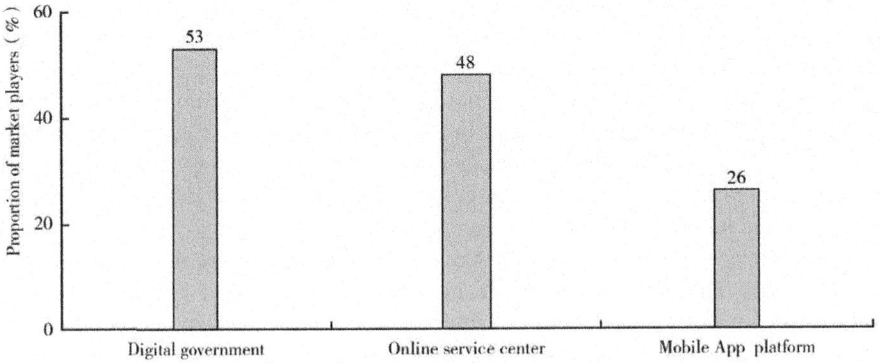

Fig. 3.5 Fifty-three percent of market players said they use digital government

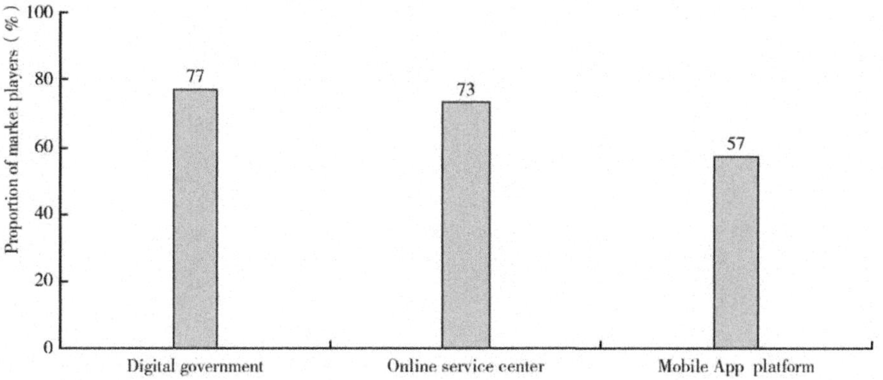

Fig. 3.6 The digital government appeal rate was 77%

In this study, the appeal rate is defined as the proportion of market players aware of digital government who find using it appealing, that is, the ratio of the digital government usage rate to awareness rate. As Fig. 3.6 shows, the nationwide appeal rate of digital government was seventy-seven percent (53% ÷ 69%), that is, among market players who were aware of digital government, seventy-seven percent said they choose to use it. More specifically, the appeal rate of online service halls was seventy-three percent (48% ÷ 66%), and that of the mobile app was fifty-seven percent (26% ÷ 46%).

(6) **Thirty to forty percent of market players commonly use a business service system**

At the 2018 press conference, Premier Li Keqiang proposed the "Six Ones" reform goals. Among them, "one network" signifies single-network access for government services. As shown in Fig. 3.7, thirty-one percent of market players nationwide said they only needed to use the computer-based service system when handling business affairs, while forty-four percent said they only needed to use the mobile service system. The fewer computer or mobile systems needed to handle business affairs, the more intensive the functions of the online processing system, the easier it is to operate, and thus the higher the market players' sense of fulfillment.

(7) **Forty-six percent of market players use the digital government service functions**

As shown in Fig. 3.8, the three online service office functions of processing business-related tasks, inquiry and reservation show imbalanced development. Among the market players who use online office halls, most use it for specific services, accounting for forty-six percent, while market players who inquire about service information and make reservations respectively account for thirty-four percent and eighteen percent.

Meanwhile, the development of the same three functions in the mobile apps is relatively balanced. The numbers of market players who handle specific business affairs

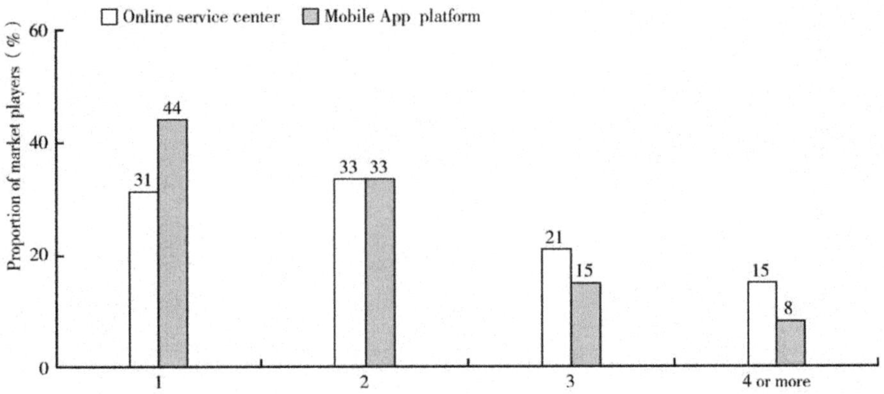

Fig. 3.7 Thirty to forty percent of market players said they use the digital government services system

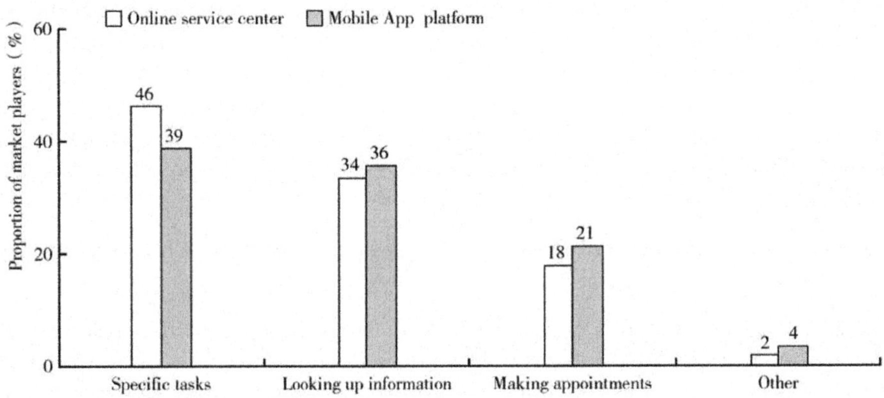

Fig. 3.8 Market players mainly use digital government to process business-related tasks and make inquiries and reservations

and inquire about service information are roughly equal, respectively accounting for thirty-nine percent and thirty-six percent, while twenty-one percent use the mobile platforms to make reservations.

(8) Sixty-eight percent of market players believe that digital government cannot completely replace physical service windows

As shown in Fig. 3.9, when market players were asked if they believed that digital government could completely replace window processing, a national average of sixty-eight percent said they believed that it could not. This shows that, while ninety-three percent of market players believe that digital government is the general trend, and ninety-two percent are willing to use it, most believe that physical service halls are still irreplaceable.

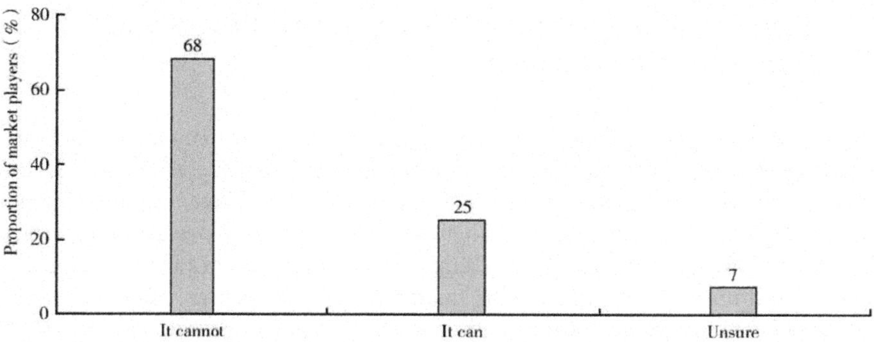

Fig. 3.9 Sixty-eight percent of market players said they believe that digital government cannot completely replace physical service windows

Market players believe that physical service windows are more reliable and caring when doing business affairs, and thus cannot be completely replaced. For example, in Xianning, Hubei, some market players who were unaware of or did not use digital government said they preferred to deal with staff compared to machines and online services. In Hanzhong, Shaanxi, a market player who had not chosen to use online services told us, "I'll just take a look at what I need online. Having someone to guide you in person is much more reassuring."

(9) **Summary of this section**

The above analysis shows that digital government possesses great potential demand, and is currently in a stage of potential rapid development. At this stage, the demand-side construction of digital government is in the large-scale awareness stage, and is progressing toward the stage of large-scale use. The details are as follows.

A total of ninety-three percent of market players said they think that digital government is the general trend, and ninety-two percent were willing to use it.

The awareness rate of digital government was sixty-nine percent, showing that it has entered the large-scale awareness stage. Specifically, the awareness rate of online service halls was sixty-six percent, while that of mobile apps was forty-six percent. A total of sixty-one percent of market players had learned about digital government through active publicity and promotion by government departments.

The usage rate of digital government was fifty-three percent, thus having entered the stage of large-scale use. Specifically, the online service hall usage rate was forty-eight percent, and the mobile app usage rate was twenty-six percent. The digital government appeal rate was seventy-seven percent, that is, seventy-seven percent of market players who knew about digital government used it.

In terms of the development relationship between digital government and physical service windows, sixty-eight percent of market players said they believe that digital government cannot completely replace physical service windows.

3.2 Progress of the "Nationwide Administrative Services Platform" Construction

The nationwide government service platform refers to the nationally integrated administrative service platform that was put into trial operation by the General Office of the State Council in June 2019. Its goal is to accelerate the implementation of single-network access and offsite processing of business-related government services nationwide, thus offering convenience to market players and improving their sense of fulfillment. According to the market players' responses, after one month, the awareness rate reached twenty-eight percent, and the usage rate reached sixteen percent.

(1) **Twenty-eight percent of market players are aware of the nationwide government service platform**

As shown in Fig. 3.10, twenty-eight percent of China's market players are aware of the nationwide government service platform. In the one month from its launch in June 2019 to the time of the survey in July 2019, nearly thirty percent of all market players knew about the nationwide government service platform, a remarkable result.

(2) **Sixteen percent of market players use the nationwide administrative service platform**

As shown in Fig. 3.10, sixteen percent of market players use the nationwide administrative service platform. This study defines the appeal rate as the proportion of market players who know about the nationwide government service platform to those who use it, that is, the ratio between the usage rate and awareness rate of the nationwide government service platform. The appeal rate of the nationwide government service platform was fifty-seven percent (16% ÷ 28%), which means that, among market

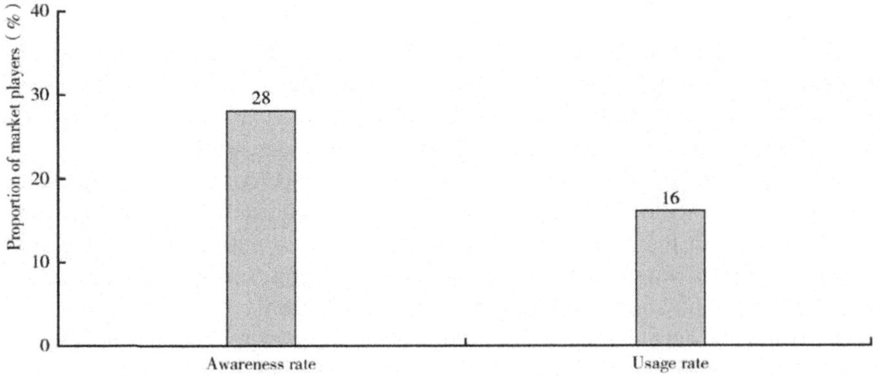

Fig. 3.10 The awareness rate of the nationwide government service platform was twenty-eight percent, and the usage rate was sixteen percent

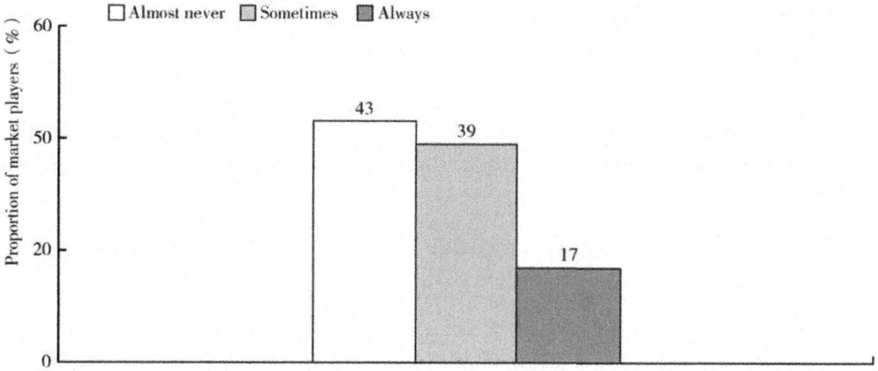

Fig. 3.11 Among market players who knew about the nationwide government service platform, seventeen percent always used it

players who knew about the nationwide government service platform, fifty-seven percent chose to use it.

(3) **Among the market players who know about the nationwide government service platform, seventeen percent always use it**

As shown in Fig. 3.11, among the market players who knew about the nationwide government service platform, seventeen percent used it every time they needed to complete business-related tasks, while thirty-nine percent used it occasionally, and forty-three percent seldom used it.

(4) **Summary of this section**

According to the above analysis, in the one month from the trial operation in June 2019 to the research period in July 2019, the nationwide government service platform achieved remarkable results. The details are as follows.

The awareness rate of the nationwide government service platform reached twenty-eight percent. Although a recent innovation, the nationwide administrative service platform achieved a twenty-eight percent awareness rate in just one month of trial operation, thus showing it has a strong foundation for development.

The usage rate of the nationwide government service platform was sixteen percent, and the appeal rate was fifty-seven percent, that is, fifty-seven percent of market players who know about the nationwide government service platform choose to use it.

Of the market players who know about the nationwide government service platform, seventeen percent always use it, and thirty-nine percent use it occasionally.

3.3 Progress of the "Digital Government" Construction in Various Regions

This section examines the progress of the demand-side construction of digital government in 110 cities across China, the respective scores of which are shown in Table 3.3.

(1) **The total score for the demand-side construction of digital government in various regions is mainly at level B**

As shown in Fig. 3.12 and Table 3.2, six cities reached level A (eighty-five to 100 points), accounting for about six percent of the total; fifty-nine cities were at level B (seventy to eighty-four points), accounting for fifty-six percent; twenty-three cities were at C level (sixty to sixty-nine points), accounting for twenty-two percent; and eighteen cities were at level D (below sixty points), accounting for about seventeen percent. Among the 110 cities, that which scored the highest in terms of digital government demand-side construction reached ninety-five points, while the lowest score was forty-two. The top six cities, in order, were Zhaotong, Beijing, Huzhou, Zhejiang, Pu'er, Hangzhou and Shenzhen (see Table 3.3).

(2) **The potential usage rate of digital government everywhere is mainly at level A**

As shown in Fig. 3.13 and Table 3.2, six cities achieved a perfect score of 100 in terms of the potential usage rate of digital government, namely Zhaotong, Hangzhou, Yuxi, Huanggang, Qinzhou and Yulin. A total of ninety-four cities reached level A, eleven reached level B, one was at level C, and none were at level D. In terms of proportion, cities at levels A, B, C and D respectively accounted for eighty-nine percent, ten percent, one percent and zero percent of the total, and the potential usage rate of digital government in the vast majority of cities was level A.

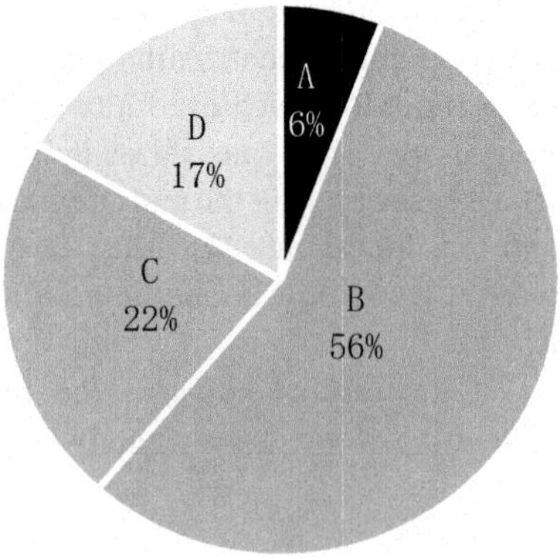

Fig. 3.12 Fifty-six percent of cities had level B demand-side construction of digital government

Table 3.2 Scores and rankings for the construction of digital government in 110 cities China

City	Score	Level	Ranking	Level 2 indicators			City	Score	Level	Ranking	Level 2 indicators		
				Potential usage	Actual awareness	Actual usage					Potential usage	Actual awareness	Actual usage
Zhaotong	95	A	1	100	94	90	Yuncheng	71	B	53	88	69	57
Beijing	89	A	2	98	90	80	Haikou	71	B	53	93	67	52
Huzhou	87	A	3	89	95	77	Zhangye	71	B	53	92	71	49
Pu'er	87	A	3	92	90	79	Hengyang	71	B	53	90	71	52
Hangzhou	85	A	5	100	83	72	Yinchuan	71	B	53	90	73	48
Shenzhen	85	A	5	99	86	70	Yancheng	70	B	61	85	71	56
Changsha	84	B	7	93	87	73	Suizhou	70	B	61	97	67	48
Pingliang	84	B	7	93	90	70	Bengbu	70	B	61	88	66	56
Baishan	84	B	7	97	89	66	Shijiazhuang	70	B	61	97	66	46
Ningbo	84	B	7	96	87	68	Jinan	70	B	61	94	66	49
Qingdao	83	B	11	93	81	76	Yichang	69	C	66	85	73	50
Xuchang	83	B	11	91	85	73	Suzhou	69	C	66	95	67	45
Jiuquan	83	B	11	94	91	64	Huaihua	69	C	66	97	59	50
Hefei	82	B	14	96	82	69	Bijie	69	C	66	94	70	42
Hanzhong	82	B	14	94	91	61	Changzhou	68	C	70	93	63	48
Fuyang	81	B	16	94	82	67	Zhoushan	67	C	71	91	65	46
Qujing	81	B	16	93	79	69	Changde	67	C	71	82	66	54
Changchun	80	B	18	96	81	63	Chongqing	67	C	71	92	63	45
Luoyang	80	B	18	95	79	66	Lanzhou	67	C	71	94	57	49
Xi'an	79	B	20	95	80	64	Taiyuan	66	C	75	91	60	48

(continued)

Table 3.2 (continued)

City	Score	Level	Ranking	Level 2 indicators			City	Score	Level	Ranking	Level 2 indicators		
				Potential usage	Actual awareness	Actual usage					Potential usage	Actual awareness	Actual usage
Yuxi	79	B	20	100	75	63	Shanghai	66	C	75	98	61	41
Putian	79	B	20	97	78	62	Quanzhou	66	C	75	92	60	46
Qinzhou	78	B	23	100	76	59	Nanjing	66	C	75	85	64	49
Wuhan	78	B	23	90	79	65	Liuzhou	66	C	75	96	63	38
Zhengzhou	78	B	23	81	83	68	Zhanjiang	65	C	80	93	63	41
Huanggang	77	B	26	100	71	60	Quzhou	65	C	80	92	63	40
Kunming	77	B	26	92	77	61	Jingmen	65	C	80	94	58	42
Guiyang	77	B	26	96	73	61	Guangdong	64	C	83	84	61	46
Binzhou	77	B	26	90	80	60	Yulin	62	C	84	83	60	42
Xinyang	76	B	30	97	74	59	Songyuan	61	C	85	94	66	24
Zunyi	76	B	30	96	74	58	Guigang	61	C	85	91	54	37
Fangchenggang	76	B	30	86	81	62	Datong	60	C	87	88	54	38
Jilin	76	B	30	96	74	58	Zibo	60	C	87	88	55	36
Xuzhou	76	B	30	90	73	65	Tangshan	59	D	89	78	57	43
Suqian	76	B	30	85	78	63	Shaoguan	59	D	89	88	52	38
Fuzhou	76	B	30	93	76	59	Dongying	59	D	89	87	59	32
Wuhu	75	B	37	96	74	56	Xining	59	D	89	93	51	32
Tianjin	75	B	37	94	74	57	Ningde	58	D	93	93	51	29
Jiayuguan	74	B	39	82	72	69	Chaozhou	57	D	94	95	39	37

(continued)

Table 3.2 (continued)

City	Score	Level	Ranking	Level 2 indicators			City	Score	Level	Ranking	Level 2 indicators		
				Potential usage	Actual awareness	Actual usage					Potential usage	Actual awareness	Actual usage
Shaoyang	74	B	39	86	78	59	Yangjiang	57	D	94	85	52	32
Zhoukou	74	B	39	95	77	50	Siping	57	D	94	91	45	33
Jinhua	74	B	39	86	74	62	Tongchuan	56	D	97	69	65	35
Taizhou	74	B	39	95	71	55	Guyuan	56	D	97	88	56	25
Ankang	74	B	39	94	78	49	Zhangjiakou	55	D	99	94	44	27
Xianning	73	B	45	80	78	61	Langfang	55	D	99	88	45	30
Yulin	73	B	45	100	70	48	Tongling	53	D	101	97	38	25
Yueyang	73	B	45	95	64	59	Hengshui	53	D	101	82	50	26
Huaibei	73	B	45	92	74	52	Wuzhong	52	D	103	74	55	26
Luohe	73	B	45	83	75	60	Chengde	52	D	103	87	39	29
Jiangmen	72	B	50	97	67	53	Sanming	47	D	105	86	39	17
Anyang	72	B	50	92	68	56	Jieyang	42	D	106	95	18	13
Longnan	72	B	50	83	73	60	Changzhi						
Nanning	71	B	53	96	63	55	Lüliang						
Lishui	71	B	53	91	77	46	Zaozhuang						
Ezhou	71	B	53	88	74	52	Chongzuo						

Note The rating criteria are as follows: level A: eighty-five to 100 points, level B: seventy to eighty-four points, level C: sixty to sixty-nine points, and level D: sixty points or less. The total score is the average of the three secondary indicators. The sample size of the following cities did not reach thirty, thus no score was calculated: Changzhi, Lüliang, Zaozhuang, and Chongzuo

Source Research Group on "Deepening the Business System Reform"

Table 3.3 Comparative analysis of digital government construction scores

Region	Score				Ranking			
	Total score	Potential usage	Actual awareness	Actual usage	Overall rank	Potential usage	Actual awareness	Actual usage
Top six (level A)								
Zhaotong	95	100	94	90	1	1	2	1
Beijing	89	98	90	80	2	8	5	2
Huzhou	87	89	95	77	3	75	1	4
Pu'er	87	92	90	79	3	56	5	3
Hangzhou	85	100	83	72	5	1	13	8
Shenzhen	85	99	86	70	5	7	11	9
Average	88	96	90	78	3	25	6	5

Source Research Group on "Deepening the Business System Reform"

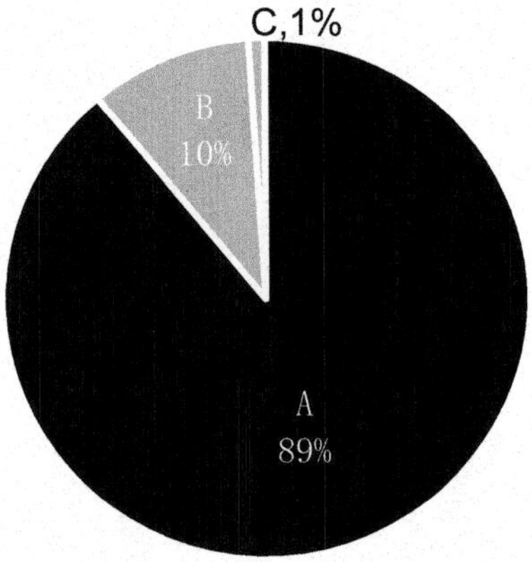

Fig. 3.13 Eighty-nine percent of cities had level A digital government potential usage rates

(3) **The actual awareness rate of digital government nationwide is mainly at level B**

As shown in Fig. 3.14 and Table 3.2, a total of twelve cities had level A digital government actual awareness rates. The highest scores were Wenzhou and Zhaotong, with ninety-five and ninety-four points, respectively. A total of forty-five cities were at level B, twenty-six were at level C, and twenty-three were at level D. In terms of proportion, cities at levels A, B, C and D respectively accounted for eleven percent, forty-two percent, twenty-five percent and twenty-two percent, thus the digital government actual awareness rate in most cities was level B.

(4) **The digital government actual usage rate of all regions is mainly at level D**

As shown in Fig. 3.15 and Table 3.2, one city had a digital government actual usage rate at level A, nine were at level B, while twenty-six were at level C, and seventy

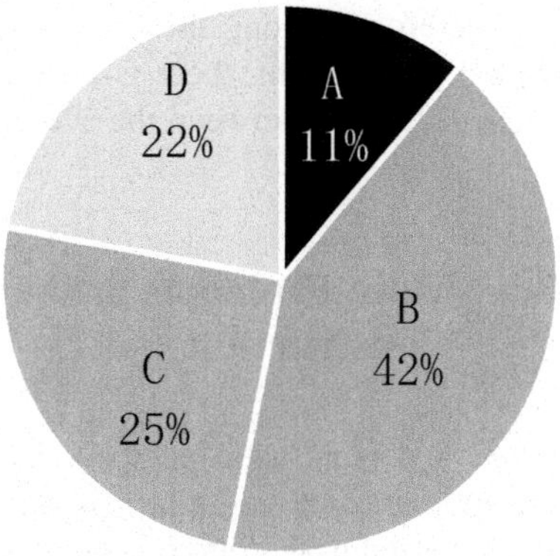

Fig. 3.14 Forty-two percent of cities had level B digital government actual awareness rates

were at level D. In terms of proportion, cities at levels A, B, C and D respectively accounted for one percent, eight percent, twenty-five percent and sixty-six percent, thus the digital government actual usage rate in the vast majority of cities was at level D.

In the city with the highest overall score, this was mainly attributed to its high actual knowledge and actual usage rates. Six prefecture-level cities had level A scores (eighty-five points and above), as shown in Table 3.3. Among these six cities, the average potential usage rate was ninety-six points, which was four points higher than the national average, ranking twenty-fifth on average. The average actual awareness rate was ninety points, twenty-one points higher than the national average, ranking sixth on average. The average actual usage rate was seventy-eight points, twenty-five points higher than the national average, ranking fifth on average. It can thus be seen that the six regions that have reached level A have significant leads in terms of actual awareness and actual usage rates.

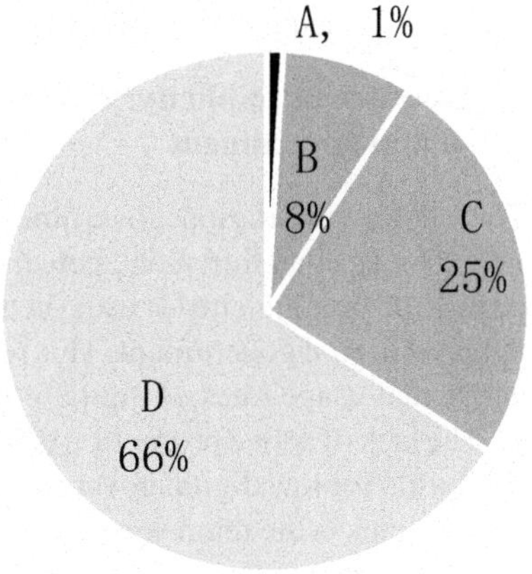

Fig. 3.15 Sixty-six percent of cities had level D digital government actual usage rates

Therefore, among these 110 cities, in the current demand-side construction of digital government, there is little difference in terms of potential usage rate, yet a great difference between the actual awareness rate and actual usage rate.

3.4 Main Problems in the "Digital Government" Construction

From a demand-side perspective, the main problems in the digital government construction now are that it is inadequate and imbalanced. It is inadequate in that the potential usage rate is ninety-two percent and the actual usage rate is fifty-three percent, meaning that thirty-nine percent of potential needs are not being met. It is imbalanced in that the actual awareness and actual usage rates in the best-performing regions are seventy-seven points higher than in the worst-performing ones, exhibiting uneven development from region to region.

(1) **Insufficient digital government demand-side construction**

The digital government demand-side construction is inadequate, with thirty-nine percent of the potential needs not being met. For demand-side construction, as shown in Fig. 3.16, the potential usage rate of digital government is ninety-two percent, while the actual usage rate is fifty-three percent, thus the potential needs of thirty-nine percent of market players are not being met. Specifically, while eighty-nine percent and eighty-five percent of market players clearly expressed their willingness to use the online service halls and mobile app platforms, their respective actual usage rates were only forty-eight percent and twenty-six percent. This shows that forty-one percent and fifty-nine percent of the respective potential needs of the online service halls and mobile app platforms are not being met.

As for demand-side digital government construction, there are four main reasons why it is inadequate throughout the country.

1. **Insufficient publicity: thirty-one percent of market players are unaware of digital government**

The nationwide digital government actual awareness rate was sixty-nine percent, which means that thirty-one percent of market players are still unaware of it. Knowledge is the prerequisite for use, yet thirty percent of market players neither knew about nor used digital government. This results in a discrepancy between the potential usage and actual usage rates of digital government.

The lack of active promotion efforts by functional government departments may be the reason for low digital government awareness rate. Active promotion by functional departments is the main way that market players learn about digital government. The low awareness rate means that active communication by service hall staff and through advertisements may still be insufficient. The results of our field survey revealed that, even if the service halls had been equipped with multiple computers, market players

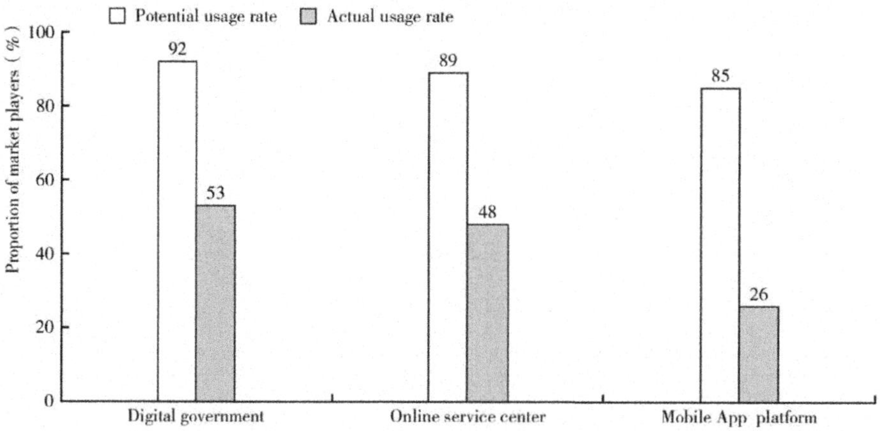

Fig. 3.16 The difference between the potential usage and actual usage rates of digital government is thirty-nine percentage points

were unaware it was possible to complete business-related tasks online. For example, in a city in the eastern region, our researchers noticed that there were four dedicated computers in the service hall, yet many market players still said they did not know they could complete tasks on a computer. In another eastern city, in addition to computers, the service hall had also posted banners advertising online government services. But when asked if it was possible to complete business-related tasks on computers or online, some market players there answered either "I don't know" or "Probably not."

2. **Insufficient service construction: thirty-four percent of market players think digital government services are inadequate**

Inadequate services is the main reason that market players do not use digital government. As shown in Fig. 3.17, due to inadequate services, thirty-four percent and thirty-six percent of market players respectively said they did not use the online service halls or mobile app platforms.

During our field study, the market players generally said that the main problem with digital government was that its services were inadequate. At a government service center in an eastern city, one market player completing a task related to foreign funds said, "There are no foreign-funded enterprise services or a way to ask questions online, so you have to come here to get information. This is a big drawback, and it's really inconvenient." In a central province, responses from market players showed that the electronic company registration system used uniformly province-wide can only process simple tasks such as registering a company, with no way to complete other tasks online, including market entry or exit, or company dissolution. In a city in the west, market players said that many government services systems could only handle company-related services, while most individual services still needed to be done in person.

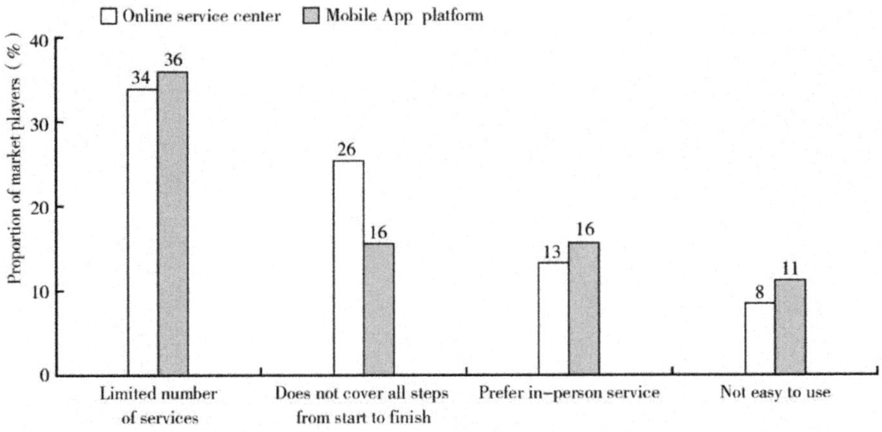

Fig. 3.17 Reasons that market players do not use digital government. *Note* Another nineteen percent and twenty-one percent of market players chose not to use the online service halls and mobile app platforms to complete business-related tasks for other reasons

3. **Insufficient process construction: twenty-six percent of market players think digital government cannot handle all steps in the process**

Some market players said they do not use digital government because not all steps can be done online, so some in-person trips still need to be made. As shown in Fig. 3.17, twenty-six percent of market players said they were unable to complete all their tasks through the online service hall and still needed to visit the physical service hall, while sixteen percent said they did not choose to use the mobile app platform for the same reason. This shows that not enabling digital government to complete all tasks has reduced its usage rate and appeal.

During the survey, many businesspeople complained that not all tasks could not be processed online. Market players in an eastern city generally said that, after submitting materials online, they still had to submit a paper-based version in person: "If it's been approved online, why do we still have to submit a paper version?" In a district in another eastern city, some market players mentioned situations where information was not up to date or incomplete, and some online forms were missing. In addition, when using the mobile app platform, there were often problems with displaying all parts of the process. In a central city, one market owner said, "The information given online is different from that on site," and further explained as follows: "The information on the website isn't up to date, and the details of the process are old. So the materials you prepare based on the website can't be used on site, and you have to do it all over again." In another central city, many market players expressed their dissatisfaction with the lack of "full digitization": "After you're done on the computer you have to do it on your phone, then you've still got to go there in person. It's such a pain." In an eastern city, market players said that sometimes the online service system also makes things more difficult: "The online system doesn't work. At first I only had to make two trips, but since my business and tax data aren't synced, I have to make a third trip." The interviewees' responses reveal that digital government has yet to reach full-process and fully-digital completion, greatly reducing market players' sense of fulfillment toward it.

4. **Insufficient guidance: thirteen percent of market players prefer to complete tasks offline**

Although ninety-three percent of market players nationwide said they believe that digital government is the general trend, sixty-eight percent think that it cannot completely replace physical service windows, and thirteen percent prefer offline processing.

They believe that in-person inquiries are more considerate and manual handling is more reassuring, thus there is no need for digital government. During our field survey, we discovered that market players were more comfortable with in-person processing and preferred not to use digital government because there is no one to guide them in completing tasks online, and no one to respond to their inquiries. In an eastern city, some market players expressed frustration that they wanted to use digital government but did not know how: "Personally, I'd really like to try using a computer system to do business tasks, like the city's one-window management system. But sometimes when there's something I want to do, I just can't find the right place. I don't know where to go to do it, so I still have to come and ask someone here." In a central city, numerous market players from manufacturing companies said, "You can ask for help in person at any time, but when processing things online you don't get answers right away." Another market player said, "There are lots of forms on the website that I have no idea how to fill out. If I call in by phone, there's often no answer, so I end up having to come here and ask in person. The materials I submitted online kept getting rejected, so in the end it's easier just to get it done at the service hall." In an eastern city, one market player also said, "When doing things online I don't know who to ask when I have a question, so I'd rather just go talk to someone in person." In Zhengzhou, Henan, the staff's helpfulness played a major role in market players' decision to use digital government. One market player who had little experience computers and was not familiar with digital government continually praised the volunteers: "The volunteers here are great. Just a few days ago, I applied for a permit here, and I had to use a computer to do it. There was this one enthusiastic young man who kept calling me 'Auntie,' and saw that I wasn't very good with computers, so he just walked me through the entire process. I was done in no time at all." With help from volunteers, market players who have never used digital government can experience how fast and convenient it makes the process. This shows that, although in the short term some market players cannot change their habit of completing tasks in person, if the service hall lacks initiative and guidance for market players to complete tasks online, then this may limit the increase in the digital government usage rate.

(2) **Imbalanced digital government demand-side construction**

Imbalanced development from region to region is a spatial manifestation of inadequate digital government construction. The best-performing city in terms of digital

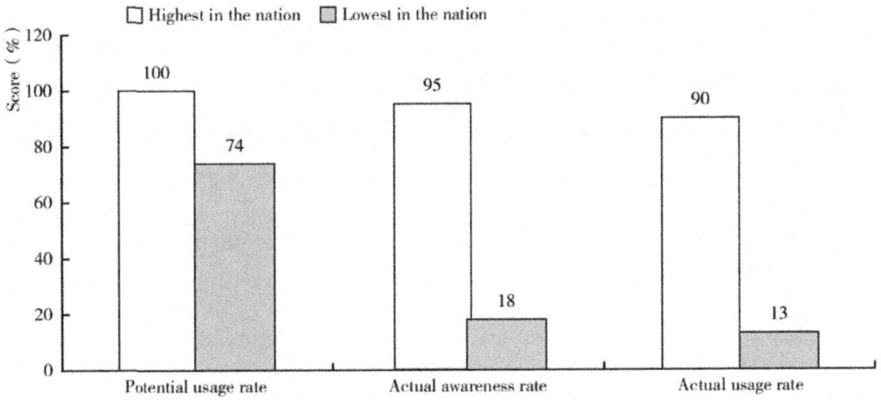

Fig. 3.18 The development of digital government between regions is imbalanced

government construction scored ninety-five points, and the lowest forty-two points, the former being more than two times the latter. As shown in Fig. 3.18, there is also a broad gap in the potential usage rate, actual awareness rate and actual usage rate, with the highest- and low-scoring regions respectively at twenty-six points, seventy-seven points and seventy-seven points, showing that interregional development is uneven.

The potential demand for digital government is generally high in all regions, yet there is a great difference between the actual awareness rate and actual usage rate. The respective ratios of the potential utilization levels A, B, C and D were eighty-nine percent, ten percent, one percent and zero percent, respectively; those of the actual awareness rate levels A, B, C and D were eleven percent, forty-two percent, twenty-five percent and twenty-two percent; and those of the actual usage rate levels A, B, C and D were one percent, eight percent, twenty-five percent and sixty-six percent. This shows that there is high potential demand for digital government in all regions, yet there is a great difference between the actual awareness rate and actual usage rate.

1. **Some functional departments do not actively notify people about digital government, leading to an imbalanced awareness rate**

As shown in Fig. 3.19, out of the 110 cities covered by the survey, in terms of people learning of digital government through staff notifications the best-performing city scored seventy-one percent, and the lowest-performing one scored twenty-one percent, the difference between the two being fifty percentage points. As for people who had learned about digital government through referral from friends, the difference between the highest and lowest was about forty-three percentage points, and that between people who had learned about it online was twenty-seven percentage points. It can be seen from this that the difference in active notification by government workers is the main reason for the interregional differences in the digital government awareness rate.

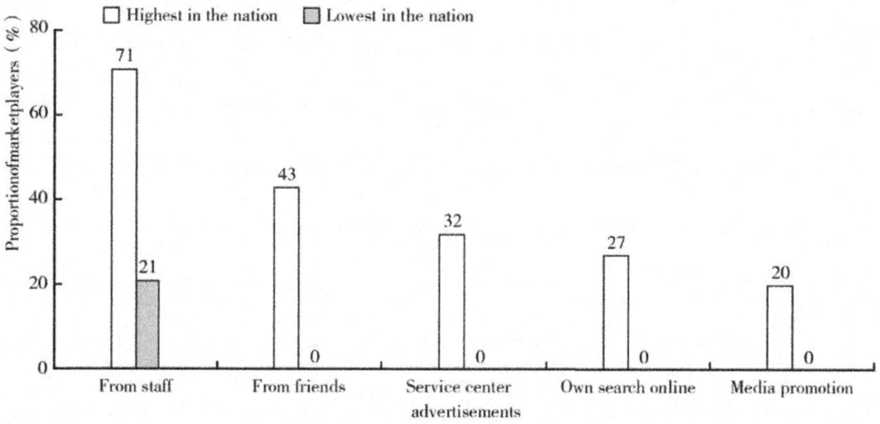

Fig. 3.19 The difference between the highest and lowest ratios of people who learned about digital government from staff was fifty percentage points

2. **Some services are missing and not all steps can be completed, thus skewing the digital government usage rate**

As shown in Fig. 3.20, out of the 110 cities covered in the survey, that with the highest proportion of market players who believe that digital government business is inadequate was sixty-four percent, and that of the lowest was six percent, for a difference of fifty-eight percentage points. As for people who think that digital government cannot process all the tasks they need, the difference between the highest- and lowest-scoring cities was fifty-three percentage points. The proportion of market players who did not use digital government and consider it difficult to use—instead preferring on-site processing—had a difference of nearly forty percentage points between the highest- and lowest-scoring regions. This shows that inadequate services and inability to process all tasks are the main reasons for the interregional differences in the digital government usage rate.

3. **Some regions do not emphasize digital government, resulting in imbalanced development**

The level of importance and practices involved with digital government in various regions have affected its actual awareness and usage rates. In one prefecture-level city which takes digital government as the focus of its work and publicity, the service hall launched a "full-process/semi-digital" service. They have made great efforts in the promotion and construction of the online service platform, thus increasing market players' awareness and usage rates. In Fuyang, Anhui, the service staff told our researchers that, for most of the business services there, all of the steps had been digitized, thereby minimizing the time businesspeople needed to spend. In Qujing, Yunnan, one staff member also said that the whole process had been digitized there, which had also led to high digital government awareness and usage rates. However, in cities that had yet to pay attention to digital government construction and use

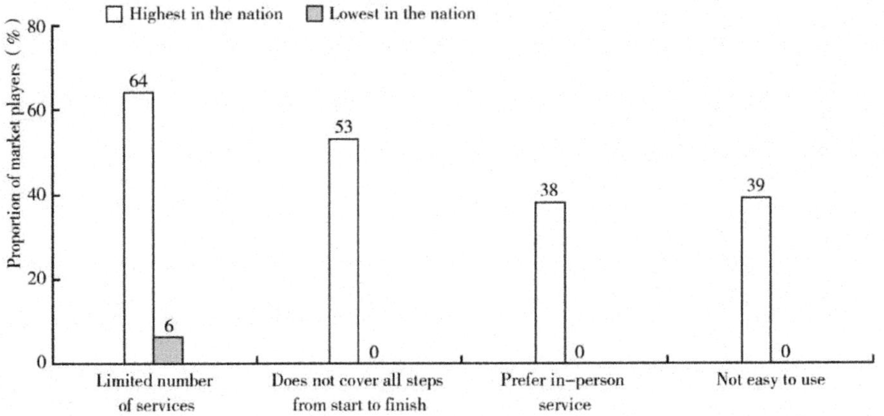

Fig. 3.20 The difference between the highest- and lowest-scoring cities in terms of people who believe digital government does not encompass all tasks is fifty-eight percentage points

digital government to supplement in-person processing, despite the computers and promotional banners in the service halls, the staff there had not actively promoted it. This resulted in low digital government awareness and usage rates, and attention to digital government in these cities remains insufficient.

3.5 Potential Directions for Deepening the "Digital Government" Construction

The challenges and difficulties faced by market players in the process of using digital government are both the starting point and foothold of digital government construction. Based on the current stage of the development of digital government construction and the main conflicts it faces, this study proposes to deepen the digital government construction to enable its large-scale use as soon as possible.

We must focus on the demand-side construction of digital government, further increase efforts to actively promote it, and raise its awareness rate. At present, ninety-two percent of China's market players are willing to use digital government. If all of these market players were aware of digital government, then even at the current appeal rate, the national digital government usage rate would increase from fifty-three percent to seventy-one percent ($92\% \times 77\% = 71\%$). This would bring the nationwide digital government construction into the stage of large-scale use. Therefore, relevant functional departments must continue to increase their efforts to actively publicize and promote the digital government and raise its awareness rate as soon as possible.

We must also accelerate the supply-side construction of digital government, increase the supply of digital government services, promote whole-process digital government, and continue to increase the digital government usage rate. The current appeal rate of digital government nationwide is seventy-seven percent. If digital government can reach the goal of 100 percent appeal, then even calculated based on the current digital government awareness rate, the nationwide usage rate would increase from fifty-three percent to sixty-nine percent ($69\% \times 100\% = 69\%$). If this happens, it will enter the large-scale use stage. Among market players who had not chosen to use digital government, thirty-four percent said they believe that not all tasks can be completed online, while twenty-six percent believe that not all steps can be processed online. Therefore, to face the difficulties in the use of these market players, we must begin by promoting whole-process digital government, then launch more digital government services, improve user experience, and strive to achieve the goal of 100 percent appeal.

We must promote the integrated development of online and offline government services. Nationwide, sixty-eight percent of market players believe that digital government should be integrated and developed with in-person processing. Among the market players who had not chosen to use the online service hall, thirteen percent preferred to complete tasks in person. Among those who had not chosen to use the mobile platform, sixteen percent also preferred to do things in person. Therefore, it is necessary to open up online and offline business channels; accelerate the construction of an online single-network access system; promote the offline implementation of single-visit and single-window services; and build a comprehensive, high-quality online and offline government services system, so as to provide market players with multi-channel government services that are convenient and easy to use.

We must promote balanced development between regions through the standardization of digital government. The uneven interregional development in terms of the awareness and usage rates of the demand-side construction of digital government stems from the large discrepancy in the level of promotion and construction of local government functions. Therefore, we must promote the standardization of digital government, refine and quantify its construction standards, narrow the gap between regions, and achieve the nationwide equalization of its demand-side construction.

Chapter 4
Performance of the Business Environment Construction

Qingmiao Bi and Xianxiang Xu

4.1 Report Overview

The construction of China's business environment enables high-quality development. The shift from rapid growth to high-quality development is a profound transformation, the achievement of which ultimately depends on many high-quality market players. In terms of market players, first, more of them must enter the market and provide a quantitative basis for high-quality development; and second, the high-quality growth of market players must be promoted, that is, market players create employment guarantee, steady growth, structural adjustment and innovation, in turn providing quality assurance for high-quality development. This report first conducts quantitative analysis based on previous data and first-hand data collected through a field survey performed in 2019, so as to systematically evaluate the macro-effects, shortcomings and directions of serving high-quality development achieved in China's business environment construction (Table 4.1).

The indicator system of this report includes the four indicators of creating job opportunities, promoting enterprise growth, optimizing the production structure, and driving innovation and development. In terms of how the construction of a business environment can match and support high-quality development, this study breaks this problem down into four areas, each constituting four tertiary indicators. **(1) The proportion of market players who created new jobs**. The 19th National Congress Report states that employment is the greatest livelihood of the people, and thus it is necessary to encourage entrepreneurship to drive employment, achieve higher-quality and more abundant employment, and provide livelihood assurance for

Q. Bi · X. Xu (✉)
Lingnan College, Sun Yat-sen University, Guangzhou, China
e-mail: lnsxuxx@mail.sysu.edu.cn

Institute of Mezzoeconomics, Sun Yat-sen University, Guangzhou, China

X. Xu et al. (eds.), *Report on the Chinese Business Environment Survey 2020*, Research Series on the Chinese Dream and China's Development Path,
https://doi.org/10.1007/978-981-99-6112-2_4

Table 4.1 Performance indicator system and most recent progress in business environment construction

Indicator	Nationwide average (%)	Maximum (%)	Minimum (%)
(1) Proportion of market players creating new jobs	34	45	22
(2) Proportion of market players with increased performance	49	58	34
(3) Proportion of market players in the service industry	70	97	50
(4) Proportion of market players who innovated	44	56	32

Note The data are from the Sun Yat-sen University Research Group on "Deepening the Reform of the Business System." Maximum and Minimum respectively refer to the maximum and minimum values at the provincial level

high-quality development. The more jobs created, the greater the support for high-quality development. **(2) The proportion of market players who had increased performance**. Maintaining and increasing the activity of market players is the key to promoting steady economic growth. Increased performance reflects the growth of market players, and provides quality support for high-quality development. **(3) The proportion of market players in the service industry**. To promote high-quality economic development, focus must be placed on promoting transformation and upgrading of the industrial structure. The more market players entering the service industry after the reform, the better the foundation for the industrial transformation in high-quality development. **(4) The proportion of market players who innovated**. Innovation is an urgent requirement and an important means of supporting the promotion of high-quality development and conversion of momentum. The higher the proportion of market players engaged in innovative activities, the more momentum provided for high-quality development. All four indicators are positive ones: More market players creating jobs, increased performance, more enterprises in the service industry, and greater innovation will all support high-quality development.

Based on the above indicator system, our research team collected first-hand data on the demand side of market players through a field survey, and quantitatively analyzed the macro-effects of the business environment construction. **The report results show that the business environment construction strongly supports high-quality development, by promoting entrepreneurship, assuring employment, stabilizing growth, restructuring, and promoting innovation**. The business environment promotes entrepreneurship, with the number of market players having doubled, among which the size of small, micro and private market players has increased dramatically. It has also assured employment, with thirty-four percent of market players having upsized. It stabilized growth, with forty-nine percent of market players performing better. It adjusted the market structure, with the proportion of market players in the service industry increasing from fifty-four percent before the business environment construction to seventy percent after the reform.

Finally, it promoted innovation, with forty-four percent of market players having innovated. At the same time, innovation has led to an increase of twenty-three percent in the proportion of market players who upsized, and an increase of twenty-five percent in the proportion of those who performed better. The survey results show that the business environment construction has achieved remarkable results in promoting entrepreneurship, assuring employment, stabilizing growth, restructuring and promoting innovation, thereby laying a solid foundation for high-quality development.

4.2 Promoting Entrepreneurship

The continuous entry of market players to the market is a prerequisite for steady growth and high-quality development. Without a steady stream of new market players, it will not be possible to create more jobs, and in turn there will be a lack of a microeconomic foundation for growth. In addition, without new market players, the market will lack the motivation to compete and innovate, and will also lack a microeconomic foundation for industrial restructuring, thus making it difficult to achieve high-quality macroeconomic development.

(1) **After 2014, the total number of market players doubled**

Among all the active market players randomly interviewed in 2019, about fifty-three percent had registered and entered the market after the 2014 business reform. A visual reflection of the business environment construction that promotes more market players to start businesses is that many of the current market players registered between 2014 and 2019. As shown in Fig. 4.1, forty-seven percent of the market players covered by the random sample in the survey had registered before 2014, while about fifty-three percent had registered between 2014 and 2019. This shows that, according to the sample from this survey, the number of new market players who registered, started businesses and entered the market after the reform surpassed that before the reform, thus accounting for more than half of all active market players.

(2) **Players in the small and micro market are increasing**

The share of players in the small and micro market is growing. Figure 4.2 divides market players into two groups: those established before the 2014 business reform, and those established after it. Then the two groups' proportions of two market players of different sizes are calculated. The results show that the proportion of small and micro market players increased. Among the market players established before the 2014 business reform, nineteen percent were micro market players with fewer than ten employees. Among the market players established after 2014, this proportion became forty-eight percent, an increase of more than two times. At the same time,

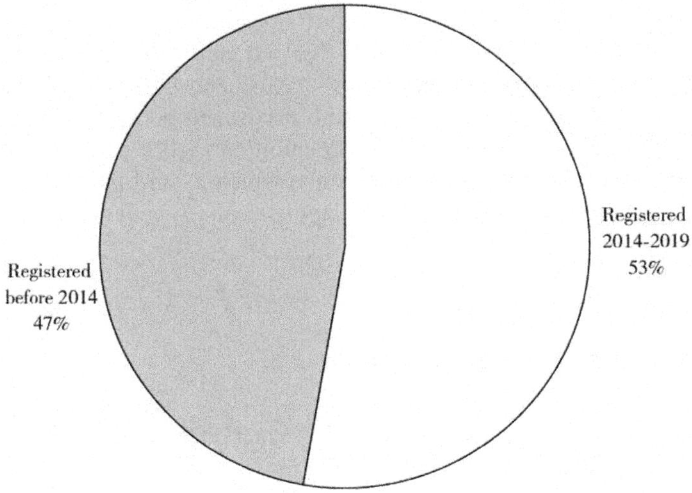

Fig. 4.1 Fifty-three percent of all market players registered between 2014 and 2019. *Data source* The China Doing Business Enterprise Survey

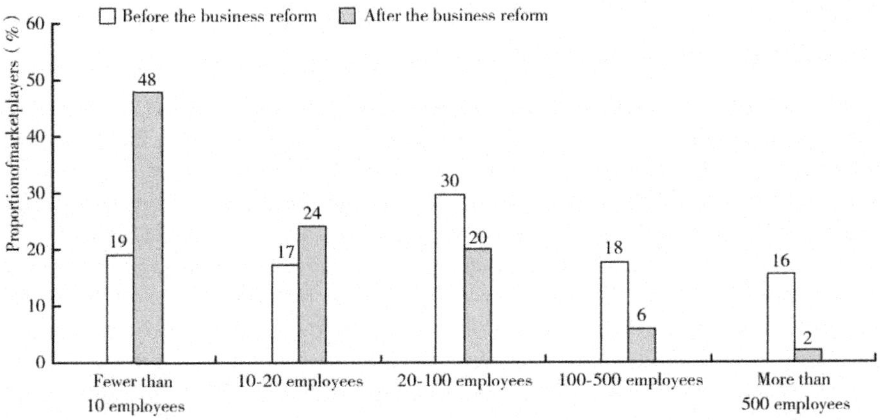

Fig. 4.2 After the business environment construction in 2014, the proportion of small and micro market players increased. *Data source* The China Doing Business Enterprise Survey

the proportion of small market players with a scale of ten to twenty employees also increased slightly after the reform, from seventeen percent to twenty-four percent. Many new small-scale market players have diluted the proportion of medium- and large-sized ones. After the reform, market players with twenty to 100, 100 to 500 and more than 500 employees respectively decreased by ten, twelve and fourteen percentage points. It can thus be seen that the business environment construction promotes widespread entrepreneurship. In terms of scale, it mainly promotes the market entry of small and micro market players.

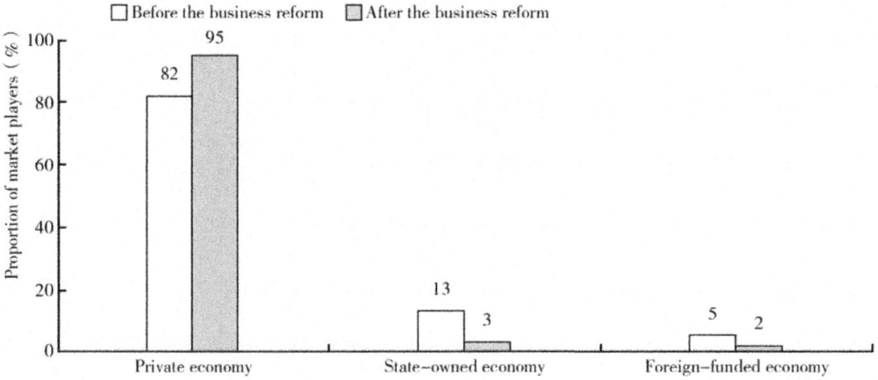

Fig. 4.3 The proportion of private economy enterprises increased after the 2014 business environment construction. *Data source* The China Doing Business Enterprise Survey

(3) **Increased share of private economy enterprises**

The share of the private economy has increased since the business reform, from eighty-two percent to ninety-five percent. Figure 4.3 divides market players into two groups: those established before and after the 2014 business reform. Then the proportions of market players with different ownership systems in each group are calculated. The results reveal that eighty-two percent of the market players established before the 2014 business reform were in the private economy, while among those established after the 2014 reform, the proportion of those in the private economy increased to ninety-five percent. Compared with the sharp increase in private economy enterprises, after the business environment construction, the proportion of foreign-funded economy enterprises dropped from five percent to two percent, while that of state-owned economy ones also dropped from thirteen percent to three percent.

4.3 Assuring Employment

Employment is the main livelihood of the people. The number of people employed reflects the ability of market players to absorb employment, and is an important foothold for maintaining stability and promoting development.

(1) **In 2019, thirty-four percent of market players created new jobs**

During the survey, our researchers asked representatives of market players if their companies had upsized or downsized over the past six months. As shown in Fig. 4.4, in the first half of 2019, thirty-four percent of companies had upsized, fifty-five percent remained the same, and eleven percent had downsized. This report defines the net increase in employment of market players as the difference between the

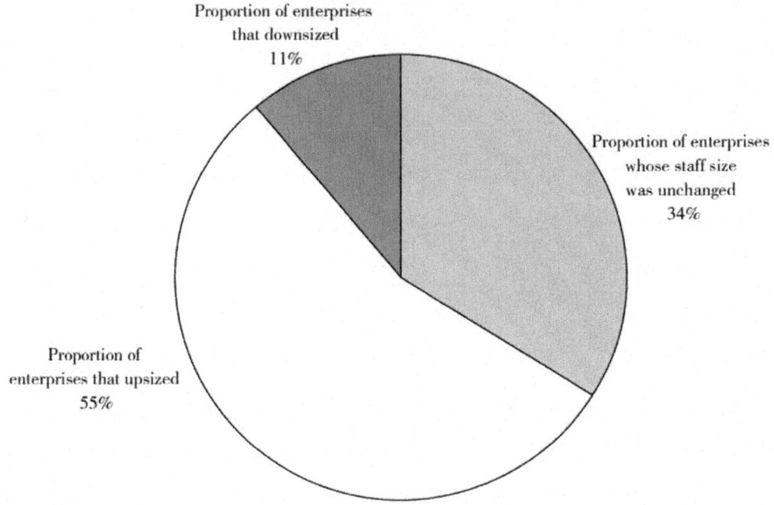

Fig. 4.4 In the first half of 2019, thirty-four percent of the market players nationwide upsized. *Data source* The China Doing Business Enterprise Survey

proportion of those who upsized and those who downsized. The difference between the two was twenty-three percentage points, that is, the net increase in employment of market players was twenty-three percent. This shows that in the first half of 2019, market players created more jobs and provided more employment opportunities.

(2) **New companies created more new jobs than old ones did**

In terms of company expansion, more new market players upsized. As shown in Fig. 4.5, thirty percent of the old market players (those registered before the 2014 business reform) had upsized, while thirty-seven percent of new market players had done so. As a result, both old and new market players have created jobs over the past six months, but, in comparison, new market players are more adept at this.

As for downsizing, many old market players did so. As shown in Fig. 4.5, seventeen percent of the old market players had downsized, while only nine percent of new market players had done so, the former being eight percentage points higher than the latter.

In terms of the net increase in employment, new market players had a higher rate. As shown in Fig. 4.5, the old market players' upsize rate was thirteen percentage points higher than the downsize rate, for a net employment increase of thirteen percent, while the new market players had a net employment increase of twenty-eight percent, fifteen percentage points higher than the former.

(3) **The service industry created many new jobs**

Many market players in the service industry upsized. As shown in Fig. 4.6, among the service industry market players, thirty-five percent had upsized, the highest among

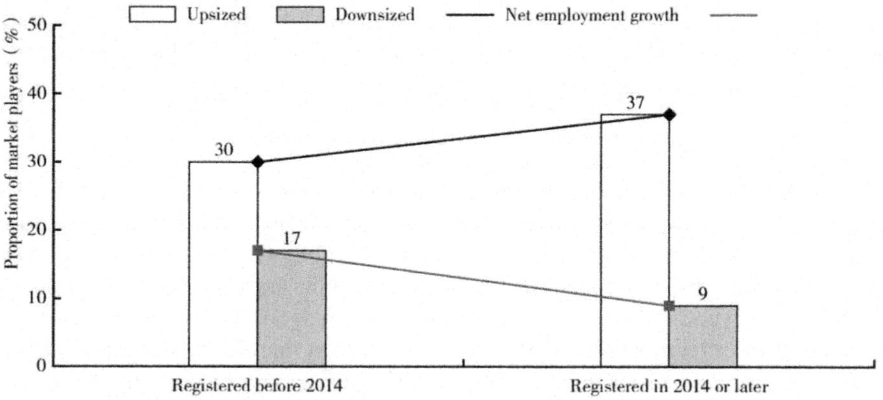

Fig. 4.5 Proportion of market players who upsized and downsized in 2019 by year of registration. *Data source* The China Doing Business Enterprise Survey

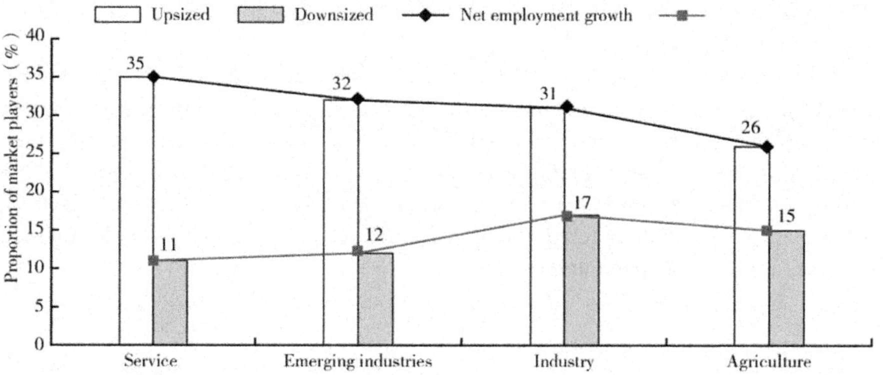

Fig. 4.6 Proportions of market players who upsized and downsized in 2019 by industry. *Data source* The China Doing Business Enterprise Survey

all types of market players. Among the main players in the emerging industry market, thirty-two percent had upsized, second only to the service sector. In the industrial market, thirty-one percent had upsized. Finally, in the agricultural market, twenty-six percent of major market players had upsized, the lowest among the four industries.

Many market players in the industrial market downsized. Among market players in the industrial market, seventeen percent had downsized, the highest among all industries. Meanwhile, those in agriculture, emerging industries, and service had respective downsize rates of fifteen percent, twelve percent and eleven percent, with no significant difference among them.

Many market players in the service sector rate increased employment. Market players in all industries had positive net employment growth. Among them, the service sector had a net employment increase of twenty-four percentage points, the highest among the four industries; this was followed by emerging industries, with twenty percentage points of net employment growth; then industry, at fourteen percentage points; and agriculture had the lowest rate, at eleven percentage points.

(4) **Large-scale market players created many new jobs**

The larger the scale, the higher the proportion of companies that upsized, with nearly half of the market players with more than 500 employees having done so. As Fig. 4.7 shows, over the past six months, among large-scale market players with more than 500 employees, fifty percent had upsized, the highest rate among all market players. Following the scale of market players from large to small, the proportion of those that upsized decreases. The lowest rate was that of micro market players (those with fewer than ten employees), who had an upsize rate of nineteen percent, less than half that of the large-scale market players.

Market players with more than 500 employees also had the highest downsize rate. As shown in Fig. 4.7, in the first half of 2019, twenty-one percent of market players with more than 500 employees downsized, while the proportions of market players of other sizes who downsized did not differ greatly, ranging between ten percent and twelve percent.

From the perspective of net employment growth, medium- and large-sized market players had high net employment increases, while micro market players had the lowest. Overall, market players of all sizes had positive net employment growth. Among them, the net employment increase of market players with 100–500 employees was thirty-three percentage points, the highest of all company sizes; and micro market players with fewer than ten employees had the lowest net employment increase, at only nine percentage points.

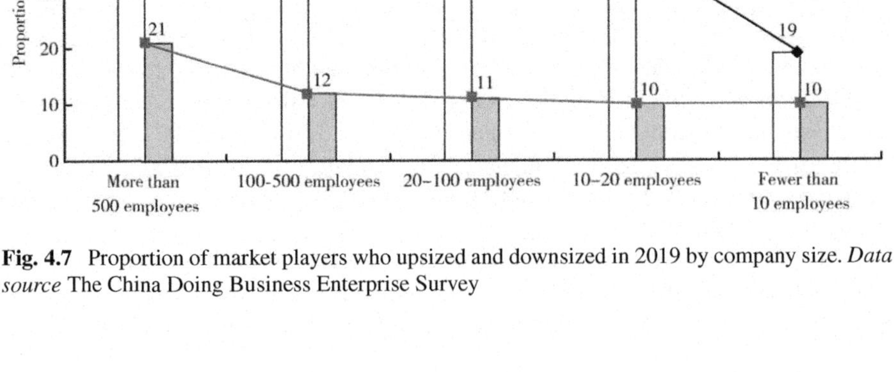

Fig. 4.7 Proportion of market players who upsized and downsized in 2019 by company size. *Data source* The China Doing Business Enterprise Survey

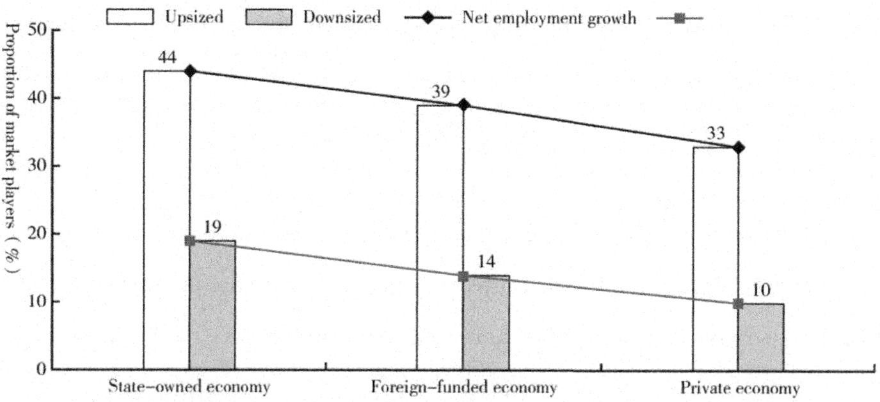

Fig. 4.8 Proportion of market players who upsized and downsized in 2019 by ownership type. *Data source* The China Doing Business Enterprise Survey

(5) State-owned economy companies created many new jobs

Many state-owned economy companies upsized. Figure 4.8 shows that in the past six months, forty-four percent of state-owned economy market players upsized, with the greatest recruitment expansion among all types of market players; thirty-nine percent of foreign-funded economy ones expanded; and thirty-three percent of private economy ones.

State-owned economy companies downsized the most. Figure 4.8 shows that in the past six months, the respective proportions of state-owned and foreign-funded economy market players who downsized were nineteen percent and fourteen percent. The lowest downsizing rate was in the private economy, at ten percent.

Market players of all forms of ownership had a net employment growth of around twenty percent. Among them, the net employment increase in the state-owned and the foreign-funded economies was twenty-five percentage points, while that in the private economy was twenty-three percentage points. Thus there was no significant difference in net employment growth among the various forms of ownership.

4.4 Stabilizing Growth

Macroeconomic growth depends not only on the number of market players, but also on their growth. The business environment construction promotes the performance improvement and growth of market players at the micro level, reflecting the performance achieved by the reform in terms of stabilizing growth.

(1) **In 2019, nearly half of the market players had increased performance**

During the survey, our researchers asked representatives of market players whether their companies' sales performance had increased, decreased, or remained unchanged over the past six months. As shown in Fig. 4.9, in the first half of 2019, forty-nine percent of market players said their performance had increased, that of thirty-two percent had not changed, and nineteen percent had decreased. This shows that in the first half of 2019, nearly half of the market players performed better.

(2) **More new market players improved their performance than old ones did**

Many new market players had increased performance. As shown in Fig. 4.10, forty-two percent of the market players who had registered before the 2014 business reform had increased their sales performance in the first half of 2019, while fifty-three percent of those established after the reform had done so. Among market players both new and old, over forty percent of market players had increased their performance in the past six months. Between the two categories, new market players had a slightly higher increase in performance.

Many old market players had decreased performance. As shown in Fig. 4.10, twenty-six percent of old market players had decreased performance, while only sixteen percent of new ones did, ten percentage points lower than the former.

(3) **Many market players in emerging industries and service industries performed better**

Almost fifty percent of market players in emerging industries and the service industry had improved performance. As shown in Fig. 4.11, forty-nine percent of

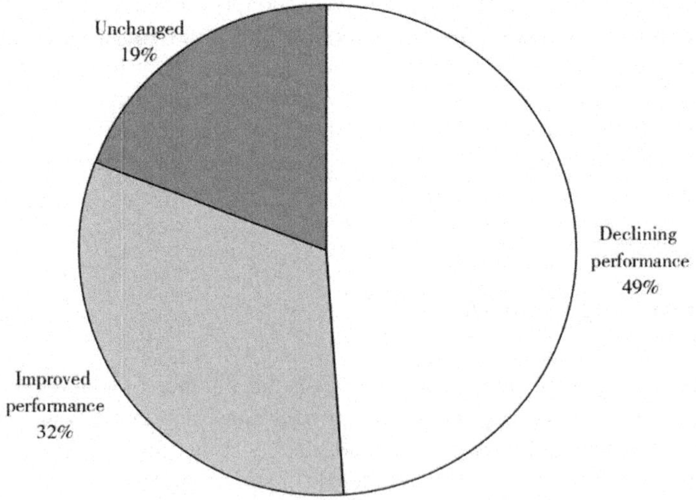

Fig. 4.9 In the first half of 2019, forty-nine percent of market players nationwide performed better. *Data source* The China Doing Business Enterprise Survey

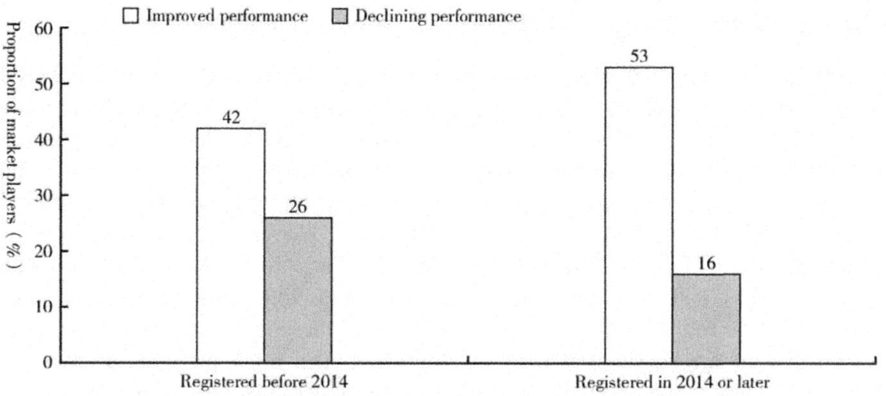

Fig. 4.10 Proportion of market players with increased and decreased performance in 2019 by year of registration. *Data source* The China Doing Business Enterprise Survey

the market players in emerging industries and the service industry performed better than before, the highest among all types of market players; meanwhile, forty-four percent of the industrial and forty percent of agricultural market players improved, the latter having the lowest rate among the four industries.

About 20% of market players in industry, agriculture, and service had decreased performance. As shown in Fig. 4.11, twenty-five percent of market players in agriculture had decreased performance. In the industrial and service sectors, eighteen percent and nineteen percent of market players respectively had decreased performance; and emerging industries had the lowest proportion of decreased performance, at thirteen percent.

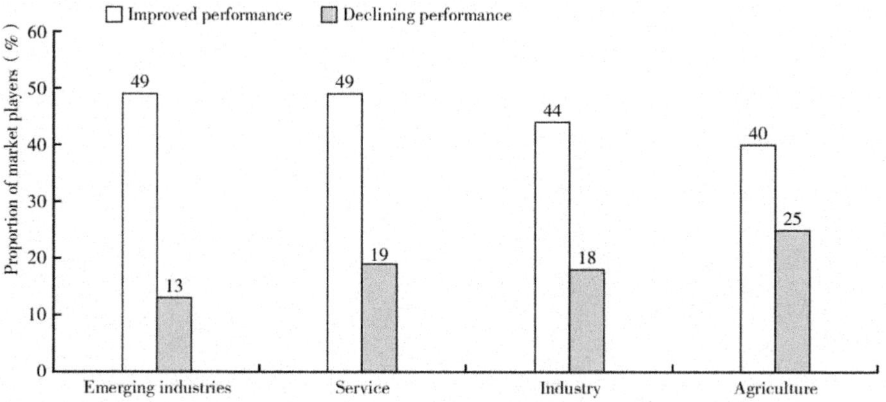

Fig. 4.11 Proportion of market players with increased and decreased performance in 2019 by industry. *Data source* The China Doing Business Enterprise Survey

(4) **Many large-scale market players had increased performance**

The larger the scale, the greater the increase in performance. Among the large-scale market players, sixty-three percent performed better than before, while only thirty-seven percent of the micro market players did so. As shown in Fig. 4.12, in the past six months, large-scale market players (those with more than 500 employees) had the highest rate of increased performance, at sixty-three percent. With the decrease in size, the proportion of market players with improved performance decreases. The lowest was that of micro market players (those with fewer than ten employees), with only thirty-seven percent of them improving their performance in the past six months, about half the proportion of the large-scale market players.

Small and micro market players decreased the most in performance. As Fig. 4.12 shows, in the first half of 2019, twenty-two percent of micro market players had decreased performance. Meanwhile, about seventeen percent of market players of other sizes had decreased performance, with no significant difference among the various sizes.

(5) **Many foreign-funded companies had better performance**

Looking at the proportion of companies who had improved performance, fifty-nine percent foreign-funded economy market players performed better than before, while those in the private economy had the lowest rate of improvement, at forty-five percent. As Fig. 4.13 shows, in the past six months, fifty-nine percent of the foreign-funded economy market players performed better, while fifty-three percent of those in the state-owned economy did so, both over fifty percent. Private economy had the lowest rate of performance improvement, at forty-five percent.

About twenty percent of market players with various forms of ownership had decreased performance. As shown in Fig. 4.13, in the past six months, twenty

Fig. 4.12 Proportion of market players with increased and decreased performance in 2019 by company size. *Data source* The China Doing Business Enterprise Survey

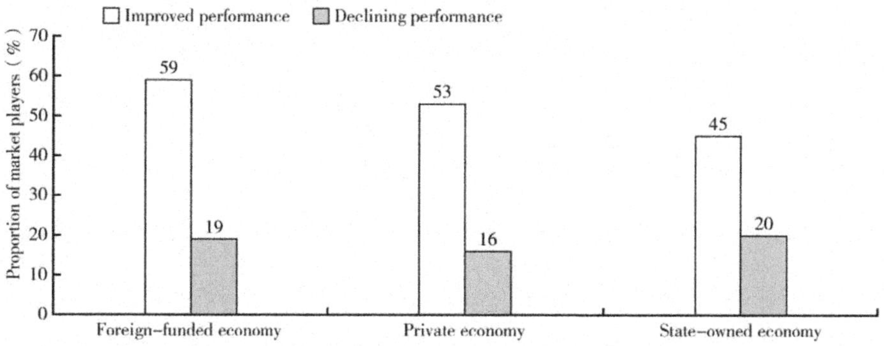

Fig. 4.13 Proportion of market players with increased and decreased performance in 2019 according to ownership type. *Data source* The China Doing Business Enterprise Survey

percent of market players in the private economy had decreased performance, the highest among all types; this was followed by those in the foreign-funded economy, at nineteen percent; and the performance decrease rate of market players in the state-owned economy was around sixteen percent. The proportion of market players with decreased performance of all three types of ownership economies was around twenty percent, with no significant difference among them.

4.5 Restructuring

The construction of the business environment has motivated market players to engage in entrepreneurship. The many new market players have provided an opportunity for industrial transformation, and laid the foundation for China's economy to be dominated by market players in the service industry.

(1) **Market players in the service industry increased by 16 percentage points**

After the business environment construction in 2014, the proportion of market players in the service industry increased from fifty-four percent to seventy percent. In Fig. 4.14, market players are divided into two groups: those established before and after the 2014 business reform. Then their respective proportions in different industries are calculated. The results show that fifty-four percent of the old market players were in the service industry, then after the reform the proportion increased to seventy percent, an increase of sixteen percentage points.

After the business reform, the market share of industrial market players dropped from twenty-eight percent to eleven percent. As shown in Fig. 4.14, twenty-eight percent of the old market players were industrial ones, then after the reform among the proportion of industrial market players decreased to eleven percent. After the business environment construction, the proportion of industrial market players reduced by more than half.

Fig. 4.14 Proportion of market players in various industries before and after the business reform. *Data source* The China Doing Business Enterprise Survey

After the business reform, the proportion of market players in emerging industries was fourteen percent, exceeding that of industrial market players. As shown in Fig. 4.14, thirteen percent of the old market players were in emerging industries, then after the reform the proportion became fourteen percent, which is higher than that of industrial market players after the reform (thirteen percent). Therefore, the number of emerging industry market players has now surpassed that of industrial market players.

(2) **More market players are joining the service industry**

After the reform, the proportion of service industry market players of all sizes increased, with a range of five percent to twenty-one percent. As shown in Fig. 4.15, seventy percent of the micro market players registered before the 2014 reform were in the service sector; after the reform, among the new micro market players, the proportion of those in the service industry rose to seventy-seven percent, an increase of seven percentage points. The greatest increases were in the market players with employee numbers of twenty to 100 and 100–500. The respective proportions of them in the service sector increased from forty-four percent to sixty-five percent and from forty-eight percent to sixty-nine percent, both increases of twenty-one percentage points. The smallest increase was in market players with more than 500 employees, whose proportion in the service sector rose from forty-eight percent to fifty-three percent, an increase of only five percentage points. This shows that, in terms of the scale of the new market players, the proportion of those in the service industry has increased.

(3) **More service sector market players are in the private economy**

The proportion of service sector market players in the private economy has increased dramatically. As shown in Fig. 4.16, fifty-six percent of the private economy market players registered before the 2014 reform were in the service sector.

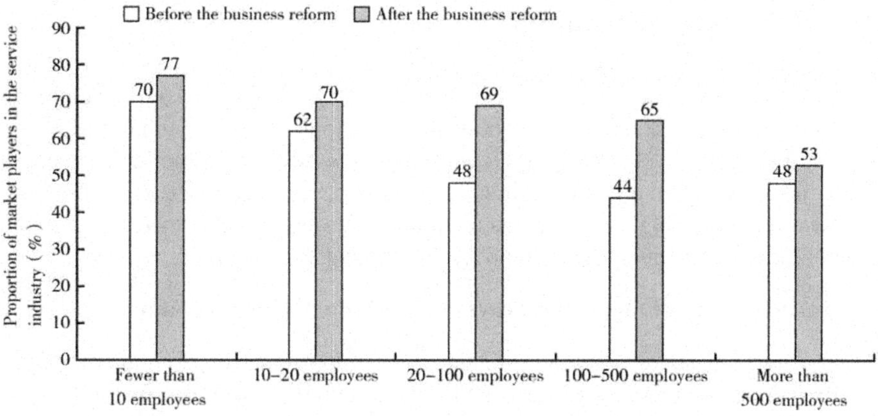

Fig. 4.15 According to scale, the proportions of market players of all sizes in the service industry increased after the reform. *Data source* The China Doing Business Enterprise Survey

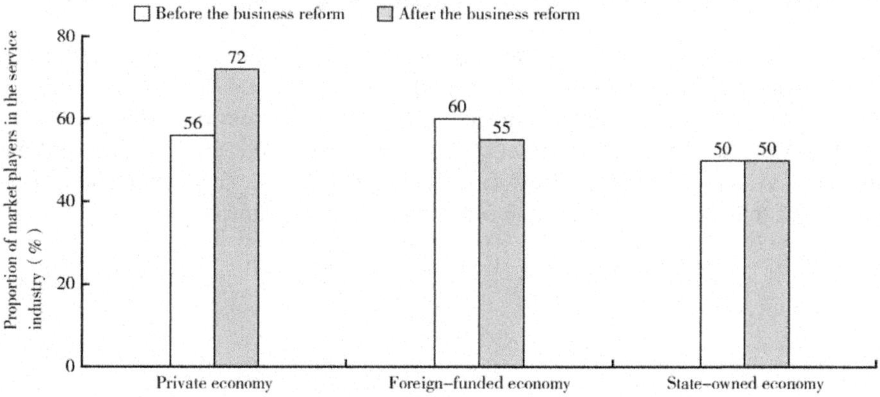

Fig. 4.16 In terms of ownership, the proportion of service industry market players in the private economy has increased. *Data source* The China Doing Business Enterprise Survey

Then, between 2014 and 2019, the proportion rose to seventy-two percent, an increase of sixteen percentage points. Meanwhile, the service sector accounted for about fifty percent of the state-owned economy, with almost no change after the reform. The proportion of market players in the service sector in the foreign-funded economy decreased slightly, from sixty percent to fifty-five percent. This shows that the private economy has played a major role in the transformation of China's economy toward becoming dominated by the service industry.

4.6 Promoting Innovation

In recent years, China has attached importance to innovation-driven development by cultivating high-quality market players, so as to achieve high-quality development at the macro level. The 2019 Government Work Report pointed out the necessity of insisting on innovation leading development, cultivating and expanding new momentum, enhancing scientific and technological support capabilities, and further promoting entrepreneurship and innovation among the people.

(1) **In 2019, nearly half of all market players launched new products or services**

During the field survey, our researchers asked representatives of market players whether their companies had launched new products or services in the past six months. As Fig. 4.17 shows, in the first half of 2019, forty-four percent of market players had launched new products or services. In other words, over forty percent of China's market players have innovated in the past six months.

(2) **44% of both new and old market players innovated**

Looking at the years of registration of market players, as shown in Fig. 4.18, in the past six months, forty-four percent of market players established both before and after the 2014 business reform launched new products or services. This means that the business environment construction has benefited market players both old and new. In terms of promoting innovation among the people, this is reflected in the consistent innovation ratio between old and new market players.

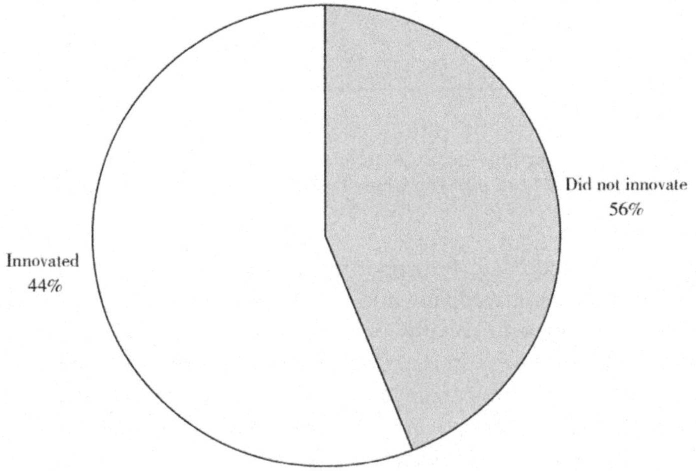

Fig. 4.17 In 2019, forty-four percent of China's market players launched new products or services. *Data source* The China Doing Business Enterprise Survey

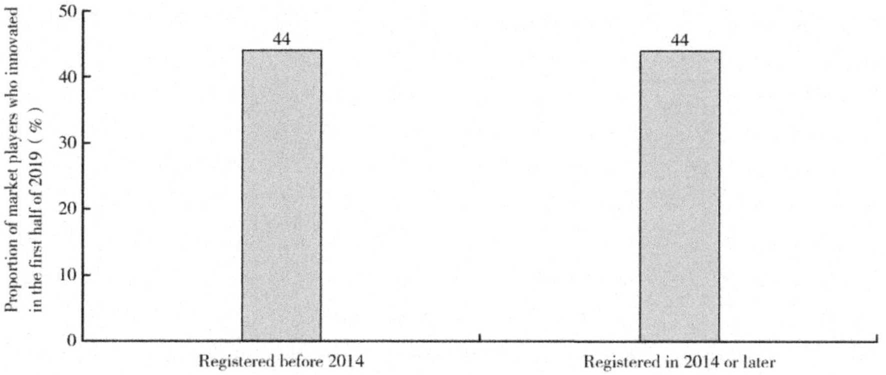

Fig. 4.18 In 2019, forty-four percent of both old and new market players innovated. *Data source* The China Doing Business Enterprise Survey

(3) **Market players in service and emerging industries were more innovative**

Looking at the industries to which market players belong, as shown in Fig. 4.19, many of those in the service industry and emerging industries innovated, with forty-six percent having launched new products or services in the past six months; among the industrial market players, thirty-nine percent had innovated and launched new products in the past six months; while the agricultural market players innovated the least, at thirty-three percent.

(4) **Large-scale market players innovated the most**

In the past six months, at least thirty percent of market players of all sizes innovated, and the larger their scale, the more they did so. As Fig. 4.20 shows, large-scale market players (those with more than 500 employees) had the highest

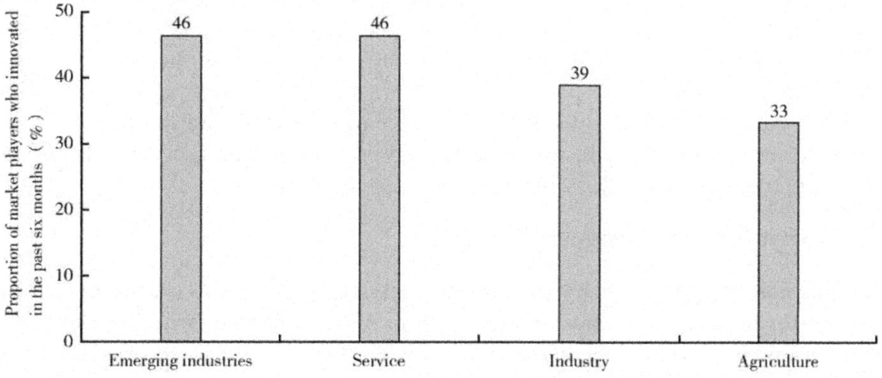

Fig. 4.19 Proportion of market players who innovated in 2019 by industry. *Data source* The China Doing Business Enterprise Survey

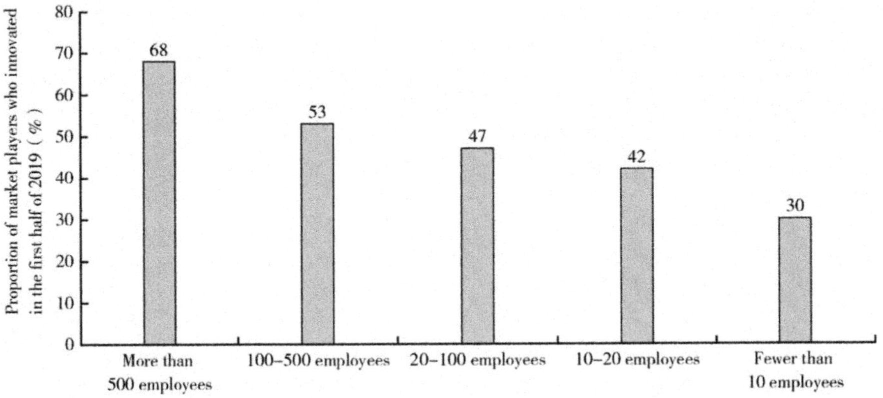

Fig. 4.20 Proportion of market players who innovated in 2019 by company size. *Data source* The China Doing Business Enterprise Survey

rate of innovation, at sixty-eight percent. The larger the market player, the stronger its foundation for innovation. As the scale decreases, the proportion of innovative market players gradually decreases. The least innovative were micro market players, with only thirty percent of them having launched new products or services in the past six months. Therefore, in terms of scale division, there is a large gap in the rate of innovation among large, medium, and micro market players, with small and micro market players not innovating enough. Overall, the respective proportions of all types of market players innovating over the past six months exceeded thirty percent.

(5) **Foreign-funded economy companies were very innovative**

In terms of ownership system, over forty percent of market players of different types innovated. The proportion of innovation in the foreign-funded economy was the highest, and that in the state-owned economy was lowest. As Fig. 4.21 shows, market players in the foreign-funded economy had the highest rate of launching new products or services, at sixty-nine percent; this was followed by the state-owned economy, at fifty-seven percent; and the private economy had the lowest innovation rate, at forty-one percent. This shows a great difference in the innovation ratio among market players of different ownership systems, and innovation in the private economy is clearly insufficient. Overall, the innovation ratios of all types of market players exceeded forty percent.

(6) **Innovation led to company upsizing**

Among market players who innovated, forty-seven percent created new jobs, twenty-three percentage points higher than market players who did not innovate. In Fig. 4.22, market players are divided into two groups: those who innovated and those who did not. Then the changes in number of employees of the two groups over the past six months are calculated. Of the market players who did not innovate, twenty-four percent upsized, while forty-seven percent of the innovative market

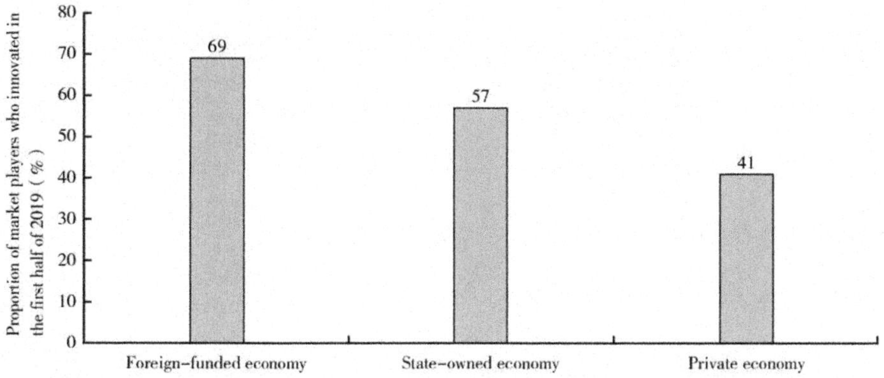

Fig. 4.21 Proportion of market players who innovated in 2019 in terms of ownership type. *Data source* The China Doing Business Enterprise Survey

players upsized in the past six months. This shows that innovation increased the proportion of new jobs created by market players by twenty-three percentage points, which is conducive to market players creating new jobs, and further contributes to high-quality development.

(7) **Innovation led to better performance**

Among the market players who innovated, sixty percent had increased performance, twenty-five percentage points higher than those who did not innovate. In Fig. 4.23, market players are divided into two groups: those who innovated and those who did not. Then the sales performance changes of the two groups over the past six months are calculated. Among the market players who did not innovate, thirty-five percent had increased performance, while sixty percent of those who innovated had

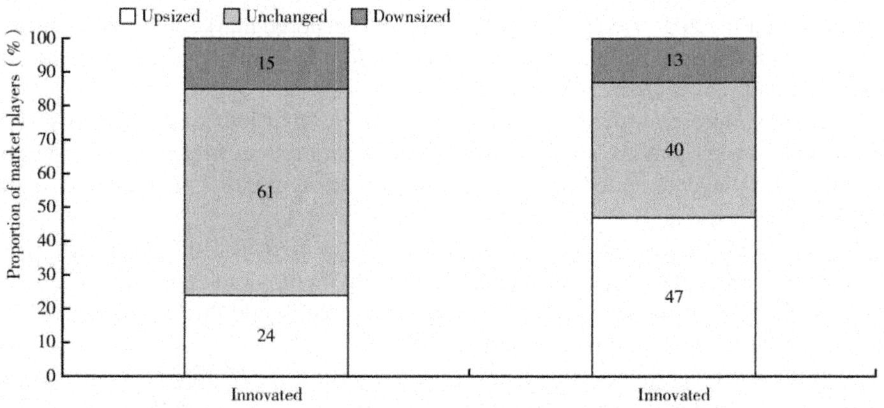

Fig. 4.22 Among the market players who innovated, 47% upsized. *Data source* The China Doing Business Enterprise Survey

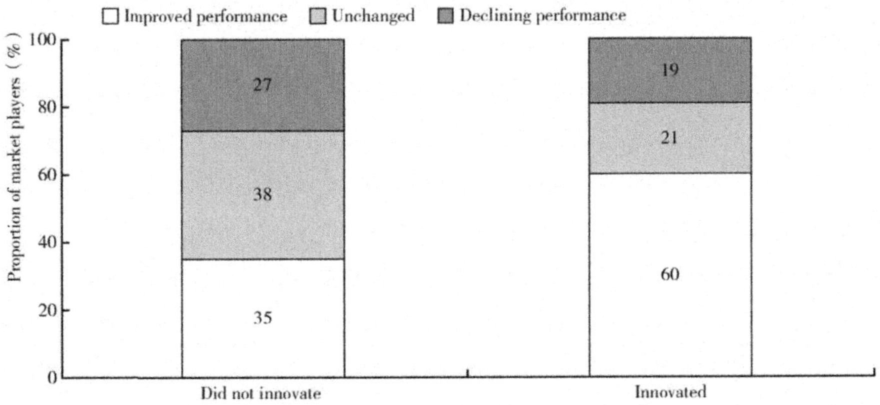

Fig. 4.23 Sixty percent of market players who innovated performed better. *Data source* The China Doing Business Enterprise Survey

increased performance in the past six months. At the same time, the proportion of non-innovative market players who had decreased performance was twenty-seven percent, while this was true for only nineteen percent of market players who innovated. As a result, non-innovative market players face a higher risk of elimination from the market. This shows that innovation is conducive to market players' growth, and further aids high-quality development.

(8) **Summary**

The study results show that the business environment construction strongly supports high-quality development by promoting entrepreneurship, assuring employment, stabilizing growth, restructuring, and promoting innovation. The details are as follows.

The business environment construction promotes entrepreneurship among the people. After the 2014 reform, the proportion of registered market players exceeded fifty percent, the total number of market players doubled, and the share of small and micro market players increased.

It creates more employment opportunities. In the first half of 2019, thirty-four percent of market players upsized. Among them, more than fifty percent of large-scale market players created new jobs, while only thirty percent of small and micro market players did so.

It promotes the growth of market players. In the first half of 2019, forty-nine percent of market players performed better. Among them, more than sixty percent of large-scale market players had increased performance, while this was true for only forty percent of small and micro market players.

It promotes industrial transformation. The proportion of new entrants to the market in the service industry increased from fifty-four percent to seventy percent. This dramatic increase in private economy market players in the service sector has played a major role in China's transformation to being dominated by the service industry.

It promotes widespread innovation. A total of forty-four percent of market players innovated in the first half of 2019. In turn, innovation has helped market players to increase their proportion of new jobs created by twenty-three percentage points, and their performance ratio by twenty-five percentage points, thus further promoting high-quality development.

4.7 Potential Directions for Increasing the Performance of the Business Environment Construction

Beginning from the overall situation in which business environment construction serves high-quality development, China's business environment construction can be divided into three stages. Stage one: business environment construction at the enterprise market entry stage. Stage 2: the enterprise growth stage. Stage 3: the high-quality enterprise development stage. At present, China's business environment construction is in a transition period between the first and second stages. There is an urgent need to reduce the institutional costs of market players throughout their life cycle, support their growth, and transform their quantitative foundation into a qualitative one. Based on the macro effects already achieved and new problems faced by China's business environment construction, and combined with the new economic development situation in China, this report proposes three possible directions for improving the macro effects of the business environment construction.

The first is the organizational dimension, by adhering to the leadership of the Party and establishing new government agencies. For example, the establishment of an approval bureau, a government service data regulation bureau, and so on, is expected to generate natural reactions through the functional restructuring and reengineering of enterprise-related processes, thereby reducing the institutional costs in market players' operations.

The second is the legal dimension, namely constructing a legalized business environment. For example, to promote a profound transformation in government functions, accelerate the creation of a stable, fair, transparent and predictable business environment, and further stimulate market vitality and social creativity, the "Regulations on Optimizing the Business Environment" were introduced in October 2019, and came into effect on January 1, 2020. We hope to reduce institutional costs in market players' operations by further broadening the scope of market access, promoting fair regulation, simplifying government services, and providing convenience for the people.

The third is the technical dimension, namely constructing a digital government. Local governments have launched various mobile apps or mini-programs, such as Guangdong Provincial Affairs, the Zheli Office mobile app, and the Suishen Office mobile app. In June 2019, the General Office of the State Council also launched the trial operation of the nationwide government service platform. In addition, it is necessary to experiment with hardware, by launching automated machines for government services. For example, Guangdong Province's all-in-one government services machine consolidates common government service matters from provincial and municipal departments, including public security, justice, society, civil affairs, housing and construction, agriculture, health planning, market regulation, taxation and disability federations. In addition, for enterprises in Dongguan, full-process intelligent service automated robots are available, which integrate market regulation, taxation, public security and other departments, so that a single machine can provide full-process services for starting a company. The automated machine integrates the approval business of multiple functional departments, achieving standardized services through its built-in standardized approval process. These are all new explorations aimed at deepening the business environment construction. The results of the reforms require further observation, but this report gives us an overview of the general trends.

Part II
Progress in Select Provinces

Chapter 5
The Business Environment of Zhejiang Province

Huirong Huang, Zijun Li, and Guangjun Shen

5.1 Overview on the Report of Zhejiang Province

Following up on the survey performed in Zhejiang Province in 2018, the following year our researchers visited seven cities in the province, namely Hangzhou, Jinhua, Lishui, Ningbo, Quzhou, Huzhou and Zhoushan. In fifteen districts of these cities, our research team randomly interviewed businesspeople at the government service halls, and collected a total of 648 valid questionnaires. Table 5.1 shows the business environment indicator system and the latest progress in Zhejiang Province.

5.2 Progress of Zhejiang Province's Business Environment Construction (2018–2019)

(1) **Sixty-four percent of market players completed registration in one day, the fastest nationwide**

Zhejiang has a short registration processing turnover. As shown in Fig. 5.1, the proportion of market players in Zhejiang who completed registration of their companies in one day increased from 53% in 2018 to 64% in 2019, the fastest nationwide. In 2018, 53% of market players in Zhejiang completed registration within one day, which was significantly higher than the national average for the same period (19%), and the best nationwide. In 2019, 64% of market players said they completed registration within one day, higher than the national average for the same period (25%), maintaining a leading position among the provinces and cities surveyed. The average

H. Huang · Z. Li · G. Shen (✉)
Lingnan College, Sun Yat-sen University, Guangzhou, China
e-mail: shengj6@mail.sysu.edu.cn

X. Xu et al. (eds.), *Report on the Chinese Business Environment Survey 2020*, Research Series on the Chinese Dream and China's Development Path,
https://doi.org/10.1007/978-981-99-6112-2_5

Table 5.1 Business environment indicator system and latest achievements in 2019

Level 1 indicators	Level 2 indicator	Level 3 indicators	Province-wide mean	Nationwide average	Nationwide maximum	Nationwide minimum
Main progress	Market entry	Number of days needed to register a company	4.8	6.9	9.3	3.0
		Number of service windows needed to visit	1.9	1.8	3.1	1.4
		Number of permits needed to process	1.0	1.8	2.7	1.0
	Credit regulation	National enterprise credit information publicity system usage rate (%)	58	66	79	47
	Internet + government services	Online service hall awareness rate (%)	77	66	84	47
		Online service hall usage rate (%)	58	48	73	27
	Service efficiency	Number of visits needed to complete a task in the past six months	1.6	1.9	2.7	1.6
		Number of service windows visited to complete a task in the past six months	1.3	1.4	2.2	1.2

(continued)

Table 5.1 (continued)

Level 1 indicators	Level 2 indicator	Level 3 indicators	Province-wide mean	Nationwide average	Nationwide maximum	Nationwide minimum
		Vote rate of out-of-province market players in evaluating the province's business environment (%)	33		48	0
Macro effectiveness	Employment	Ratio of market players who upsized in the past six months (%)	30	34	45	22
	Growth	Ratio of market players with increased performance in the past six months (%)	51	49	58	34
	Innovation	Ratio of market players who innovated in the past six months (%)	42	44	56	32
	Structure	Ratio of market players in the service sector who registered after the business reform (%)	77	70	97	50

Note Nationwide maximum and Nationwide minimum are the maximum and minimum values at the provincial level
Data source Sun Yat-sen University Research Group on "Deepening the Reform of the Business System"

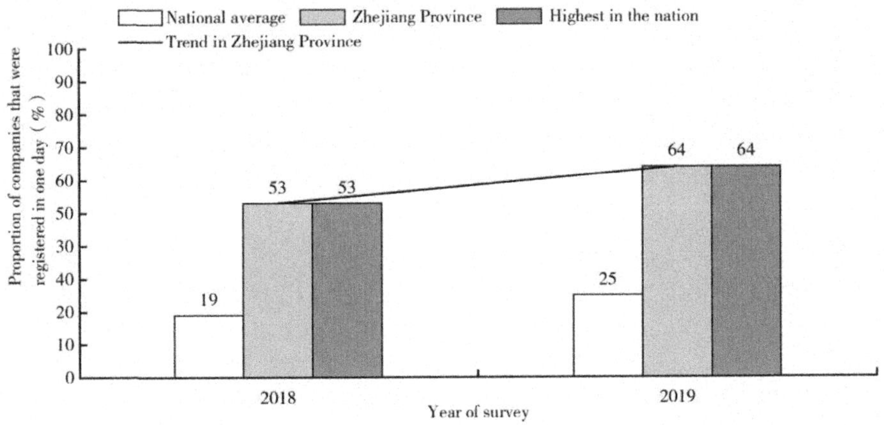

Fig. 5.1 In Zhejiang, the proportion of market players who completed registration in one day increased from 53% in 2018 to 64% in 2019

number of days that market players in Zhejiang needed to complete registration was 4.8 days, which was 2.1 days faster than the national average of 6.9 days.

(2) Market players needed an average of one permit, the best nationwide

In 2019, the average number of permits required for market players in Zhejiang was 1.0, a reduction of 1.3 from 2018. As shown in Fig. 5.2, in Zhejiang in 2018, market players required an average of 2.3 permits to register a business, 0.3 higher than the national average. In 2019, the number of documents required to register a business there was reduced to 1.0, less than the national average of 1.8, reaching the best level nationwide.

(3) More market players viewed the national enterprise credit information publicity system

The starting point of credit regulation is market players accessing the national enterprise credit information publicity system to view the credit information of relevant market players. As shown in Fig. 5.3, in 2019, 58% of market players in Zhejiang chose to view the credit information of their trading partners on the national enterprise credit information publicity system, up nine percentage points from 49% in the previous year. This indicates that the construction of the demand side of credit regulation in Zhejiang has progressed, and is one step closer to entering the widespread use phase of the national enterprise credit information publicity system.

(4) Digital government: the online office hall awareness and usage rates both exceeded the national averages

As shown in Fig. 5.4, 77% of market players in Zhejiang clearly stated they were aware of the online service hall in their location. (In Zhejiang Province, the online service hall is called the Zhejiang Government Services Platform.) Nationwide, 66%

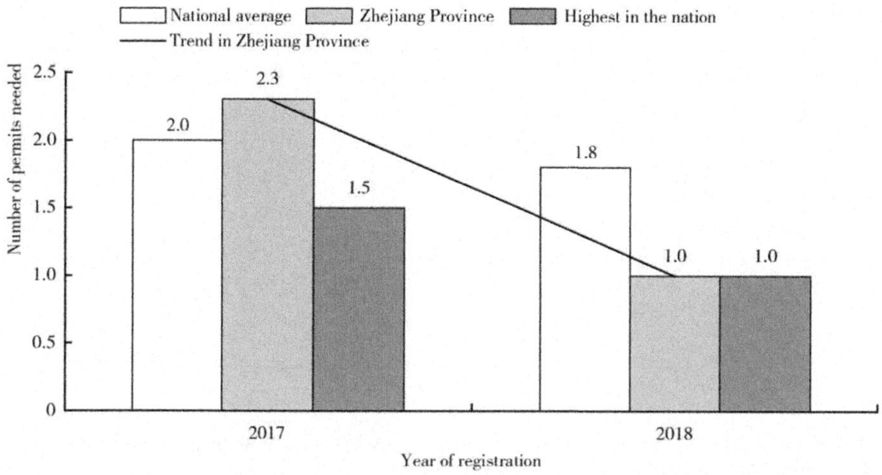

Fig. 5.2 The number of documents required for business registration in Zhejiang dropped significantly

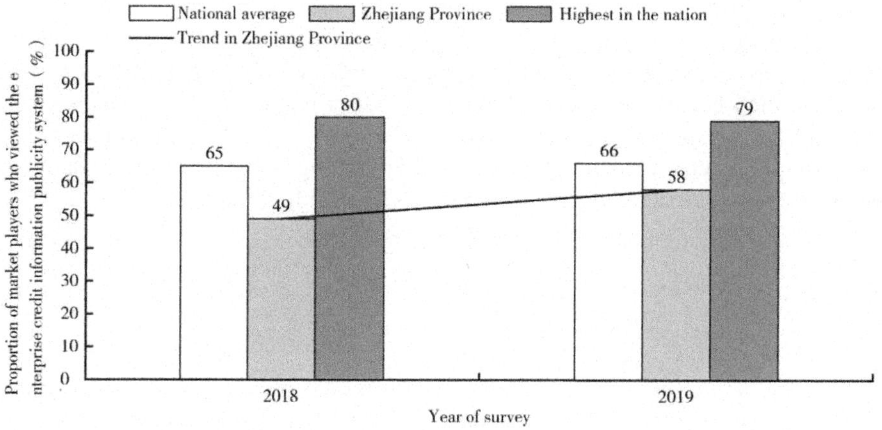

Fig. 5.3 In Zhejiang, the proportion of market players who viewed the national enterprise credit information publicity system increased from 49% in 2018 to 58% in 2019

of market players said so. Therefore, the proportion of market players in Zhejiang who knew about the online service hall was about eleven percentage points higher than the national average. In 2019 in Zhejiang, the awareness and usage rates of the online office system both increased significantly. From 2018 to 2019, the online service hall awareness rate in Zhejiang increased from 50 to 77%, and the usage rate increased from 38 to 58%. This shows that Zhejiang's digital government has moved from the stage of large-scale awareness to large-scale use.

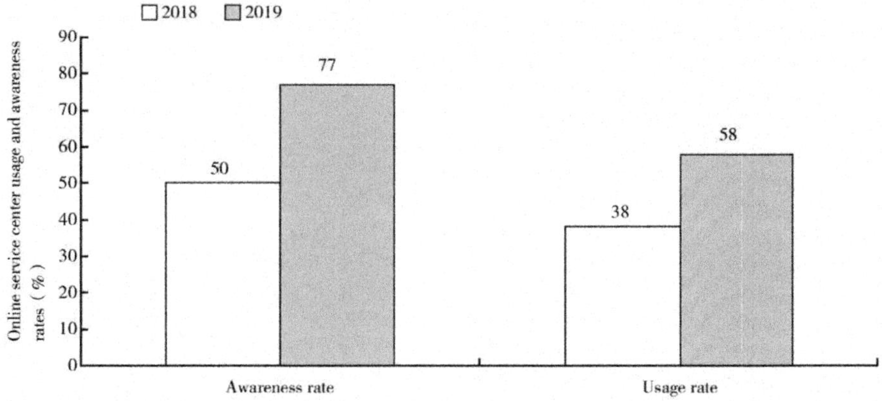

Fig. 5.4 In Zhejiang in 2019, 77% of market players said they knew about the online service hall, and 58% said they used the online service system

As shown in Fig. 5.5, in Zhejiang's construction of single-platform processing, the number of online service systems commonly used by market players was reduced from 2.1 in 2018 to 1.4 in 2019, exhibiting significant results.

In 2019, our research team further investigated the awareness and use of mobile app platforms for business affairs, including "Zheli Office." In August 2014, Zhejiang launched the Zhejiang Government Services Platform, and in 2018 it was renamed the Zheli Office mobile app. After updating, developing and integrating the Zheli Office app's functions, then optimizing and upgrading it, the platform's awareness and usage rates respectively reached 65 and 38% (see Fig. 5.6).

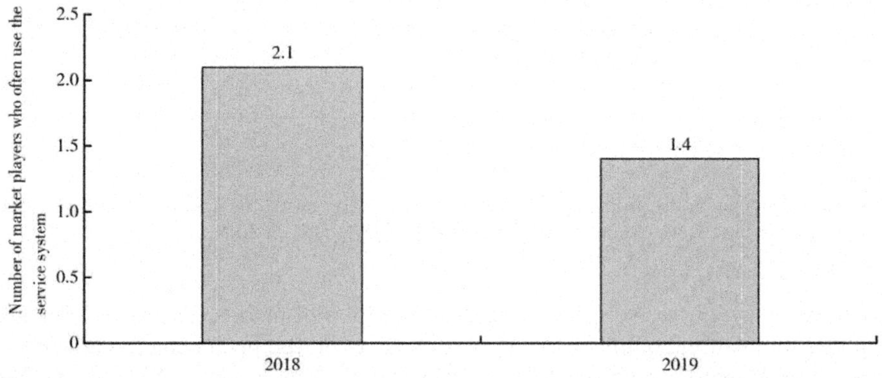

Fig. 5.5 In Zhejiang, the number of online service systems commonly used by market players was reduced from 2.1 in 2018 to 1.4 in 2019

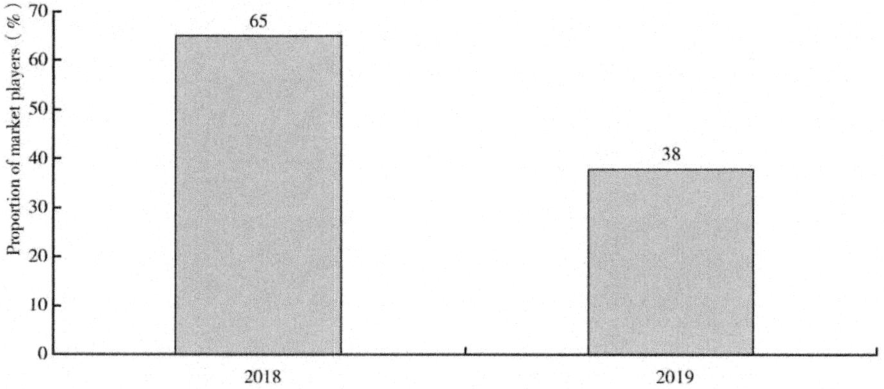

Fig. 5.6 Zhejiang's "Zheli Office" mobile app usage rate was 38%

(5) The completion in one visit rate exceeded the national average

The goal of the business environment construction proposed by the Central Government at the beginning of 2018 was for enterprises and businesspeople to complete all business-related tasks in one visit. This commitment on behalf of the government is also a demand of the market players. As shown in Fig. 5.7, in 2019, 57% of Zhejiang market players completed all of their tasks in a single visit, fifteen percentage points higher than the national average, and thirteen percentage points higher than Zhejiang's rate the previous year. The completion in one visit reform has made great progress from 2018 to 2019.

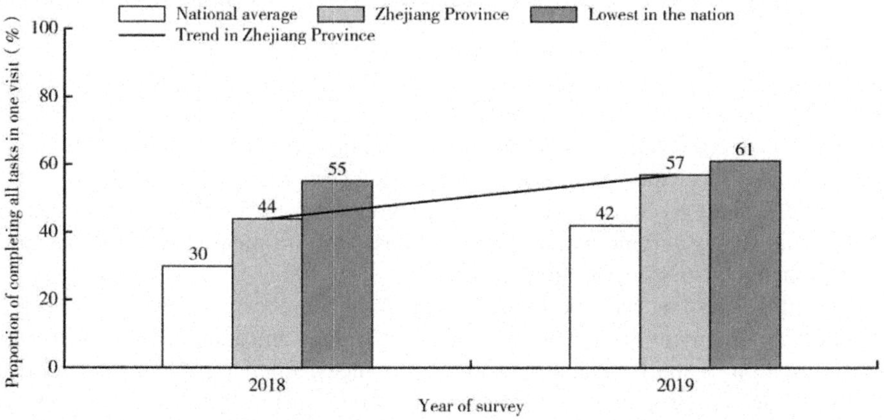

Fig. 5.7 In 2019, 57% of Zhejiang's market players completed all tasks in one visit

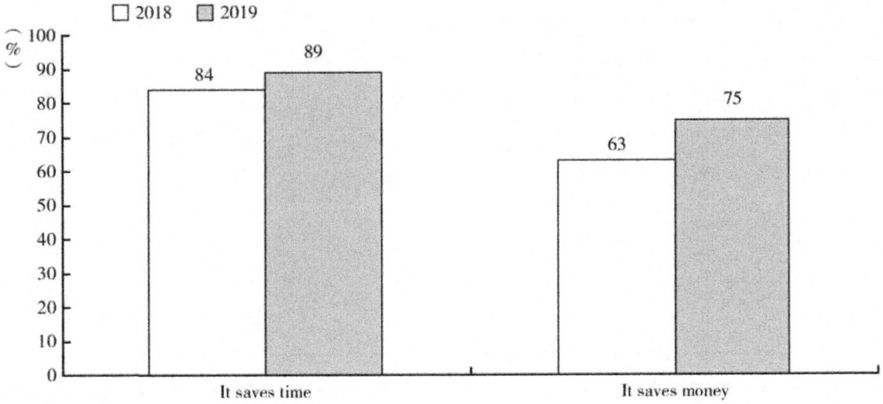

Fig. 5.8 In 2019, more market players believed that the business reform had reduced the cost of completing government-related tasks

(6) **Many market players said that both time and fees had been reduced**

Figure 5.8 shows that, in Zhejiang Province, the proportion of businesspeople who think that the business reform measures had reduced the time needed for government-related tasks increased from 84% in 2018 to 89% in 2019 (five percentage points). Meanwhile, the proportion of businesspeople who think that business reform measures had reduced the fees needed for such tasks increased from 63% in 2018 to 75% in 2019 (twelve percentage points). This shows that the business environment has made progress in reducing fees and saving time.

(7) **Seventy percent in-province approval rate, and third-highest out-of-province vote rate**

Recognition from market players is the most direct affirmation of this. The improvement of the business environment and the recognition of market players are important dimensions of the business environment construction. Figure 5.9 shows that, within Zhejiang Province, the proportion of market players who think that the business reform has had a positive impact on them increased from 59% in 2018 to 68% in 2019. This shows that the market players' sense of fulfillment toward the business environment construction has improved.

Outside the province, the poll results of other market players show that Zhejiang's business environment had a vote rate of 33%, ranking third nationwide. Based on the evaluation of market players in other provinces, Zhejiang has made progress in its business environment construction. As shown in Fig. 5.10, in 2018, 19% of market players outside Zhejiang considered it a good environment for doing business; in 2019, this percentage increased to 33%, an increase of fourteen percentage points. This is a strong affirmation of market players nationwide regarding Zhejiang's business environment construction.

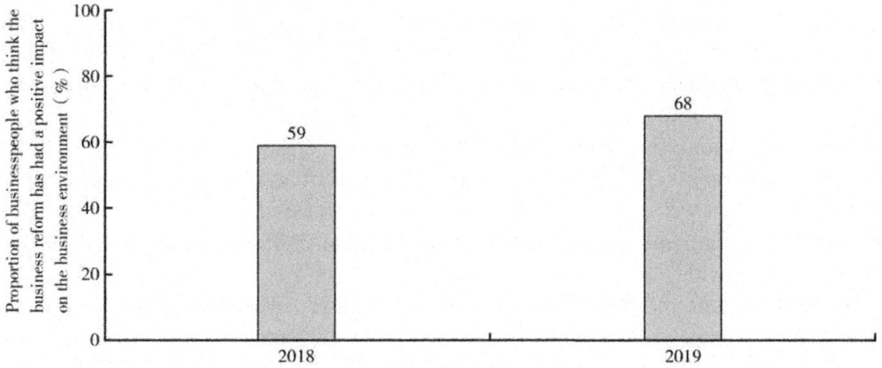

Fig. 5.9 In 2019, the proportion of market players who think that the business reform has positively impacted their operations increased from 59% in 2018 to 68%

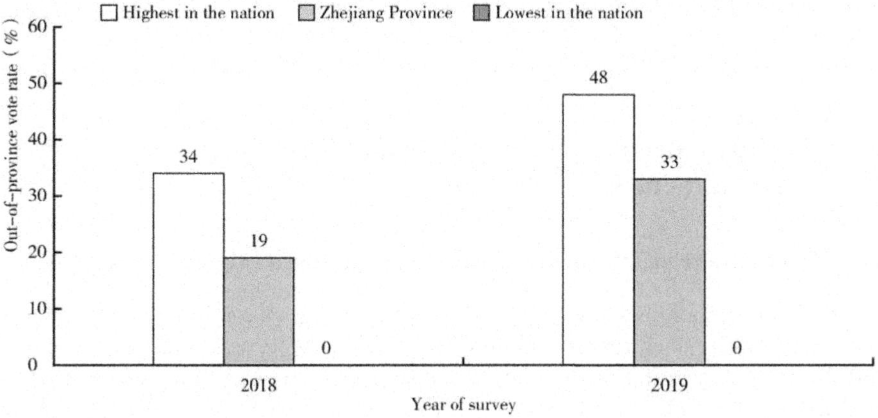

Fig. 5.10 In 2019, Zhejiang Province's business environment received 33% of the votes, up from 19% the previous year

(8) **Summary**

Compared with 2018, Zhejiang's business environment construction in 2019 made significant progress, detailed as follows.

First, the ease of market entry there has continuously improved. It took an average of 4.8 days and 1.9 windows to register a business, with a 64% one-day registration rate, and the number of permits needed was reduced from 2.3 to 1.0, both the best nationwide.

Second, Zhejiang's credit regulation construction is at the national forefront. In Zhejiang, 58% of market players access the credit information of their trade partners through the national enterprise credit information publicity system, thus credit regulation is about to enter the stage of large-scale use.

Third, the improvement of efficiency and use of digital government are among the best nationwide. In Zhejiang, the proportion of market players completing all tasks in one visit was 57%; that of one-window processing was 72%; and the online service hall awareness and usage rates were 77% and 58%, respectively, all among the best nationwide.

Fourth, the fees and time required have been reduced. Most market players recognize that the business environment construction has effectively reduced the fees and time they need, with respective recognition rate increases of 63 to 75% and 84 to 89%.

Fifth and finally, the market players have a high sense of fulfillment. Within the province, 68% of market players think that the business environment construction has had a positive impact on their business operations, and 33% of market players outside the province think positively of Zhejiang's business environment.

5.3 Performance of Zhejiang Province's Business Environment Construction

(1) **Fifty-six percent of market players registered after the business reform**

A visual manifestation of how the business system reform has promoted more market players to engage in entrepreneurship is that many of them registered between 2014 and 2019. As shown in Fig. 5.11, in the research sample of Zhejiang Province, 44% registered before 2014, while 56% registered between 2014 and 2019. This shows that the number of new market players registered companies, started businesses and entered the market after the reform has exceeded that before the reform, accounting for more than half of all current market players.

(2) **In 2019, 30% of market players in Zhejiang created new jobs**

During the field survey, our research team asked the representatives of the market players completing tasks whether they had upsized, downsized or remained the same size over the past six months. As shown in Fig. 5.12, in the first half of 2019, 30% of market players had upsized, 62% remained unchanged, and 8% downsized. This report defines the net increase in employment of market players as the difference between the proportion of market players who upsized and those who downsized. The difference between the two in Zhejiang was twenty-two percentage points, that is, their net increase in employment was 22%. This shows that in 2019, market players in Zhejiang created more jobs and provided more employment opportunities.

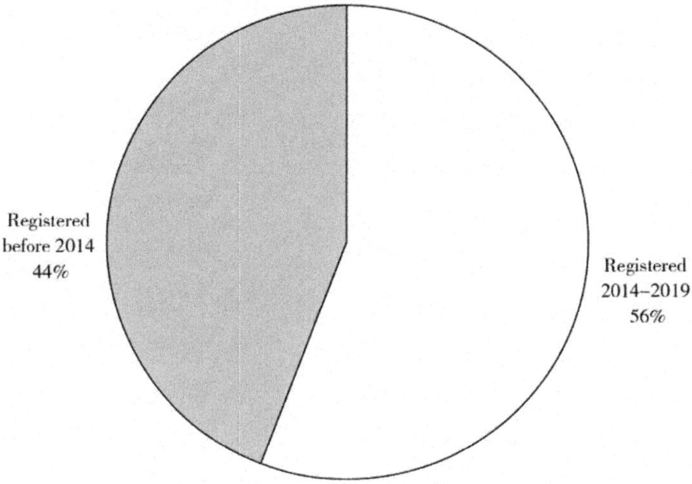

Fig. 5.11 56% of market players in Zhejiang Province registered between 2014 and 2019

Fig. 5.12 In 2019, 30% of the market players in Zhejiang upsized

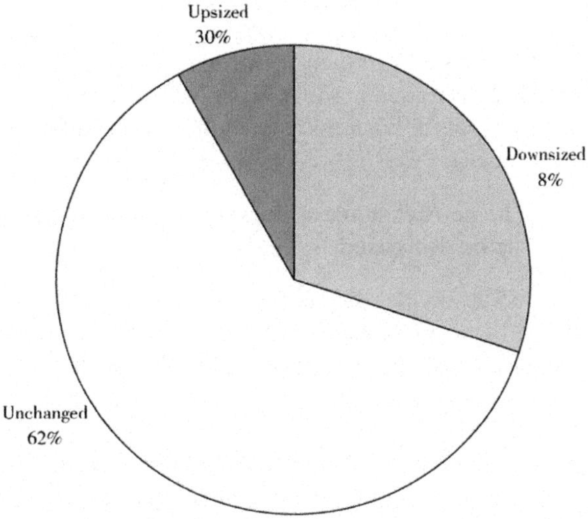

(3) **In 2019, more than half of the market players in Zhejiang had increased performance**

During the field survey, our research team asked the representatives of market players whether their companies' sales performance had increased or decreased in the past six months. As shown in Fig. 5.13, in the first half of 2019, 51% of the market players

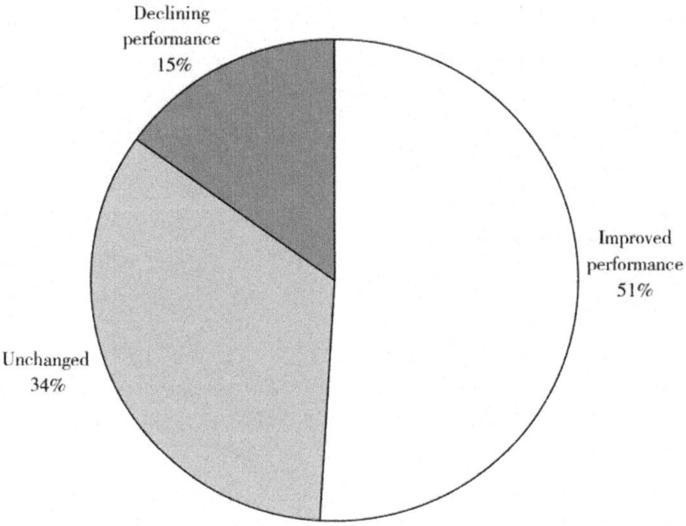

Fig. 5.13 In 2019, 51% of market players in Zhejiang had increased performance

in Zhejiang said that their performance had increased, 34% remained the same, and 15% had decreased performance. This indicates that in 2019, along with the further deepening of the business reform, more than half of the enterprises enjoyed increased performance.

(4) **The market share of the service sector increased, while that of the industry sector decreased**

Figure 5.14 divides the market subjects into two groups: those who registered before the 2014 business reform and those who registered after it. Then the respective proportions of the two are calculated. The results show that 51% of the market players registered in Zhejiang before the 2014 business reform were in the service industry, while 77% of new market players were in the service industry, an increase of twenty-six percentage points. Meanwhile, the proportion of industrial market players dropped from 33 to 13%, and market players in emerging industries fell from 11 to 7%.

(5) **In 2019, more than 40% of market players in Zhejiang launched new products or services**

During the field survey, our research team asked the representatives of the market players whether their companies had launched new products or services in the past six months. As shown in Fig. 5.15, 42% of market players launched new products or services in the first half of 2019. This shows that more than 40% of Zhejiang's market players innovated in the past six months.

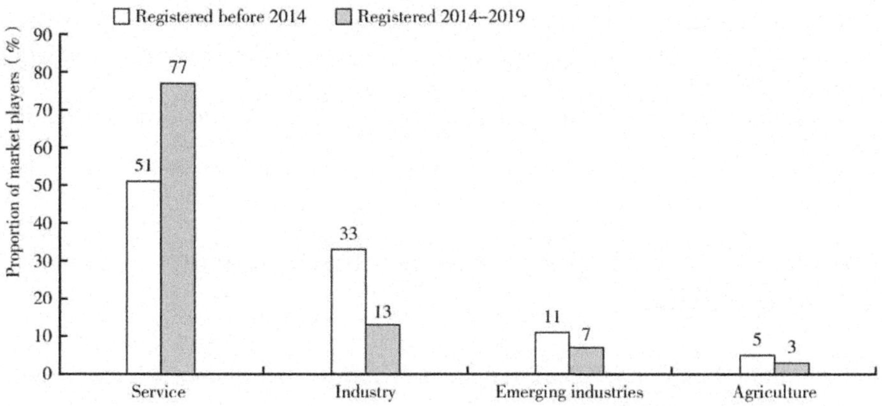

Fig. 5.14 Market share of each industry in Zhejiang Province before and after the business reform

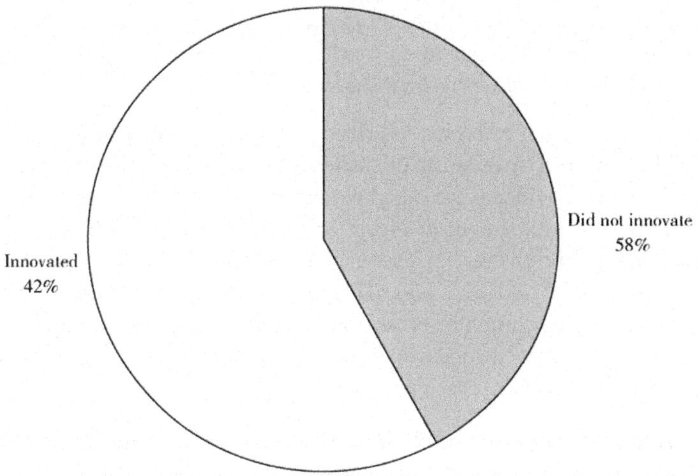

Fig. 5.15 In 2019, 42% of market players in Zhejiang launched new products or services

(6) **Summary**

The survey results show that Zhejiang's business environment construction has strongly supported high-quality economic development, by promoting entrepreneurship, assuring employment, stabilizing growth, adjusting the business structure, promoting innovation, and improving the business environment. The details are as follows.

The business environment construction promoted entrepreneurship: 56% of market players registered after the reform, doubling the total number.

It created more jobs: 30% of market players upsized in the first half of 2019.

It promoted the growth of market players: 51% of market players' performance increased in the first half of 2019.

It promoted widespread innovation: 42% of market players innovated in the first half of 2019.

5.4 Problems in Zhejiang's Business Environment Construction

(1) **Zhejiang has not yet achieved single-window processing, which urgently needs improvement**

The number of windows required to register a business in Zhejiang Province in 2019 was 1.9, slightly higher than the national average of 1.8. This shows that Zhejiang, which was voted third among China's provinces in terms of business environment, still has room for improvement in its market access, being slightly lower than the national average, and single-window processing is insufficient.

Although the number of permits required for market entry in Zhejiang in 2019 was 1.0, the best nationwide, some permits still take much time to process. Market players in Zhejiang Province were asked which permits took the longest time and how much time they took. As shown in Fig. 5.16, permits related to fire, environmental protection, venues, foreign trade and security took more than one month, respectively at 58.1, 50.4, 45.0, 45.0 and 38.2 days. The ones needing the longest time were those related to fire and environmental protection, at almost two months. Therefore, this area of market entry permit processing efficiency urgently needs improvement, so as to enhance market players' experience.

(2) **The credit information publicity system usage rate has improved, but is still lower than the national average**

Market players viewing credit information is the starting point of credit regulation. In 2019, the usage rate of the national enterprise credit information publicity system in Zhejiang increased to 58% from 49% in 2018. However, Fig. 5.17 shows that in 2019, 58% of market players in Zhejiang used the national enterprise credit information publicity system to check the credit information status of other enterprises before doing business with them. This is lower than the national average of 66%, and over twenty-one percentage points lower than the best in the country. This shows that Zhejiang's credit information system construction needs to be accelerated.

(3) **"Internet + government services" construction is insufficient**

Looking at the demand side, as of the end of July 2019, the main problem faced by Zhejiang's digital government construction is the conflict between the people's strong need for digital government and its current inadequate construction. The digital

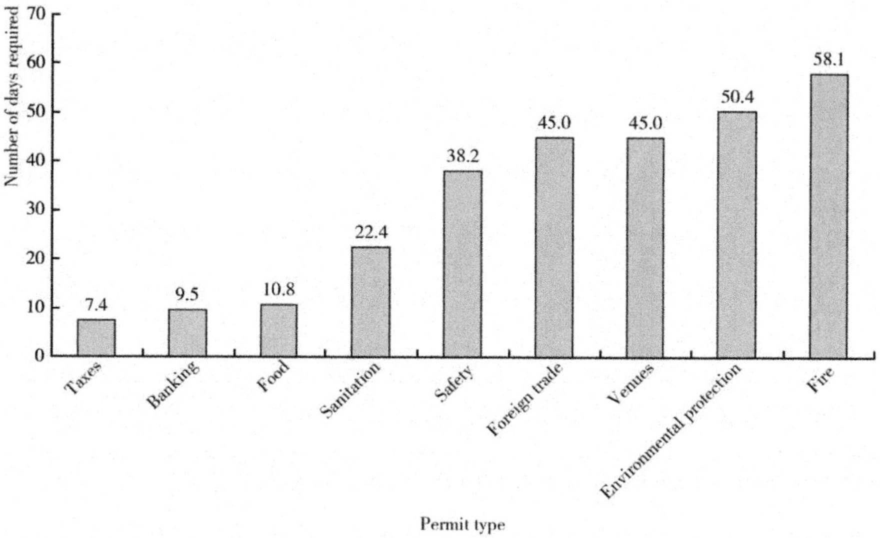

Fig. 5.16 The most time-consuming licenses of various types as described by market players in Zhejiang

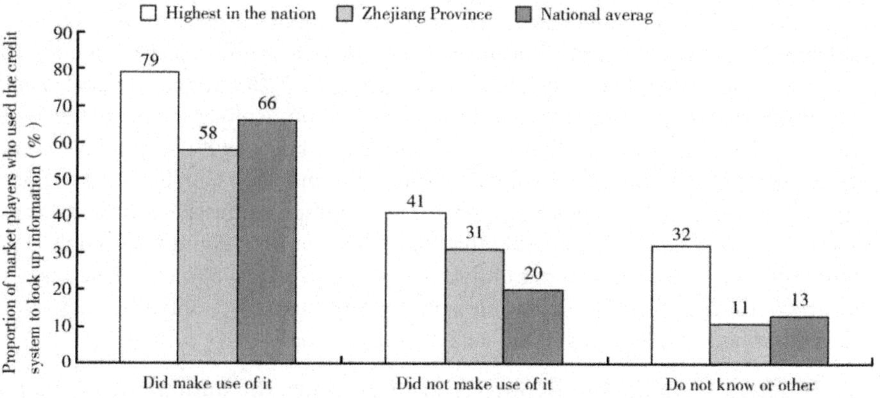

Fig. 5.17 In Zhejiang, about 58% of market players check the national credit information system

government construction level does not match the people's potential demand, and thus their needs are not fully satisfied. As shown in Fig. 5.18, 93% of the businesspeople who were completing tasks said they were willing to use digital government, and 79% said they knew about it. However, the actual usage rate was only 61%, thus the potential demand for digital government in Zhejiang Province is still 32% (93% − 61% = 32%). This indicates that 32% of potential demand for digital government in Zhejiang has not yet been met. As for the online service hall and Zheli Office mobile app, 91% and 86% of the businesspeople were respectively willing to use them, but

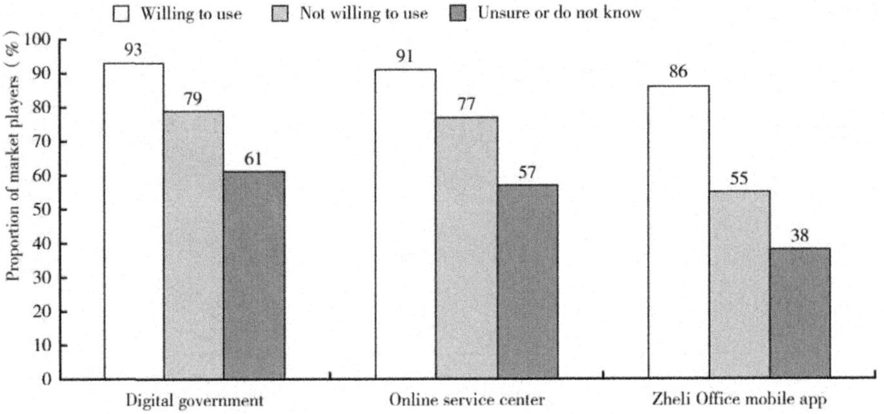

Fig. 5.18 Proportion of businesspeople in Zhejiang who are willing to use, know about and use digital government, the online service hall and Zheli Office mobile app

the actual use rates of the two were only 57 and 38%. The respective unmet demand rates of 34% (91% − 57% = 34%) and 48% (86% − 38% = 48%) are both quite high.

The two main reasons for the inadequate construction of digital government in Zhejiang are detailed below. First, the digital government services are not complete, and cannot meet all of people's business needs. As shown in Fig. 5.19, among the businesspeople who did not use the online service hall, 29% said they did so because they think it cannot perform all the tasks they need to do. Among the people who did not use the Zheli Office mobile app, 32% said it was because it did not have all the services they needed. Second, digital government is unable to handle all the required steps in the process. As shown in Fig. 5.19, among the businesspeople who did not use the online service hall, 24% said that this was because it could not complete the entire process, so after beginning online they would still have to complete tasks in person. As for the Zheli Office mobile app, 18% of businesspeople said they chose not to use it because they never had never used it before.

(4) **Zhejiang's completion in one visit rate is above the national average, but has yet to reach 100%**

Figure 5.20 shows that in 2019, 57% of Zhejiang market players only needed to make one visit to complete a task, fifteen percentage points higher than the national average, but still four percentage points behind the nationwide best level. A total of thirty-three of market players needed to make two visits to complete a task. On average, businesspeople needed to make 1.6 trips to complete a task, thus the goal of completing all tasks in one visit has not yet been achieved. This means that Zhejiang has both achievements and shortcomings in the reform of completing all tasks in one visit.

The survey responses show that the completion in one visit reform still needs work. In one city, when asked about the ease and speed of processing business permits and

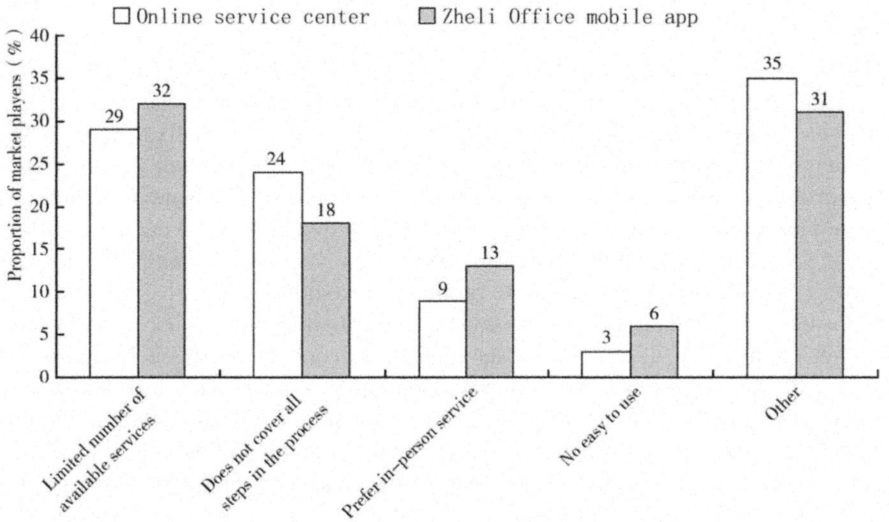

Fig. 5.19 The reasons that businesspeople in Zhejiang people did not use the online service hall and Zheli Office mobile app

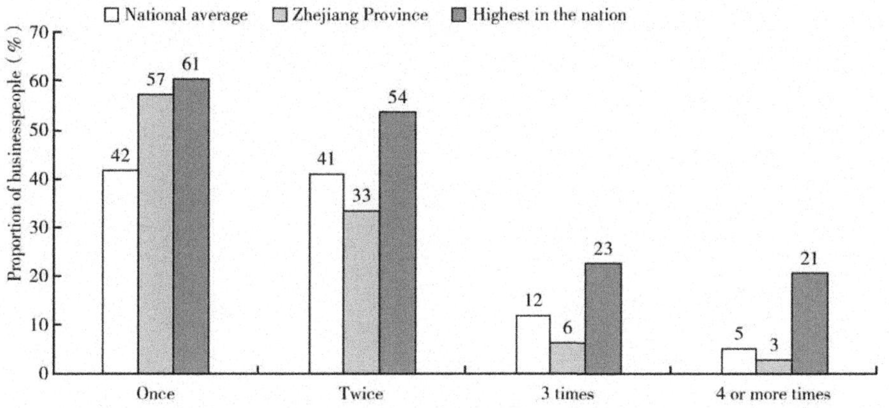

Fig. 5.20 In 2019, 57% of Zhejiang market players completed all their tasks in one visit

other licenses, one person told us, "They said it would only take one trip, so that's what I expected. But actually I still had to make several trips, which kind of bothered me.... And the website said what materials I should bring, but when I got here, they needed different ones." In another city, some people said that although the service hall has tried to implement the completion in one visit reform, in most cases people still have to make several trips, first to consult, then to bring the materials, only to find they are not the right ones, then come back again.

(5) Fierce market competition in the greatest challenge

The business system reform has centered on solving the problems in obtaining licenses and permits, exiting the market, and so on; however, the market players' responses show that these are no longer the main problems they face. When asked about the main difficulties encountered in doing business in their area, the respective proportions of Zhejiang market players who said starting a business, obtaining a license and exiting the market were 2, 4 and 2%, all quite low, showing that these are no longer the main challenges they face. At the national level, 3, 7 and 3% of market players respectively mentioned these problems, also quite low.

Instead, Zhejiang market players said the main challenges they face now are fierce market competition, high labor costs and recruitment, as respectively mentioned by 27, 22 and 17% of market players. Although market players nationwide also commonly face these three challenges, the proportions in Zhejiang are all slightly higher than the national averages, showing that the situation in Zhejiang is somewhat more severe. Clearly, the current business environment construction has not been able to directly resolve these major issues (Fig. 5.21).

It should be pointed out that these new difficulties are inevitable phenomena accompanying the process of Zhejiang's business environment construction while it continues to achieve formidable results. As of the end of December 2019, in Zhejiang Province there were 7,242,500 market players of all kinds, up 10.7% year on year. In 2019, 1,435,600 new market players of all kinds were registered, up 16.35% year on

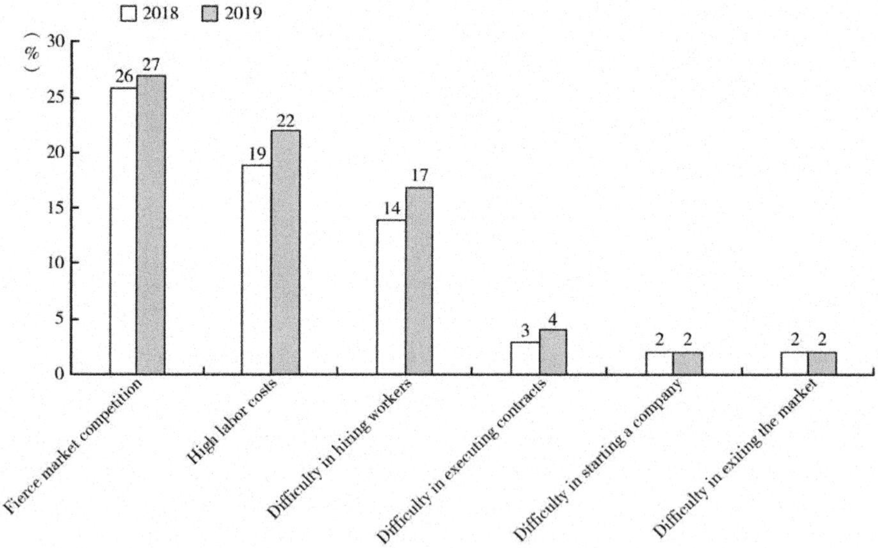

Fig. 5.21 The main challenges faced by market players in 2018 and 2019 are basically the same

year, including 497,900 newly registered ones, up 12.32% year on year. The number of market player per 10,000 people was 1262, an average of one in just under eight people, the highest nationwide ratio of market players per capita. This rapid increase in market players is an achievement in the business environment construction, yet at the same time it also creates a new challenge for it. More market players means that in the product market the market supply may be increased, inevitably leading to more intense competition. Meanwhile, in the production factor market the market demand may increase, which will inevitably lead to greater difficulties in recruitment, along with rising production factor and enterprise costs. Therefore, the challenges currently faced by Zhejiang market players are rooted in the increase of market players brought about by the business environment construction, and it is necessary to further optimize the business environment, so as to promote market players' growth.

Chapter 6
The Business Environment of Jilin Province

Bingyu Yang, Yining Su, and Xianxiang Xu

6.1 Overview of the Report on Jilin Province

In 2019, our research team conducted a second survey of Jilin Province. Through stratified random sampling, five cities were investigated in Jilin Province: Changchun, Jilin, Siping, Baishan and Songyuan. A total of 354 valid questionnaires were collected during random interviews. Table 6.1 shows Jilin Province's business environment indicator system and latest achievements.

6.2 Progress of Jilin Province's Business Environment Construction

The focuses of the business system reform are "streamlining government services, delegating power and strengthening regulation." The research results show that in 2019 the average registration time in Jilin Province decreased, the credit regulation system began entering the stage of large-scale use, and the fee reduction work has been recognized by market players.

(1) **More convenient company registration**

Jilin Province maintains the fastest registration time in the country. As shown in Fig. 6.1, in 2018 the average time required for market players in Jilin Province to register a company was 7.5 days. In 2019, this dropped to 4.2 days, better than the national average.

B. Yang · Y. Su · X. Xu (✉)
Lingnan College, Sun Yat-sen University, Guangzhou, China
e-mail: lnsxuxx@mail.sysu.edu.cn

X. Xu
Institute of Mezzoeconomics, Sun Yat-sen University, Guangzhou, China

X. Xu et al. (eds.), *Report on the Chinese Business Environment Survey 2020*, Research Series on the Chinese Dream and China's Development Path,
https://doi.org/10.1007/978-981-99-6112-2_6

Table 6.1 Business environment indicator system and latest achievements in 2019

Level 1 indicators	Level 2 indicators	Level 3 indicators	Province-wide average	National average	Nationwide maximum	Nationwide minimum
Key accomplishments	Market entry	Number of days needed to register a company	4.2	6.9	9.3	3.0
		Number of service windows needed to visit	1.9	1.8	3.1	1.4
		Number of permits needed to process	2.1	1.8	2.7	1.0
	Credit regulation	National enterprise credit information publicity system usage rate (%)	55	66	79	47
	Internet + government services	Online service hall awareness rate (%)	71	66	84	47
		Online service hall usage rate (%)	48	48	73	27
	Service efficiency	Number of trips taken to complete a task in the past 6 months	1.9	1.9	2.7	1.6
		Number of service windows visited to complete a task in the past 6 months	1.5	1.4	2.2	1.2
		Votes received from out-of-province market players in assessing the province's business environment (%)	0		48	0
Macro results	Employment	Proportion of market players who upsized in the past 6 months (%)	27	34	45	22
	Growth	Proportion of market players with increased performance in the past 6 months (%)	39	49	58	34
	Innovation	Proportion of market players who innovated in the past 6 months (%)	39	44	56	32
	Structure	Proportion of market players in the service sector who registered after the business reform (%)	66	70	97	50

Source Sun Yat-sen University Research Group on "Deepening the Reform of the Business System." The nationwide maximum and nationwide minimum are the maximum and minimum values at the provincial level

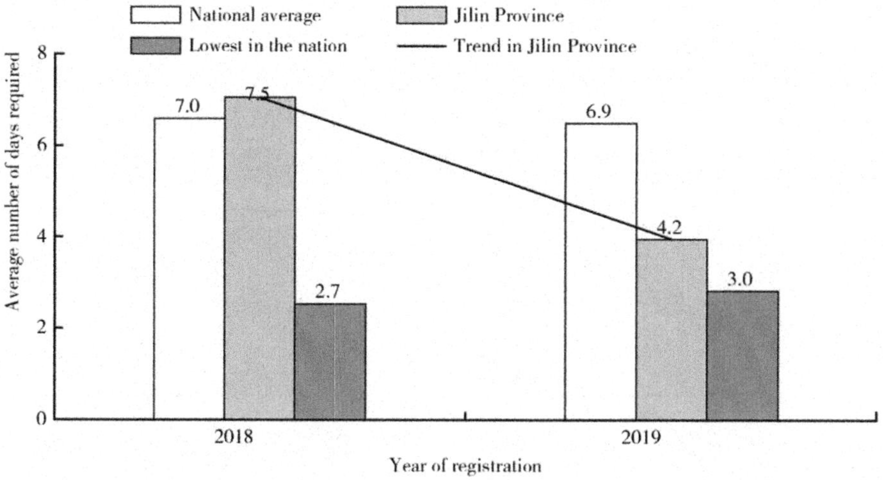

Fig. 6.1 In 2019, the time required to register a company in Jilin was 4.2 days, which is 3.3 days less than the previous year

(2) **More market players used the credit information system**

The starting point of credit regulation is for market players to access the national credit information system to check the credit information of related enterprises. As shown in Fig. 6.2, in 2018, 49% of market players in Jilin said that, before trading with other market players, they checked their credit information through the National Enterprise Information Publicity System. This rate is 16% points lower than the national average of 65%. In 2019, 55% of Jilin market players chose to check the credit information of their trading partners on the national credit information system. The national average was 66%, which Jilin was still below, but the gap between the two narrowed to 11% points. Credit regulation in Jilin Province from 2018 to 2019 was effectively promoted, drawing nearer the national average.

(3) **Reduced fees**

Fee reduction was one of 2019's key tasks. As shown in Fig. 6.3, in 2019, 79% of market players in Jilin Province believed that the business reform measures had reduced the fees for dealing with other market players and the government, an increase of 14% points compared with 2018. This shows that in terms of fee reduction work, Jilin market players' sense of fulfillment increased significantly in 2019.

(4) **Summary**

Compared with 2018, the accomplishments made in Jilin Province's business environment construction in 2019 are as follows:

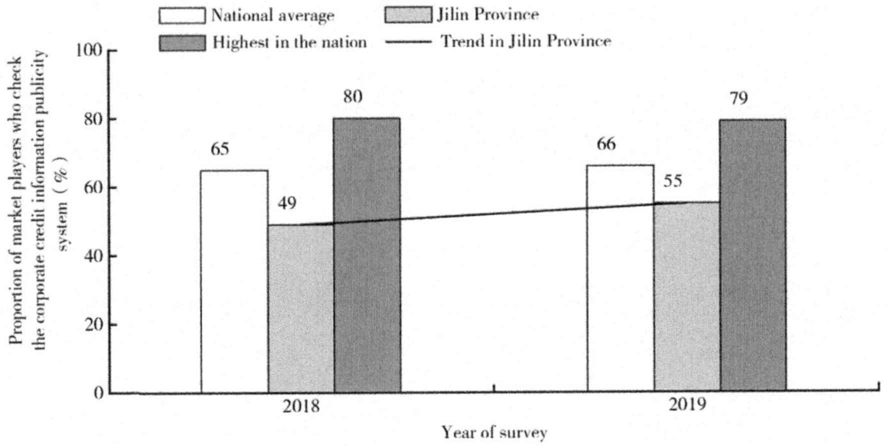

Fig. 6.2 In Jilin, the proportion of market players who checked the national credit information system rose from 49% in 2018 to 55% in 2019

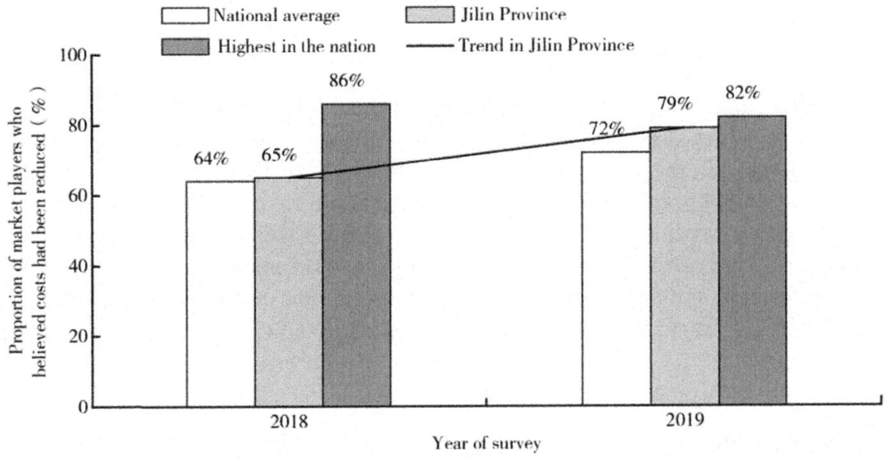

Fig. 6.3 In Jilin, the proportion of market players who said they think that the business reform had reduced costs rose to 79% from 65% in 2018

First, the average time that market players there needed to register a company dropped from 7.5 days in 2018 to 4.2 days in 2019, exceeding the national average.

Second, in 2019, 55% of Jilin market players checked the credit information of their trading partners through the national credit information system, an increase of 6% points over 2018.

Third, in terms of fee reduction work, the number of market players who recognized that fees had been reduced increased from 65 to 79%, signifying a vast majority.

6.3 Performance of Jilin Province's Business Environment Construction

Does Jilin's business system reform promote the province's economic development? The business system reform supports economic development, as reflected in promoting the entry of new market players, creating jobs, increasing performance, promoting structural transformation, promoting innovation, and improving the business environment. The survey results show that Jilin's business system reform has strongly promoted the province's economic development.

(1) **Forty-eight percent of market players had registered after the business reform**

As shown in Fig. 6.4, in the random survey sample of Jilin Province, 54% of market players had registered there before 2014, while 48% had registered between 2014 and 2019. This shows that the number of new market players who registered, started businesses, and entered the market after the reform accounted for nearly half of all active market players.

(2) **After the business reform, Jilin market players in the service industry increased**

In Fig. 6.5, market players are divided into two groups: those who registered before the 2014 business reform and those who registered after it. Then the respective proportions of different industries in each group are calculated. The results show that among the Jilin market players registered before the 2014 business reform, 49% were in the service industry, while among the newly registered market players, 66% were in the service industry, an increase of 17% points.

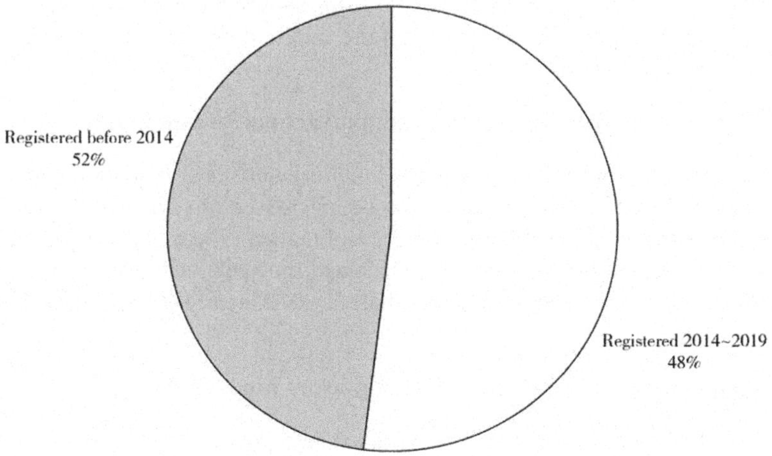

Fig. 6.4 After the business reform, the total number of market players in Jilin Province doubled

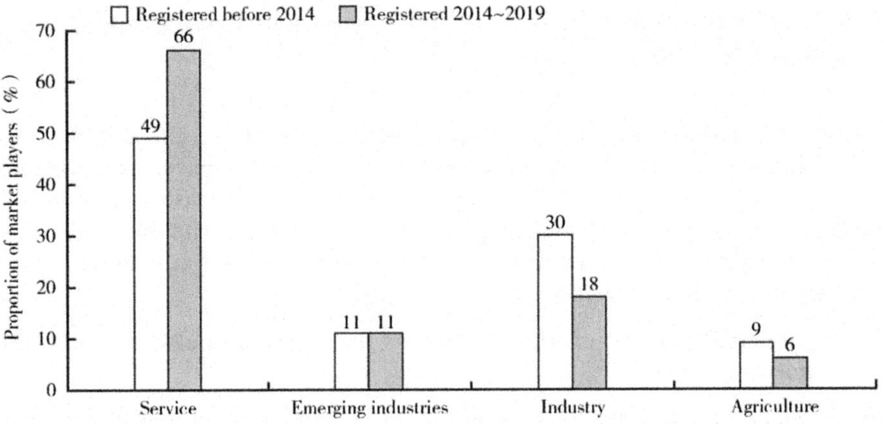

Fig. 6.5 The proportion of Jilin market players in various industries in before and after the business reform

In addition, the proportion of industrial market players dropped from 30% to 18%, while that of agricultural market players dropped from 9% to 6%. The proportion of market players in emerging industries was 11%, the same as in 2018.

(3) **Twenty-seven percent of Jilin market players created jobs**

During the field survey, our research team asked the representatives of market players if their companies had upsized or downsized in the past 6 months. As shown in Fig. 6.6, in the first half of 2019, 27% of market players upsized, 57% had no change, and 15% downsized. This report defines the net increase in employment of market players as the difference between the proportion of market players who upsized and downsized. The difference between the two was 12% points, that is, the net increase in employment of market players was 12%. This shows that in the first half of 2019, market players in Jilin Province created more jobs and provided more employment opportunities than before.

(4) **Thirty-nine percent of Jilin market players performed better**

During the survey, our research team asked representatives of market players if their companies' sales performance had increased, decreased or remained the same over the past 6 months. As shown in Fig. 6.7, 39% of market players in Jilin Province said their performance had increased, 27% remained the same, and 34% had decreased performance. This shows that in the first half of 2019, nearly 40% of market players performed better.

(5) **Thirty-nine percent of Jilin market players innovated**

During the field survey, our research team asked representatives of market players if their companies had launched new products or services in the past 6 months. As Fig. 6.8 shows, in the first half of 2019, 39% of market players there launched

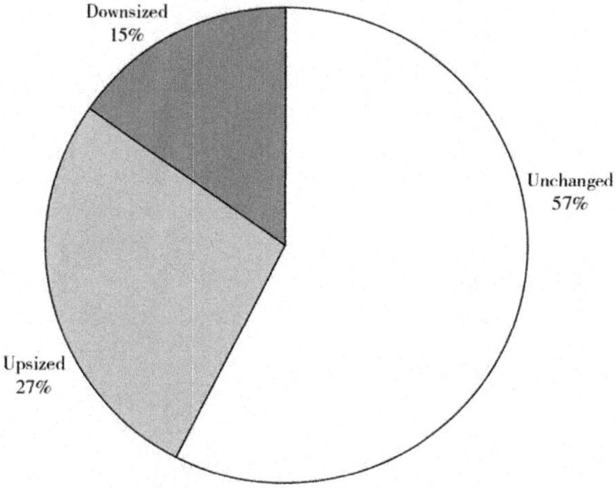

Fig. 6.6 In 2019, 27% of market players in Jilin Province upsized

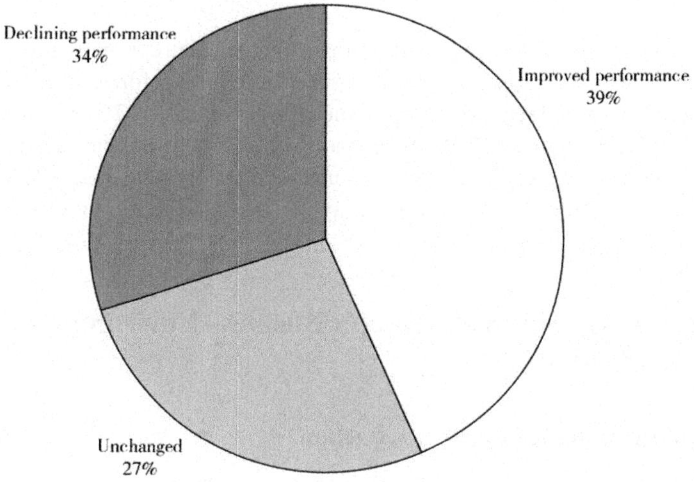

Fig. 6.7 In 2019, the performance of 39% of market players in Jilin Province improved

new products or services. This shows that nearly 40% of the market players in Jilin Province innovated in the past 6 months.

(6) **Summary**

The research results show that the business environment construction in Jilin Province has strongly supported high-quality economic development by promoting entrepreneurship, assuring employment, stabilizing growth, restructuring, promoting innovation, and improving the business environment. The details are as follows:

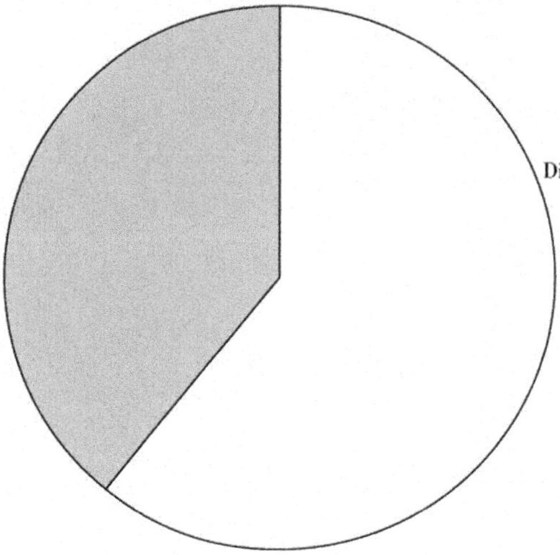

Fig. 6.8 In 2019, 39% of market players in Jilin Province launched new products or services

The business environment construction promotes entrepreneurship among the people: 48% of market players had registered after the reform, thereby doubling the total number. It creates more employment opportunities: 27% of market players upsized in the first half of 2019. It promotes the growth of market players: 39% of market players had improved performance in the first half of 2019. It promotes widespread innovation: 39% of market players innovated in the first half of 2019.

6.4 Problems in Jilin Province's Business Environment Construction

(1) **No progress made in permit reduction**

As Fig. 6.9 shows, in 2018, Jilin market players needed to apply for an average of 2.1 permits, which was close to the national average; by 2019, the number remained at 2.1, but the gap between the national average grew, thus Jilin has not made progress in permit reduction.

(2) **Service efficiency declined**

The Central Government's business environment construction goal in early 2018 was that market players would only have to visit one place, and only need to make one trip. This is also a desire of the market players. As shown in Fig. 6.10, judging from the 2018 survey results, 49% of the market players in Jilin Province completed all their tasks in one visit, which was higher than the national average. By 2019, this rate had dropped from 49% to 39%, a decrease of 10% points, putting it lower than the

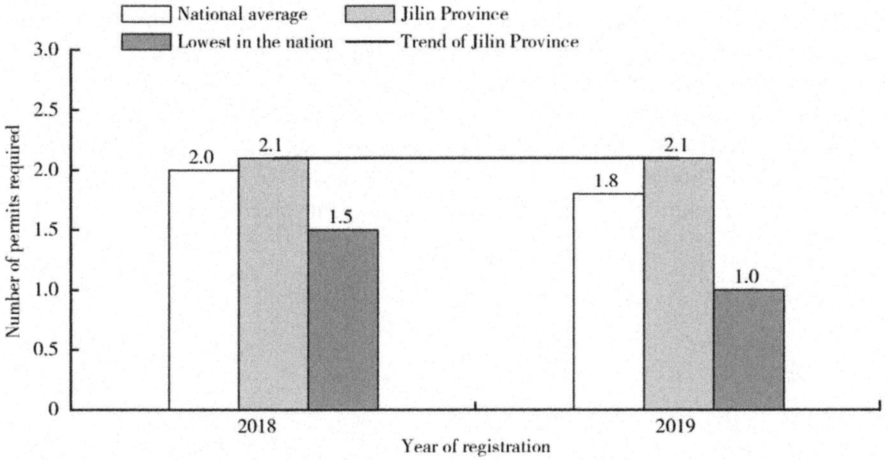

Fig. 6.9 In Jilin, the number of permits that market players needed to register a company in 2019 was the same as in 2018 (2.1)

national average. This shows that the completion in one visit reform in Jilin Province lost speed in 2019.

(3) **Reduced sense of fulfilment**

The improvement of the business environment and recognition of market players are important dimensions for evaluating the business environment construction. As shown in Fig. 6.11, judging from the evaluation of market players in the province,

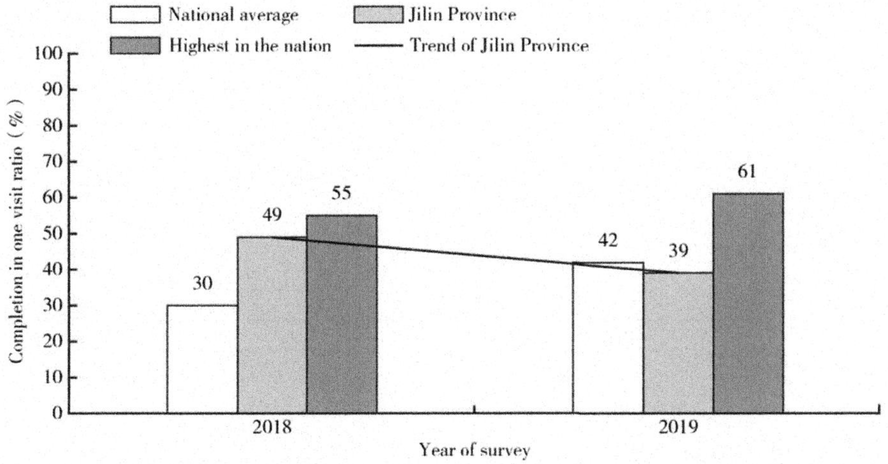

Fig. 6.10 In Jilin, the proportion of market players who completed all tasks in one visit dropped from 49% in 2018 to 39% in 2019

the proportion of those who said they thought that the business reform had a positive impact on them dropped from 71% in 2018 to 66% in 2019, thus the sense of fulfillment of market players there has decreased.

As shown in Fig. 6.12, the voting results of out-of-province market players reveal that Jilin received 0% of the votes for their business environment, ranking the lowest nationwide. This reflects the fact that the Jilin's business environment has not yet been recognized nationwide, and efforts to optimize it must be strengthened.

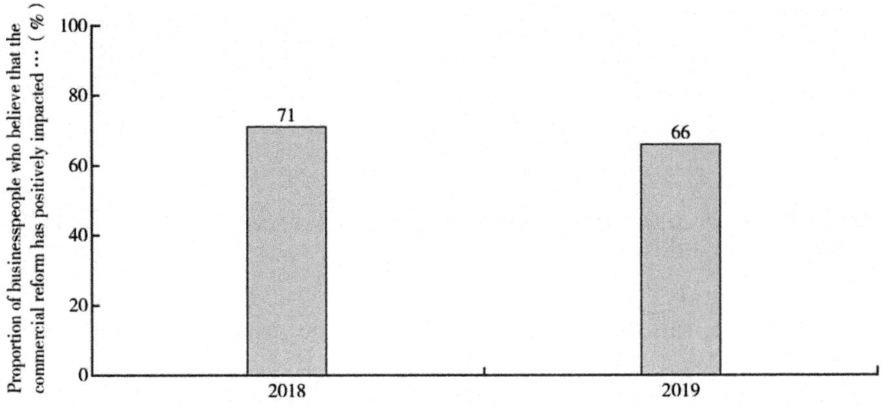

Fig. 6.11 In Jilin, the proportion of businesspeople who believe that the business reform has had a positive impact on them fell from 71% in 2018 to 66% in 2019

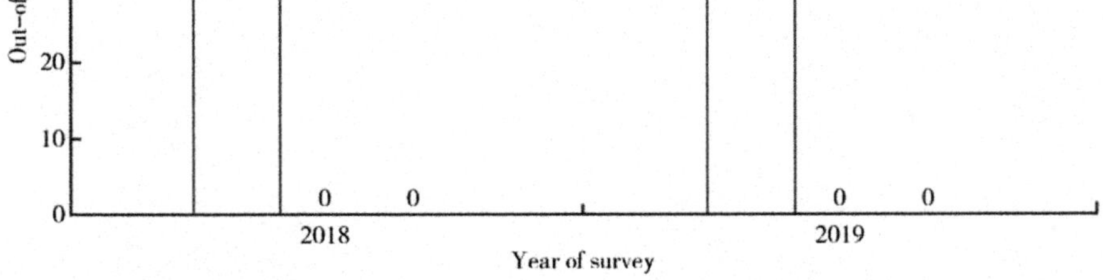

Fig. 6.12 The vote rate for Jilin's business environment was 0%

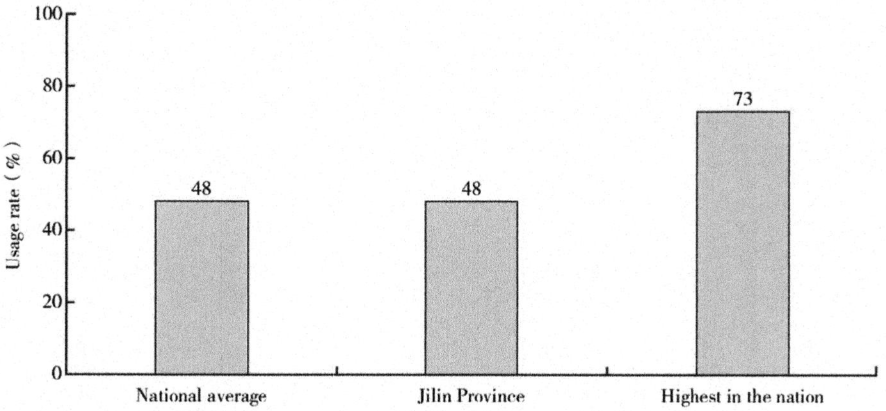

Fig. 6.13 In 2019, the usage rate of online office halls in Jilin was 48%

(4) Low online service hall usage and single-network access rates

"Internet + government services" is an inevitable trend in the information age. However, judging from the market players' responses, both the online service hall usage rate and single-network access rate in Jilin were low.

The usage rate of the online service system in Jilin was on par with the national average. As Fig. 6.13 shows, Jilin's online service hall usage rate was 48%. In Fig. 6.14, the main reason that market players gave for not using the online service system was that not all services are included, with 28% of market players believing that the online system lacks some services.

During the field survey, many market players stated that they were unable to complete tasks online. For example, one businessperson said, "It's inconvenient to handle it online? The online system approval process and real-name verification are a pain, and it's hard to get it to work. So it's still more convenient to do it at the service window." Based on the researchers' interviews, if the online service system were easy to use, then most businesspeople would choose to use it. The reason for the current low usage rate may be that they do not know how to use it. Another businessperson said, "Of course, it's faster to do it online, it's just that I don't know how to do it." In another city, our research team learned that many older businesspeople lacked experience with computers. This means that they are unable to operate a computer to complete tasks, and also encounter much difficulty in communicating with the staff. Problems such as incorrect data formats often occur, and the staff must explain the operation process on the computer several times, causing great inconvenience and decreasing efficiency.

Meanwhile, the single-network access rate in Jilin in 2019 was lower than in 2018. Figure 6.15 shows that, in 2018, 60% of market players in Jilin said they regularly used the online services system; in 2019, this rate dropped to 32%.

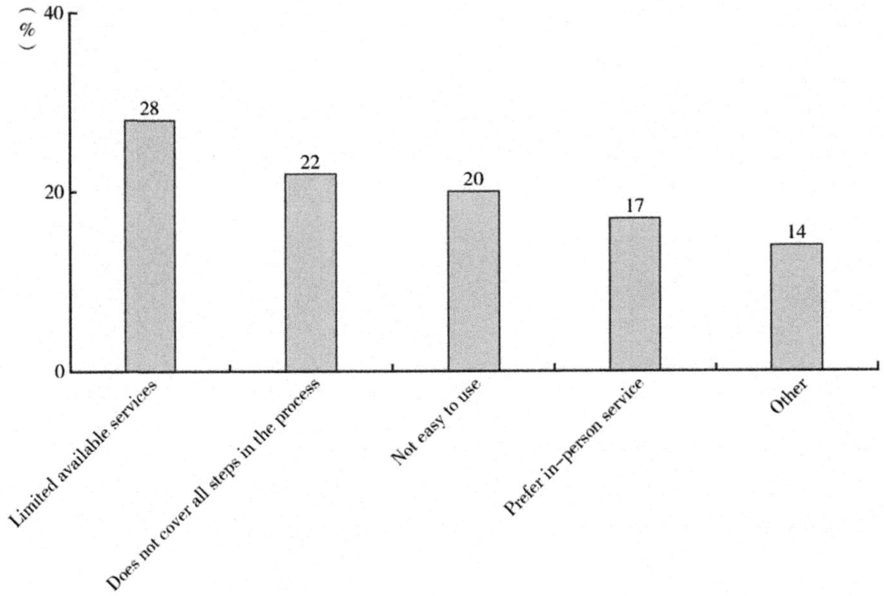

Fig. 6.14 The reasons that market players in Jilin Province did not choose to complete tasks online

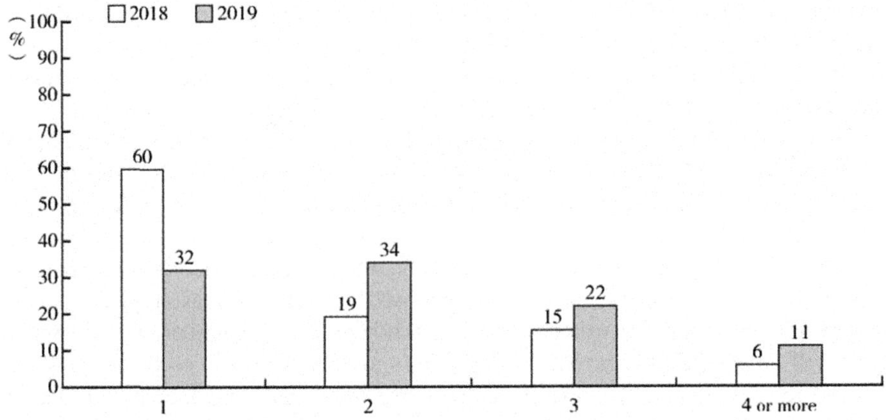

Fig. 6.15 In Jilin, the single-network access rate dropped from 60% in 2018 to 32% in 2019

(5) **Inadequate credit regulation**

As shown in Fig. 6.16, in 2019, 83% of market players in Jilin Province reported that they had been inspected on-site in the past year, which was slightly higher than the national average. Among them, 35% said the number of on-site inspections had increased, while 42% said the number had not changed, and 6% said it had decreased.

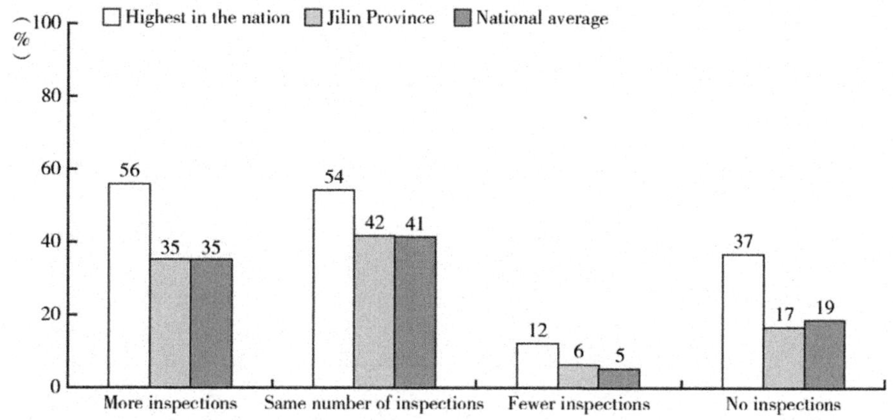

Fig. 6.16 83% of market players in Jilin underwent on-site inspections in the past year

This shows that in Jilin, market players have been inspected many times, showing that credit regulation is inadequate.

(6) Main challenges: fierce market competition, high labor costs, recruitment

The challenges faced by market players in Jilin Province are basically the same as those faced by market players nationwide. The business environment construction has always revolved around resolving difficulties such as obtaining licenses and permits, and exiting the market. However, judging from market players' responses, these are no longer the main challenges they face. As shown in Fig. 6.17, market players in Jilin reported that their main challenges in 2019 were fierce market competition, high labor costs, recruitment and financing, with respective response rates of 25%, 16%, 13% and 13%. These four challenges are also commonly faced by market players nationwide.

Compared to 2018, the issue of high labor costs was further exacerbated in 2019. As shown in Fig. 6.18, compared to 2018, the problems faced by market players in 2019 intensified. These included fierce market competition, rising labor costs, difficulties in financing, heavy tax burdens, frequent market inspections, and difficulties in contract execution. In a district in a city in southern Jilin, an Internet café owner who was completing business-related tasks told us, "It's hard to hire people in our district. Recruitment's tough here. Most young people go overseas to pursue their careers, and not enough of them stay here." He also told us that after young people in cities reach adulthood, they typically choose to work in cities with strong business environments, while few return to support their hometown's development. The mass exodus of young people from the city has led to problems such as a large local labor gap and difficulty in recruitment.

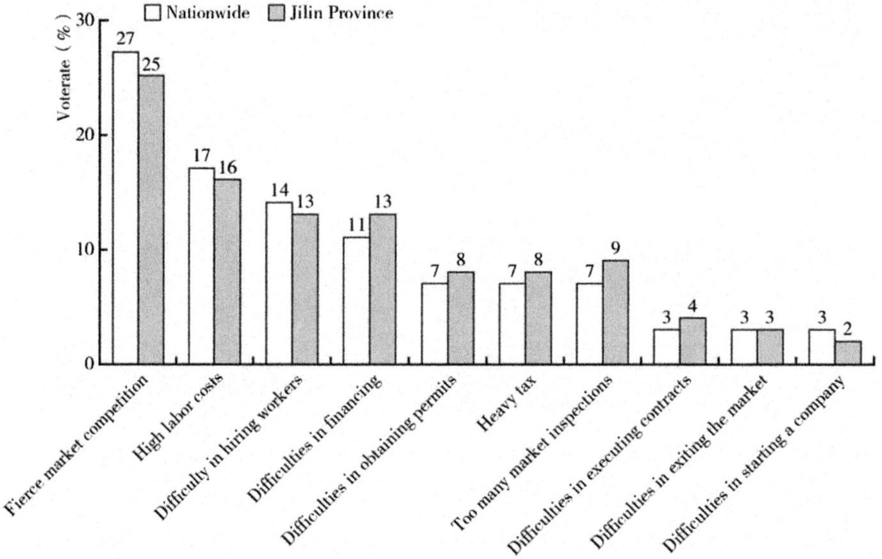

Fig. 6.17 Fierce market competition, high labor costs, and recruitment are the main challenges faced by enterprises in Jilin

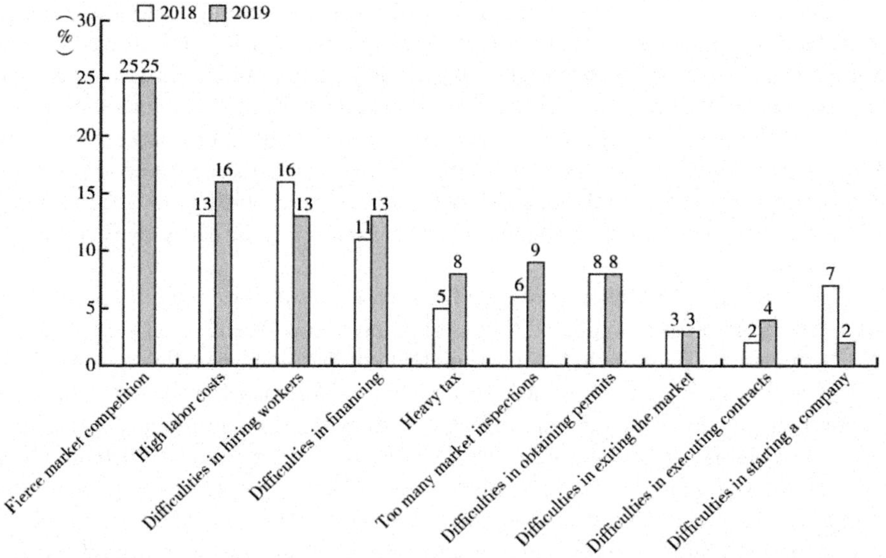

Fig. 6.18 Comparison of the main challenges faced by market players in Jilin Province from 2018 to 2019

Chapter 7
The Business Environment of Gansu Province

Zhe Liu, Jingyuan Sui, and Xiaoying Li

7.1 Overview of the Report on Gansu Province

In Gansu Province, our research team randomly studied eight districts in six cities, and collected a total of 329 valid questionnaires. The six cities were Lanzhou, Zhangye, Jiuquan, Jiayuguan, Pingliang and Longnan. After the survey, the research group compiled first-hand data and public opinion feedback regarding the business environment construction both nationwide and in Gansu, then examined the new accomplishments, challenges and directions of Gansu's business environment construction from a national perspective (see Table 7.1).

7.2 Progress of Gansu Province's Business Environment Construction (2018–2019)

The focuses of the business system reform are "streamlining government services, delegating power and strengthening regulation." The survey results show that, in 2019, Gansu Province's market entry became more convenient, with the time and number of licenses and permits both decreasing. In addition, the credit regulation system has entered the stage of large-scale use, and service efficiency, represented by

Z. Liu · J. Sui
Lingnan College, Sun Yat-sen University, Guangzhou, China

X. Li (✉)
Institute of Guangdong, Hong Kong and Macao Development Studies, Guangzhou, China
e-mail: lixy36@mail.sysu.edu.cn

X. Xu et al. (eds.), *Report on the Chinese Business Environment Survey 2020*, Research Series on the Chinese Dream and China's Development Path,
https://doi.org/10.1007/978-981-99-6112-2_7

Table 7.1 Business environment indicator system and latest achievements for Gansu Province in 2019

Level 1 indicators	Level 2 indicators	Level 3 indicators	Province-wide mean	Nationwide average	Nationwide maximum	Nationwide minimum
Main progress	Market entry	Number of days needed to register a company	5.1	6.9	9.3	3.0
		Number of service windows needed to visit	1.6	1.8	3.1	1.4
		Number of permits needed to process	2.2	1.8	2.7	1.0
	Credit regulation	National enterprise credit information publicity system usage rate (%)	56	66	79	47
	Internet + government services	Online service hall awareness rate (%)	72	66	84	47
		Online service hall usage rate (%)	56	48	73	27
	Service efficiency	Number of trips taken to complete a task in the past six months	2.1	1.9	2.7	1.6
		Number of service windows visited to complete a task in the past six months	1.3	1.4	2.2	1.2

(continued)

Table 7.1 (continued)

Level 1 indicators	Level 2 indicators	Level 3 indicators	Province-wide mean	Nationwide average	Nationwide maximum	Nationwide minimum
		Vote rate of out-of-province market players in evaluating the province's business environment (%)	1		48	0
Macro effectiveness	Employment	Proportion of market players who upsized in the past six months (%)	24	34	45	22
	Growth	Proportion of market players with increased performance in the past six months (%)	40	49	58	34
	Innovation	Proportion of market players who innovated in the past six months (%)	32	44	56	32
	Structure	Proportion of market players in the service sector who registered after the business reform (%)	73	70	97	50

Note Nationwide maximum and Nationwide minimum are the maximum and minimum values at the provincial level
Source Sun Yat-sen University Research Group on "Deepening the Reform of the Business System"

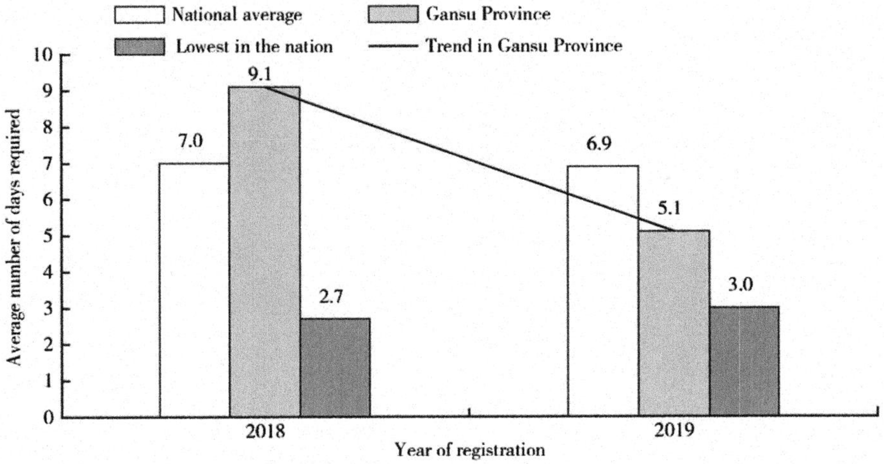

Fig. 7.1 In Gansu, the time required to register a company dropped from 9.1 days in 2018 to 5.1 days in 2019

completing all tasks in one visit, has been greatly improved, while the fee reduction work has been recognized by market players.

(1) Registering a company became easier

Gansu's average registration time was better than the national average. As shown in Fig. 7.1, in 2018, the average time required for market players to register a company in Gansu was 9.1 days, longer than the national average of 7.0 days. However, in 2019, the average registration time there was roughly 5.1 days, a reduction of four days compared to 2018, and better than the national average.

As for the number of windows required to visit, Gansu was among the best provinces in the country in 2019. Figure 7.2 shows that in Gansu, registering a company in 2018 required visiting an average of 2.0 windows, which by 2019 dropped to 1.6, better than the national average. This indicates that, compared with 2018, registering a business in Gansu in 2019 was more efficient and convenient, thus further facilitating market entry.

(2) Highly efficient service

Figure 7.3 shows that in the 2018 study, thirty percent of market players in Gansu Province completed all their tasks within thirty minutes, on par with the national average; by 2019, the proportion of thirty-minute completion increased from thirty percent to fifty-six percent, an increase of twenty-six percentage points, and only one percentage point below the country's best level. This shows that in 2019 Gansu Province has made significant progress in the reform reducing the processing time and improving efficiency.

During the survey and interviews conducted in Jiayuguan City, many businesspeople said that completing business-related tasks had indeed become faster and

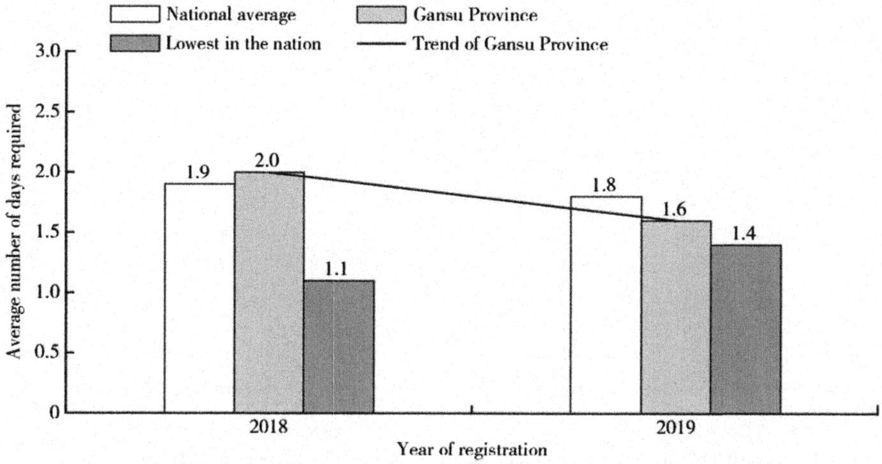

Fig. 7.2 In Gansu, the number of windows required to visit to register a company decreased from 2.0 in 2018 to 1.6 in 2019

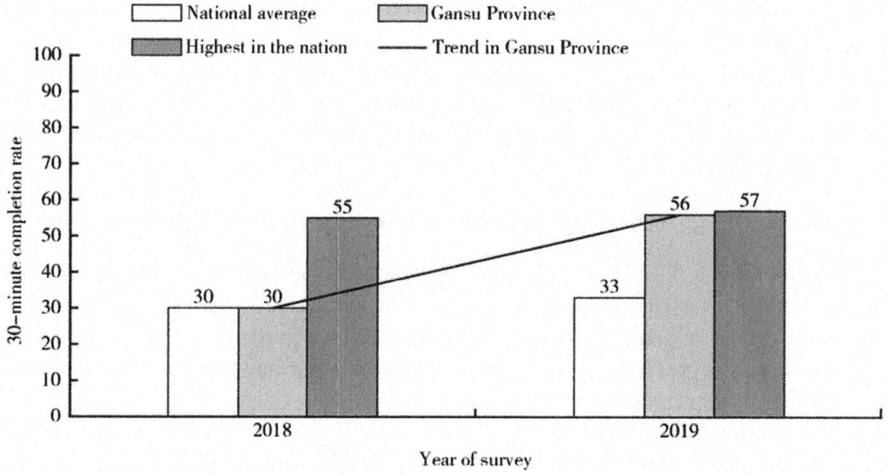

Fig. 7.3 In Gansu, the 30-min completion rate rose from 30% in 2018 to 56% in 2019

more convenient: "You never have to wait, and you're done in half an hour." The Jiayuguan service hall is quite limited in size, but it has a very logical layout, thus effectively alleviating the "rush hour" there. In addition, the staff are very diligent and responsible, and carefully guide visitors so as to ensure that their time is not wasted.

At the same time, compared with 2018, Gansu's rate of completing all tasks in one visit also rose. As shown in Fig. 7.4, in 2018, twenty-five percent of Gansu's market players completed all tasks in one visit, while fifteen percent needed to make

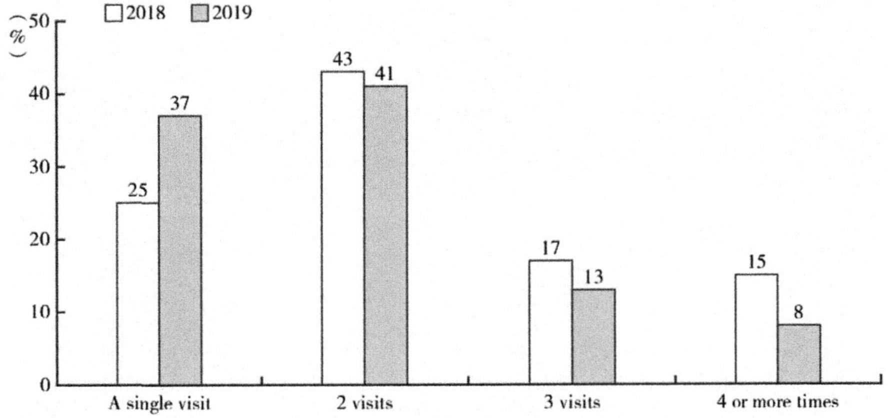

Fig. 7.4 Compared with 2018, Gansu's completion in one visit rate increased

four or more trips; in 2019, the completion in one visit rate rose by twelve percentage points, reaching thirty-seven percent. That is to say, nearly forty percent of market players only needed to make one visit. At the same time, the proportion of needing to make four or more visits dropped to eight percent. This shows that the promotion of the business reform in Gansu Province has made the process much more convenient for market players.

(3) **The digital government awareness rate exceeded the national average**

As shown in Fig. 7.5, in Gansu Province, seventy-two percent of market players said they knew there was an online service hall in their location, which is higher than the national average of sixty-six percent, and only twelve percentage points below the best province's score. It can thus be seen that, from a nationwide perspective, Gansu ranks quite high in terms of online service hall awareness.

The interviewees in Pingliang generally said, "If it weren't for the staff's patient guidance, we'd have no idea how convenient it was to do things online!" At the Pingliang City service hall, there many are online service manuals and information boards to be found, along online self-serve terminals staffed with professional guides, and other such elements, thus increasing efficiency in completing tasks, creating a good atmosphere, and improving businesspeople's opinion of the service hall and their behavior.

(4) **Reduced fees**

Fee reduction was one of 2019's priorities. As shown in Fig. 7.6, in 2019, eighty percent of market players in Gansu Province said they thought that the business reform measures had reduced the fees involved in dealing with the government, an increase of twenty-four percentage points compared to 2018. This shows that in

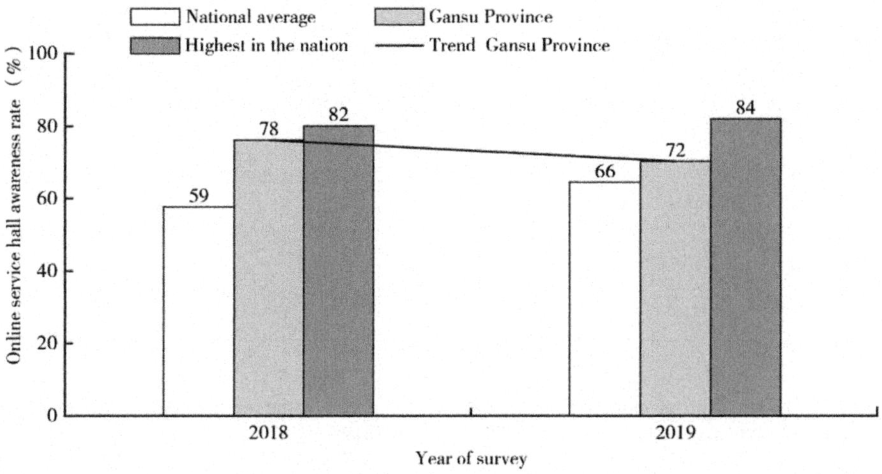

Fig. 7.5 Gansu's online service hall awareness rate exceeded the national average

2019 Gansu market players felt that the fee reduction work had been significantly improved.

(5) **Breakthrough from zero percent to one percent of out-of-province votes**

Within the province, seventy-six percent of market players said that the business reform had had a positive impact on them, the best nationwide, and eight percentage points higher than the national average (core data). The improvement of the business environment and recognition from market players are important dimensions of the business environment construction. As shown in Fig. 7.7, the proportion of market

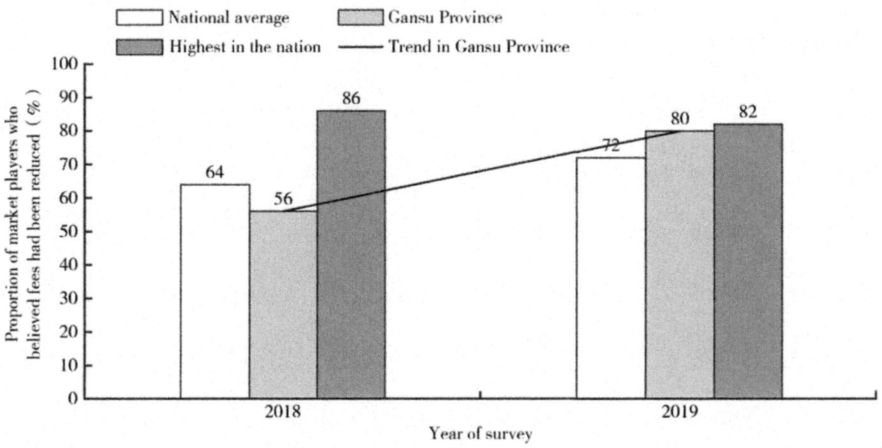

Fig. 7.6 In Gansu, the proportion of market players who believed that costs had been reduced increased from 56% in 2018 to 80%

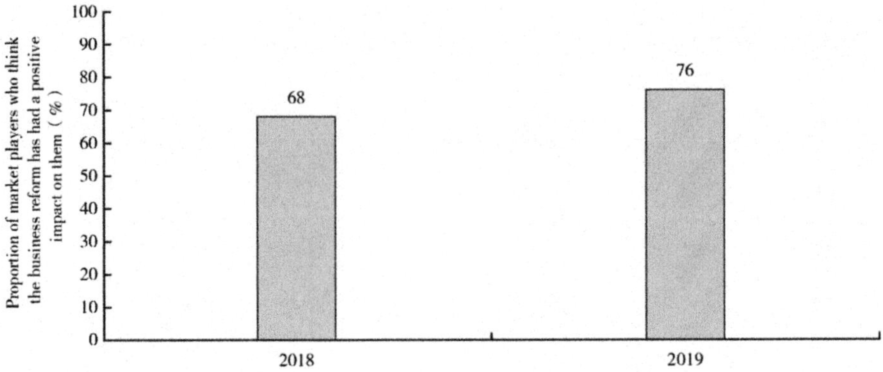

Fig. 7.7 In Gansu, the proportion of market players who believe that the business reform positively impacted them increased from 68% in 2018 to 76% in 2019

players in Gansu who said they thought that business reform had positively impacted them increased from sixty-eight percent in 2018 to seventy-six percent in 2019, thus their sense of access to the business environment construction has increased.

Outside the province, Gansu's business environment received one percent of the total votes, which is a breakthrough from zero percent the previous year. This is a strong affirmation from nationwide market players regarding Gansu's business environment construction (Fig. 7.8).

(6) **Summary**

Compared with 2018, Gansu Province made significant progress in its business environment construction in 2019, detailed as follows.

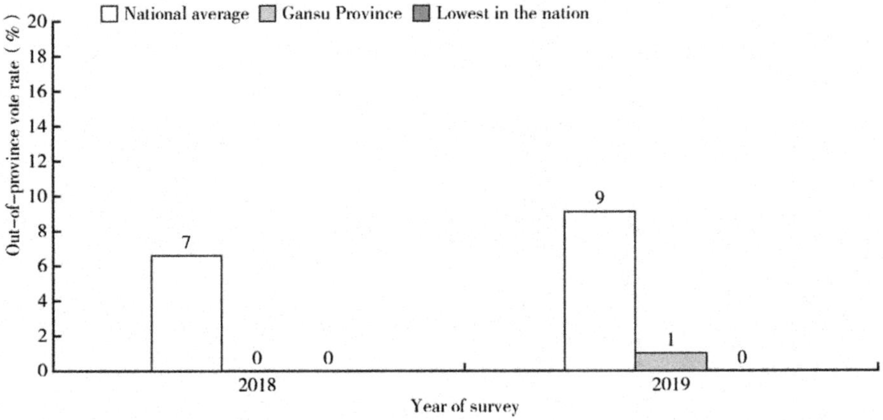

Fig. 7.8 Gansu's business environment vote rate increased from 0% in 2018 to 1% in 2019

First, its ease of market entry has continuously improved. It took an average of 5.1 days and 1.6 windows to complete registration of a company, which is close to the national average.

Second, Gansu's efficiency in completing business-related tasks has significantly improved, with the thirty-minute completion rate rising from thirty percent in 2018 to fifty-six percent in 2019.

Third, Gansu's Internet + government services has been widely popularized, with an awareness rate of seventy-two percent, higher than the national average.

Fourth, the recognition of the reduction in fees rose from fifty-six percent to eighty percent, signifying that the vast majority of market players there recognize the fee reduction work of the business environment construction.

Fifth, the market players have a strong sense of fulfillment. Nearly eighty percent of market players in the province said that the business environment construction has had a positive impact on their business operations, and, for the first time, Gansu's business environment has been recognized by out-of-province market players.

7.3 Performance of Gansu Province's Business Environment

The promotion of macroeconomic reform of the business system is reflected in aspects such as the new market players creating jobs, their increased performance, structural transformation, innovation and improved business environment. The survey results show that Gansu's business system reform has effectively optimized the province's macroeconomic development environment, and strongly supported its high-quality economic development.

(1) **More than half of all enterprises there registered after the business reform**

Among all the market players in Gansu Province randomly interviewed in our 2019 survey, about fifty-three percent had registered and entered the market after the 2014 business reform. The high proportion of market players registered between 2014 and 2019 is a manifestation of the business system reform in promoting more market players to engage in entrepreneurship. As shown in Fig. 7.9, in the survey sample of Gansu Province, forty-seven percent of market players had registered before 2014, while fifty-three percent had registered between 2014 and 2019. This result shows that the number of new market players registered, started businesses and entered the market after the reform surpassed the total number of market players before the reform, accounting for more than half of all market players, and achieving a significant increase in the total number.

(2) **Twenty-four percent of Gansu market players created jobs**

During the field survey, our research team asked the representatives of the market players whether their companies had upsized, downsized or remained the same in the

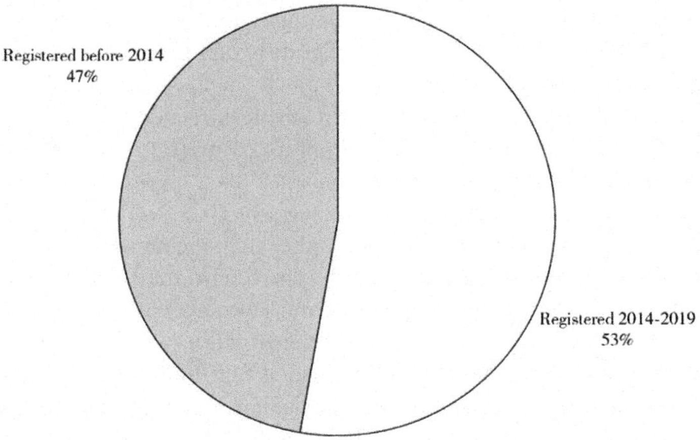

Fig. 7.9 In Gansu Province, 53% of market players registered between 2014 and 2019

past six months. As shown in Fig. 7.10, in the first half of 2019, twenty-four percent of market players upsized, sixty-one percent remained unchanged, and fifteen percent downsized. This report defines the net increase in employment of market players as the difference between the proportion of market players who upsized and those who downsized. The difference between the two was nine percentage points, for a net increase of nine percent in employment. This shows that in the first half of 2019, market players in Gansu created more jobs and provided more employment opportunities.

(3) **Forty percent of Gansu market players performed better**

During the survey, our research team asked the representatives of the market players whether their companies' sales performance had increased, decreased or stayed the

Fig. 7.10 In 2019, 24% of market players in Gansu upsized

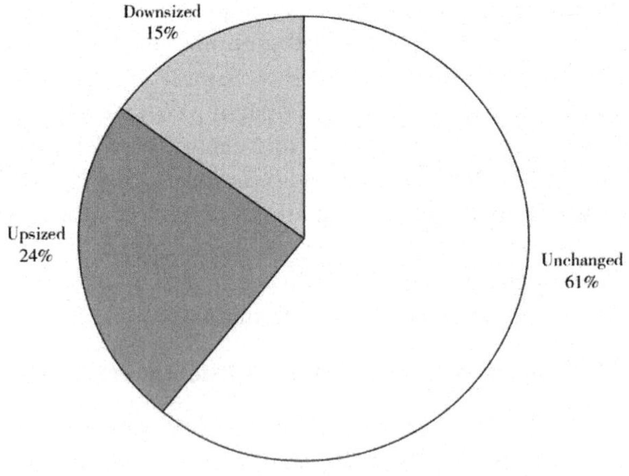

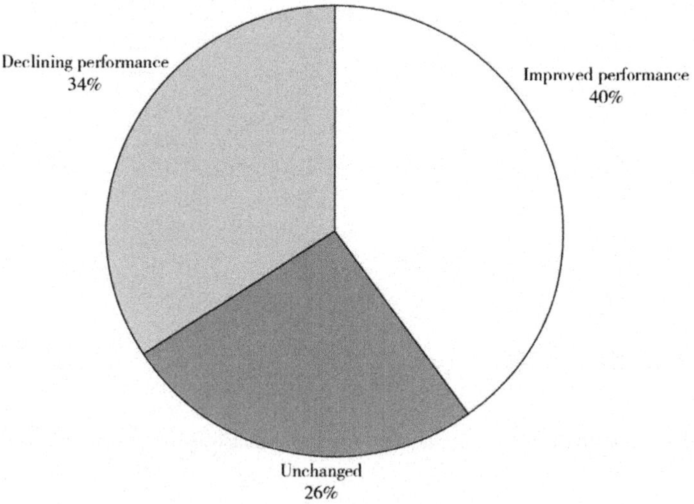

Fig. 7.11 In 2019, 40% of market players in Gansu Province had increased performance

same in the past six months. As shown in Fig. 7.11, in the first half of 2019, forty percent of market players in Gansu Province said that their performance increased, 26% did not change, and thirty-four percent had decreased performance. This indicates that forty percent of market players had better business in the first half of 2019.

(4) **Market players in the service sector increased by 19 percentage points**

After the business system reform, the proportion of Gansu market players in the service sector increased from fifty-four percent to seventy-three percent. Figure 7.12 divides the market players into two groups: those who registered before the 2014 business reform, and those who registered after it. Then the respective proportions of market subjects in different industries in each group are calculated. The results show that fifty-four percent of the market players registered in Gansu Province before the 2014 business reform were in the service industry; among the new market players, the proportion of those in the service industry was seventy-three percent, an increase of nineteen percentage points.

After the business reform, the proportion of industrial market players dropped from thirty-one percent to fourteen percent. As shown in Fig. 7.12, thirty-one percent of the market players registered before the 2014 business reform were industrial ones; among the new market players, the proportion of industrial ones decreased to fourteen percent.

After the business reform, the proportion of market players in emerging industries among all market subjects was eight percent, lower than that of industrial ones. As shown in Fig. 7.12, eight percent of the market players registered before the 2014 business reform were in emerging industries, and this proportion remained the same after the reform.

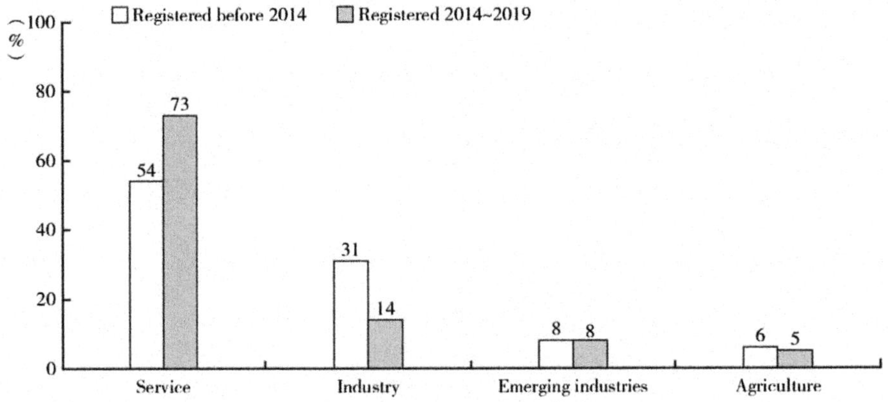

Fig. 7.12 The proportion of market players in various industries in Gansu Province before and after the reform

(5) Thirty-two percent of Gansu market players launched new products or services

During the field survey, our research team asked the representatives of the market players if their companies had launched new products or services in the past six months. As shown in Fig. 7.13, thirty-two percent of market players launched new products or services in the first half of 2019. In other words, over thirty percent of market players in Gansu innovated in the past six months.

Fig. 7.13 In 2019, 32% of Gansu's market players launched new products or services

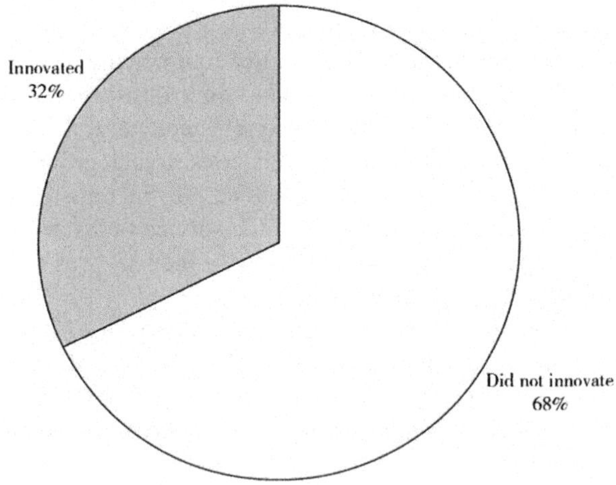

(6) **Summary**

The survey results show that Gansu Province's business environment construction has greatly supported high-quality economic development, by promoting entrepreneurship, assuring employment, stabilizing growth, adjusting the structure, promoting innovation, and improving the business environment. The details are as follows.

The business environment construction promotes widespread entrepreneurship: fifty-three percent of market players had registered after the reform, a significant increase.

It creates more jobs: twenty-four percent of market players upsized in the first half of 2019.

It promotes the growth of market players: forty percent performed better in the first half of 2019.

It promotes innovation: thirty-two percent of market players innovated in the first half of 2019.

7.4 Problems in Gansu Province's Business Environment Construction

(1) **The number of permits needed has risen**

As shown in Fig. 7.14, in 2018, Gansu's market players needed to apply for an average of 2.0 permits, which is on par with the national average. In 2019, this number rose to 2.2, an increase of 0.2 over the previous year.

(2) **The completion in one visit rate was lower than the national average**

As shown in Fig. 7.15, in 2019, thirty-seven percent of Gansu's market players only needed one trip to complete a task, five percentage points lower than the national average, and well below the national best level. Meanwhile, forty-one percent of market players needed to make two trips to complete a task. This means that Gansu is significantly behind in the reform to complete all tasks in one visit.

In one city, a member of the staff told us, "We can complete all their tasks within a day, as long as they bring all the materials they need." Some of the businesspeople confessed that they needed to make several trips because they had neglected to read all the instructions. This shows that the reason some of the market players had to make two or more trips was because their materials were incomplete. To solve this problem, first, the relevant departments must formulate logical and effective publicity methods so as to provide advance notice; at the same time, the businesspeople must also do their due diligence in carefully reading the instructions.

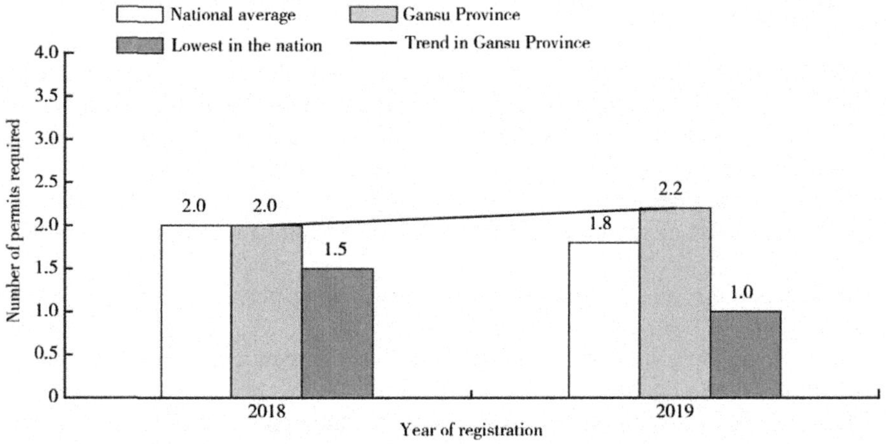

Fig. 7.14 In Gansu, the number of permits required by market players rose from 2.0 in 2018 to 2.2 in 2019

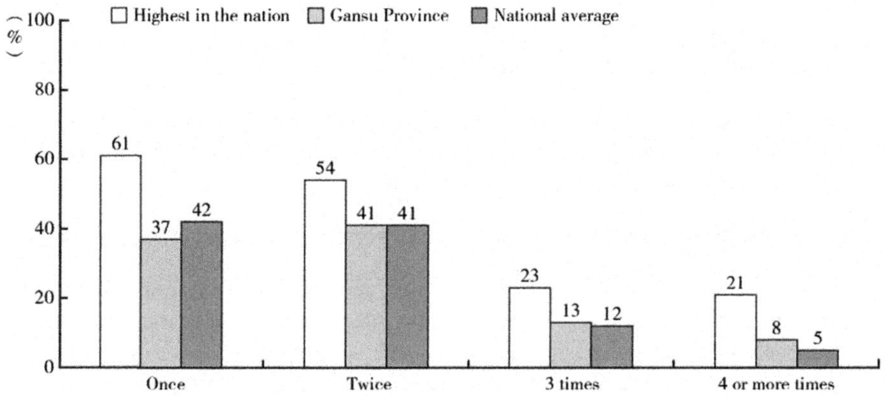

Fig. 7.15 In 2019, 37% of Gansu's market players completed all tasks in one visit

(3) Challenges: fierce competition, financing, high costs

Previously, the business environment construction has centered around deepening the resolution of problems such as acquiring licenses and permits, and dissolving companies; but market player responses show that these issues are no longer the main challenges they face. At present, the main challenges faced by market players in Gansu cannot easily be solved by the business system reform.

As shown in Fig. 7.16, when asked about the main challenges they faced in doing business locally, only two percent, two percent and four percent of Gansu market players respectively mentioned the difficulty of starting a business, exiting the market,

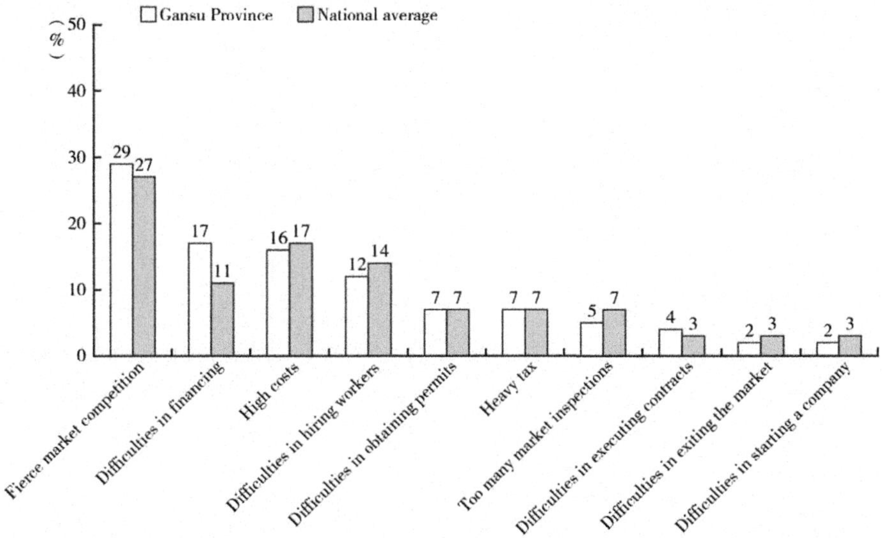

Fig. 7.16 The main challenges faced by market players today

and enforcing contracts, thus these are no longer the main challenges they face. At the national level, these three challenges all had a proportion of three percent, again showing they are no longer the main challenges market players face.

The current main challenges according to Gansu market players are fierce market competition, difficulty in financing, and high labor costs, mentioned with respective proportions of twenty-nine percent, seventeen percent and sixteen percent. These three challenges are the same as those faced by market players nationwide, but the situation in Gansu is more severe. This is mainly reflected in that Gansu market players mentioned fierce market competition and financing in proportions respectively two and six percentage points higher than the national average. Clearly, these major difficulties have not been directly addressed by the current business system reform.

Figure 7.17 shows that, in 2018, twenty-six percent of Gansu market players said that the market was highly competitive, then in 2019 this rate rose to twenty-nine percent. This indicates that over the past year, the market in Gansu Province has become increasingly competitive. Similarly, in 2018, sixteen percent of market players found it difficult to raise capital, and the following year this rate rose to seventeen percent. Consequently, in Gansu Province over the past year, the market has been highly competitive, and enterprises have faced high labor costs, financing difficulties, and other major challenges.

In addition, in 2018, six percent, two percent and four percent of Gansu market players respectively reported difficulties in contract execution, starting a business, and exiting the market. The following year, the proportions of these three indicators decreased slightly. This indicates that the main challenges faced by enterprises in

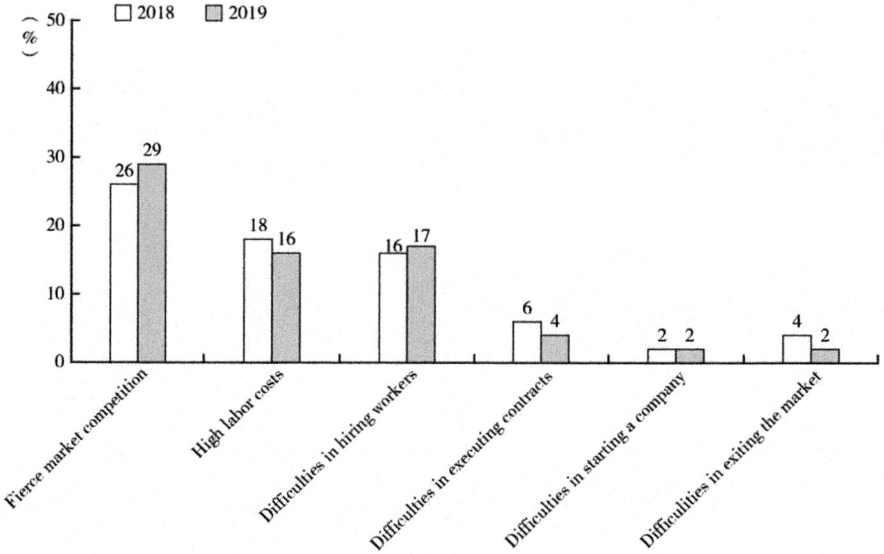

Fig. 7.17 The main challenges currently faced by market players

Gansu Province are relatively concentrated, and require further coordination and guidance from relevant departments to help them resolve their difficulties, and thus stimulate market vitality.

Chapter 8
The Business Environment of Guangdong Province

Yihan Yang, Yifei Yi, and Li Zhang

8.1 Overview of the Report on Guangdong Province

Based on the 2018 Guangdong survey, in 2019 our research team continued to conduct field research in eight cities and twenty districts in the province, and collected a total of 480 valid questionnaires. The eight cities were Guangzhou, Shaoguan, Shenzhen, Jiangmen, Zhanjiang, Yangjiang, Chaozhou and Jieyang. After the survey ended, the research group compiled first-hand data and public opinion feedback regarding the construction of the business environment both at the national and provincial levels, and examined the new progress, challenges and directions in Guangdong's business environment construction from a national perspective (see Table 8.1).

8.2 Progress of Guangdong Province's Business Environment Construction

The focuses of the business system reform are "streamlining government services, delegating power and strengthening regulation." The survey results show that, in 2019, Guangdong's market access became more convenient, with the number of licenses and permits needed and time required to process them both being reduced.

Y. Yang
School of Sociology & Anthropology, Sun Yat-sen University, Guangzhou, China

Y. Yi
Lingnan College, Sun Yat-sen University, Guangzhou, China

L. Zhang (✉)
International School of Business & Finance, Sun Yat-sen University, Guangzhou, China
e-mail: zhangL39@mail.sysu.edu.cn

Institute of Mezzoeconomics, Sun Yat-sen University, Guangzhou, China

X. Xu et al. (eds.), *Report on the Chinese Business Environment Survey 2020*, Research Series on the Chinese Dream and China's Development Path,
https://doi.org/10.1007/978-981-99-6112-2_8

Table 8.1 Business environment indicator system and latest achievements for Guangdong Province in 2019

Level 1 indicators	Level 2 indicators	Level 3 indicators	Province-wide average	Nationwide average	Nationwide maximum	Nationwide minimum
Main progress	Market entry	Number of days needed to register a company	3.0	6.9	9.3	3.0
		Number of service windows needed to visit	1.4	1.8	3.1	1.4
		Number of permits needed to process	1.4	1.8	2.7	1.0
	Credit regulation	National enterprise credit information publicity system usage rate (%)	70	66	79	47
	Internet + government services	Online service hall awareness rate (%)	52	66	84	47
		Online service hall usage rate (%)	37	48	73	27
	Service efficiency	Number of trips taken to complete a task in the past six months	1.9	1.9	2.7	1.6
		Number of service windows visited to complete a task in the past six months	1.4	1.4	2.2	1.2
		Proportion of votes received from out-of-province market players in evaluating the province's business environment (%)	41		48	0

(continued)

Table 8.1 (continued)

Level 1 indicators	Level 2 indicators	Level 3 indicators	Province-wide average	Nationwide average	Nationwide maximum	Nationwide minimum
Macro results	Employment	Proportion of market players who upsized in the past six months (%)	28	34	45	22
	Growth	Proportion of market players with increased performance in the past six months (%)	38	49	58	34
	Innovation	Proportion of market players who innovated in the past six months (%)	43	44	56	32
	Structure	Proportion of market players in the service sector who registered after the business reform (%)	71	70	97	50

Note Nationwide maximum and Nationwide minimum are the maximum and minimum values at the provincial level
Data source Sun Yat-sen University Research Group on "Deepening the Reform of the Business System."

In addition, service efficiency, represented by completing all tasks in one visit, was greatly improved, and the fee reduction work was recognized by market players. Finally, the credit regulation system entered the stage of large-scale use.

(1) Registering a company in Guangdong was the easiest nationwide

Guangdong remains the most efficient province for registering a company. As shown in Fig. 8.1, in 2018, the average time required for Guangdong market players to register a company was 2.7 days, the best nationwide. In 2019, Guangdong's average registration time was roughly three days, exhibiting no substantial change from the previous year, and still the best nationwide, being about twice as fast as the national average of 6.9 days.

In terms of the number of windows required to register a company, in 2019 Guangdong became the best nationwide. As shown in Fig. 8.2, in 2018, it took Guangdong

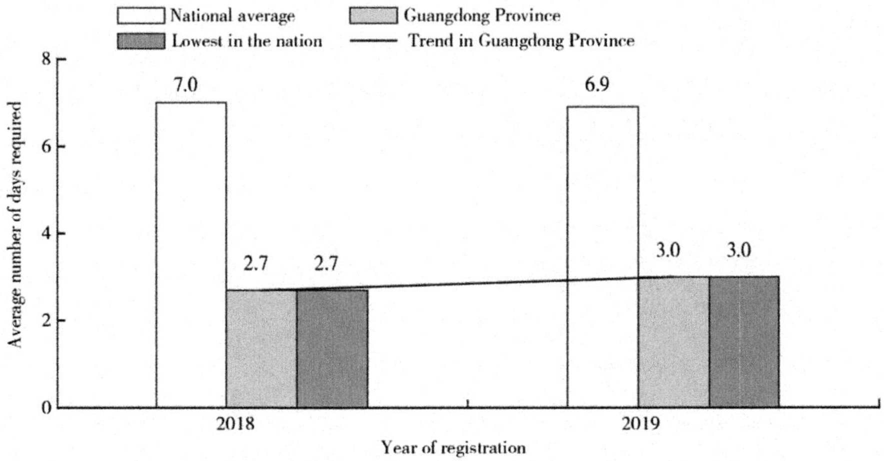

Fig. 8.1 In Guangdong in both 2018 and 2019, it took roughly three days to register a company, maintaining the highest speed nationwide

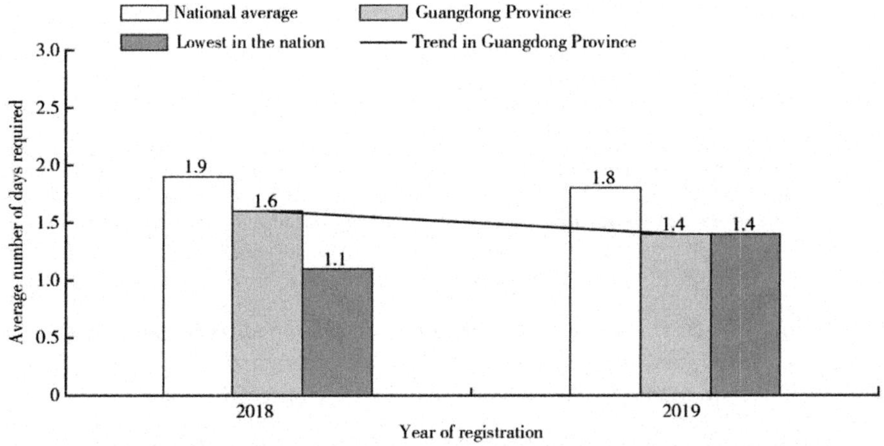

Fig. 8.2 In Guangdong, the number of windows required to register a company decreased from 1.6 in 2018 to 1.4 in 2019

market players an average of 1.6 windows to register a company. The following year, this number dropped to 1.4, making it the best in the country. This shows that, compared with the previous year, registering a company in Guangdong in 2019 became more efficient and convenient, and market access has been further facilitated.

(2) **Continued reduction in permits needed**

In 2019, the average number of permits required by Guangdong market players was 1.4, a further reduction of 0.4 from 2018. As shown in Fig. 8.3, in 2018, Guangdong

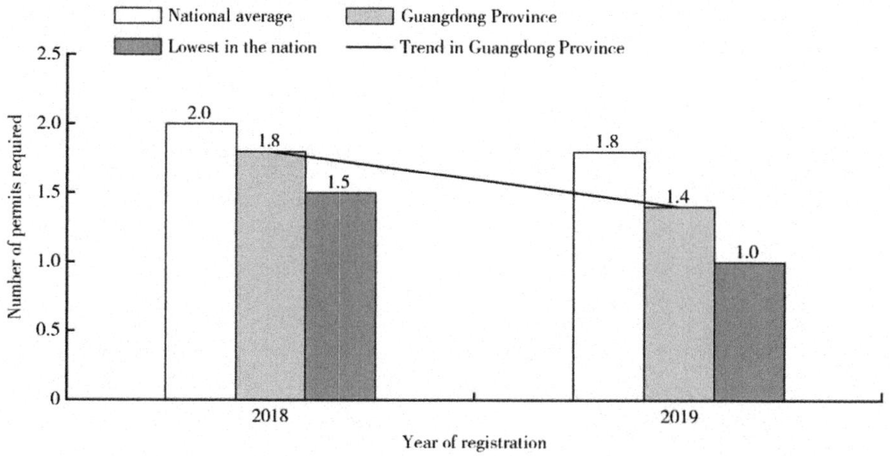

Fig. 8.3 In Guangdong, the number of permits required for market players to register a company dropped from 1.8 in 2018 to 1.4 in 2019

market players needed to apply for an average of 1.8 permits, slightly lower than the national average; by 2019, this number dropped to 1.4, 0.4 fewer than the previous year, and 0.4 lower than the 2019 national average. It can thus be seen that Guangdong Province made significant progress in its permit reduction work in 2019.

(3) **More Guangdong market players used the credit information system**

The starting point of credit regulation is that market players can easily and trustfully obtain the credit information of related enterprises. This is manifested in market players accessing the nation credit information system to check the credit information of related enterprises. From Fig. 8.4, in 2018, fifty-eight percent of Guangdong market players said that before trading with other market players they checked their credit information through the National Enterprise Information Publicity System. Guangdong Province was thus below the national average of sixty-five percent. In 2019, in Guangdong, seventy percent of market players chose to check the credit information of trading partners on the National Enterprise Credit Information Publicity System, putting the province four percentage points higher than the national average. With nearly seventy percent of market players in Guangdong already use the National Enterprise Credit Information Publicity System, the system has entered the stage of large-scale use in Guangdong.

(4) **Improved efficiency**

The Central Government's goals of the early 2018 business environment construction reform were that enterprises would only have to visit one place, and could complete all tasks in one visit. This is also the desire of market players. Figure 8.5 shows that, according to the 2018 survey results, twenty-seven percent of Guangdong market players completed all tasks in one visit, lower than the national average; by 2019, this

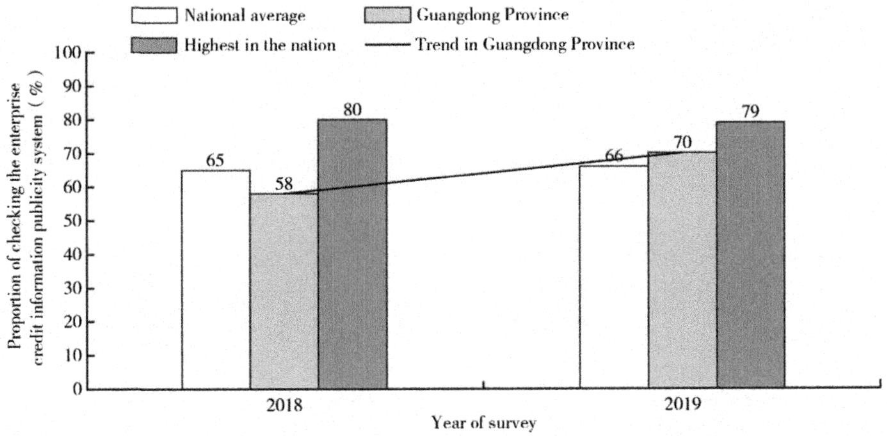

Fig. 8.4 In Guangdong, the proportion of market players who check the national credit information system rose from 58% in 2018 to 70% in 2019

number increased by fourteen percentage points to forty-one percent. This shows that in 2019 Guangdong Province achieved remarkable results in the reform of completing all tasks in one visit.

The businesspeople whom we surveyed and interviewed in Jiangmen City generally said that it had indeed become much easier and faster to complete tasks there: "It used to take a week to process, but now you can pretty much finish it in a day or two." The service hall staff there are very diligent and responsible. If the materials

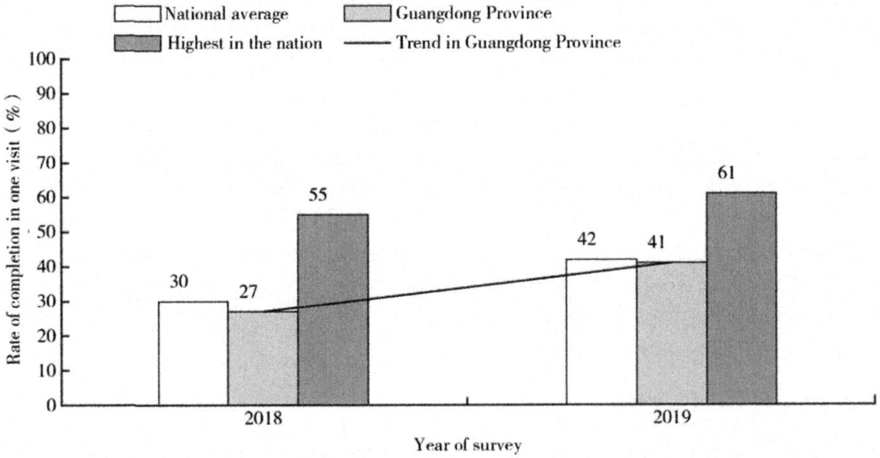

Fig. 8.5 In Guangdong, the proportion of market players who completed all tasks in one visit rose from 27% in 2018 to 41% in 2019

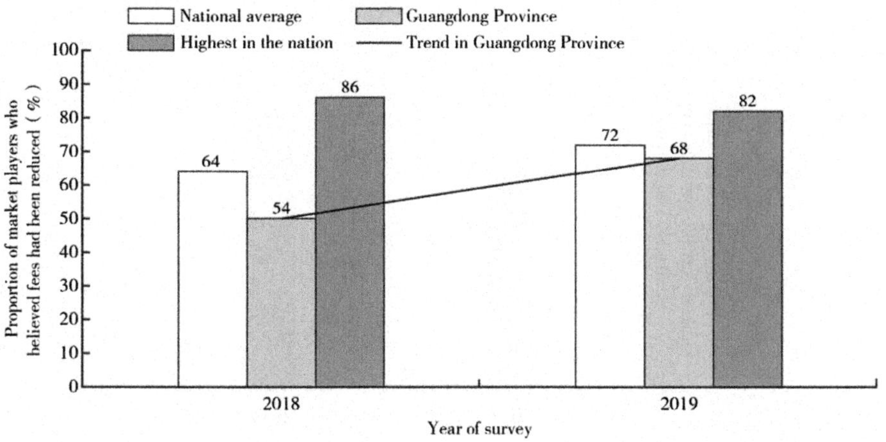

Fig. 8.6 In Guangdong, the proportion of market players who believed fees had been reduced rose to 68% from 54% in 2018

someone has brought are incomplete, the staff will patiently explain to them what materials they need, what procedures they should follow, and so on.

(5) Reduced fees

Fee reduction was one of 2019's key tasks. As Fig. 8.6 shows, in 2019, sixty-eight percent of Guangdong market players believed that the business reform measures had reduced the fees associated with dealing with the government, an increase of fourteen percentage points over the previous year. This shows that in terms of fee reduction work, Guangdong market players' sense of fulfillment increased significantly in 2019.

(6) Guangdong's business environment received the second most votes nationwide

Within the province, seventy-two percent of market players believed that the business reform had a positive impact on their operations, higher than the national average. Improving the business environment and market players' sense of fulfillment are important evaluation criteria for the success of the business system reform. As shown in Fig. 8.7, judging from the evaluation of market players in Guangdong, the proportion of those who believe that the business reform has had a positive impact on them rose from fifty-six percent in 2018 to seventy-two percent in 2019, showing that market players' sense of fulfillment toward the business system reform there continued to increase.

Outside the province, Guangdong received forty-one percent of all votes in regard to its business environment, ranking second nationwide. Judging from the evaluations of market players in other provinces, Guangdong's business environment has also made significant progress. As shown in Fig. 8.8, in 2018, thirty-one percent of out-of-province market players believed Guangdong had a good environment for doing

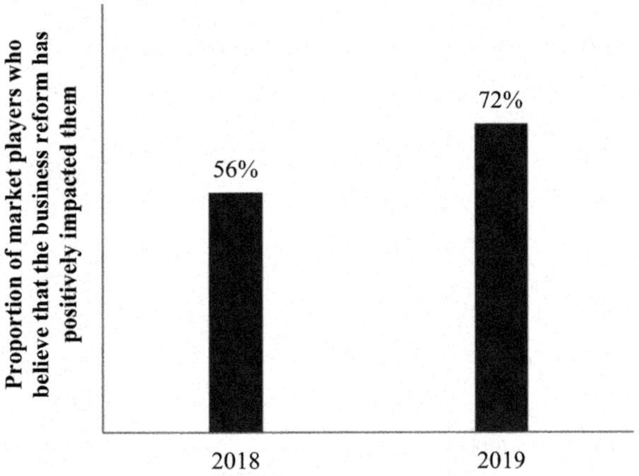

Fig. 8.7 In Guangdong, the proportion of market players who believe that the business reform has had a positive impact on them rose from 56% in 2018 to 72% in 2019

business; in 2019, this rate increased by ten percentage points to forty-one percent. This is a strong affirmation by market players nationwide regarding Guangdong's business system reform and business environment construction.

(7) **Summary**

Compared with 2018, Guangdong Province made significant progress in its business environment construction in 2019. The details are as follows.

First, Guangdong's convenience of market access has continuously improved. It takes an average of three days and 1.4 windows for market players to register

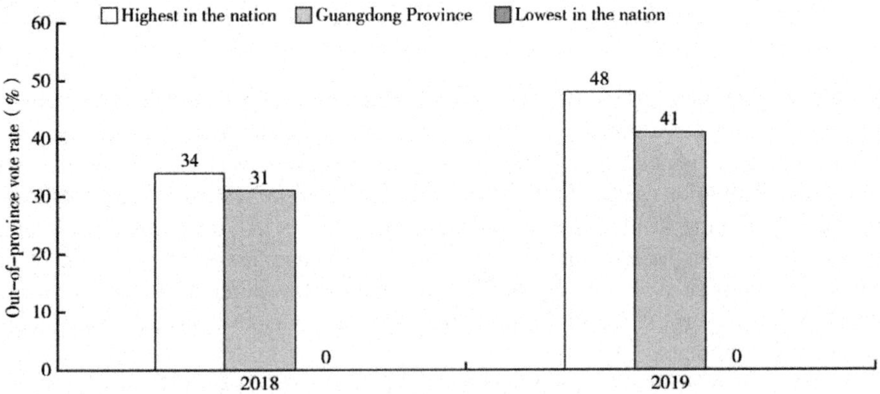

Fig. 8.8 The proportion of votes for Guangdong's business environment increased from 31% in 2018 to 41% in 2019

a company, both the best nationwide, and the number of permits needed has been reduced from 1.8 to 1.4, approaching the goal of only one permit needed.

Second, seventy percent of Guangdong market players check the credit information of their trade partners through the national credit information system, showing that the system has entered the large-scale use stage.

Third, the Guangdong's rate of completion in one visit rate increased from twenty-seven percent to forty-one percent.

Fourth, the proportion of market players who said they thought that fees had been reduced increased from fifty-four percent to sixty-eight percent, thus most market players acknowledged the effectiveness of this aspect of the business system reform.

Fifth, market players expressed a strong sense of fulfillment. About seventy percent of market players in the province said they think that the business system reform had a positive impact on them, while forty-one percent of out-of-province market players said that Guangdong has a good business environment, ranking second nationwide.

8.3 Performance of Guangdong Province's Business Environment Construction

Does Guangdong's business system reform drive the high-quality development of the economy? The business system reform promotes high-quality economic development, which is reflected in promoting the creation of jobs, encouraging innovation, increasing performance, and promoting structural transformation after new market players enter the market. Judging from the survey results, Guangdong's business environment construction has strongly supported high-quality economic development.

(1) **After the business reform, Guangdong's market players doubled**

Among all the active market players in Guangdong whom we randomly interviewed in 2019, about fifty percent had registered and entered the market after the 2014 business reform. A visual reflection of the business system's reform having a great impact on market players starting businesses is that fifty percent of market players had registered between 2014 and 2019. As shown in Fig. 8.9, in the Guangdong survey sample, fifty percent of market players had registered before 2014, and the other fifty percent had registered between 2014 and 2019. This result shows that the number of new market players who had registered, started businesses and entered the market after the reform accounted for half of all active market players, thus achieving a significant increase in the total number.

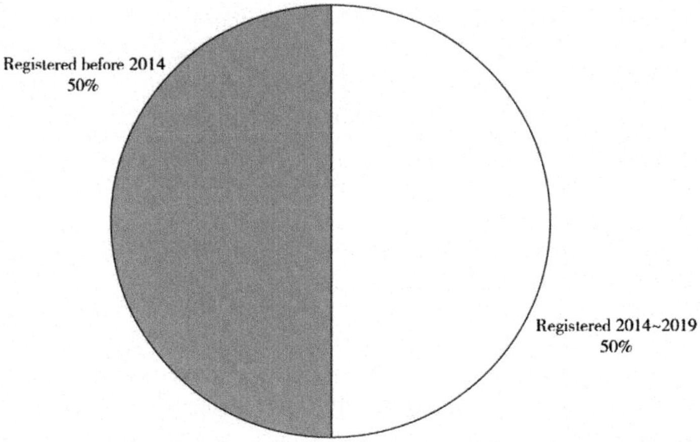

Fig. 8.9 After the business reform, the total number of market players in Guangdong Province doubled

(2) More Guangdong market players joined the service industry

After the business system, the proportion of Guangdong market players in the service industry increased from forty-seven percent to seventy-one percent. In Fig. 8.10, market players are divided into two groups: those who registered before the 2014 business reform and those who registered after it. Then the respective shares of industrial market players in the two groups are calculated. The results show that forty-seven percent of the Guangdong market players who had registered before the 2014 business reform were in the service industry; among the new market players, the proportion of those in the service industry was seventy-one percent, an increase of twenty-four percentage points over the previous year.

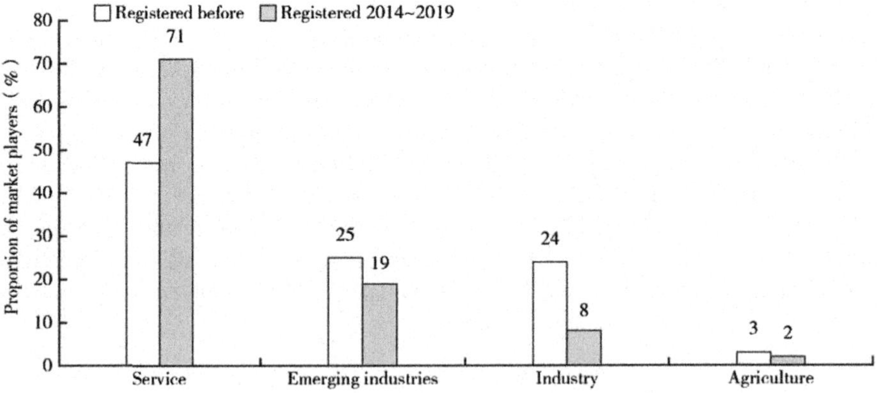

Fig. 8.10 The proportion of market players in various industries in Guangdong Province before and after the business reform

After the business reform, the proportion of industrial market players fell from twenty-four percent to eight percent. As shown in Fig. 8.10, among the market players registered before the 2014 commercial reform, twenty-four percent were industrial ones; among the new market players, the proportion of industrial ones decreased to eight percent.

After the business reform, the proportion of market players in emerging industries was nineteen percent. As shown in Fig. 8.10, twenty-five percent of the market players registered before the 2014 business reform were in emerging industries; among the new market players, this proportion was nineteen percent, a decrease of six percentage points.

(3) **Twenty-eight percent of Guangdong market players created new jobs**

During the field survey, our research team asked the representatives of market players if their companies had upsized, downsized or remained the same in the past six months. As shown in Fig. 8.11, in the first half of 2019, twenty-eight percent of market players upsized, fifty-seven percent remained unchanged, and fifteen percent upsized. This report defines the net increase in employment of market players as the difference between the proportion of market players who upsized and those who downsized. The difference between the two was thirteen percentage points, that is, the net increase in employment was thirteen percent. This shows that in the first half of 2019, market players in Guangdong created more jobs and provided more employment opportunities.

(4) **Thirty-eight percent of Guangdong market players performed better**

During the survey, our research team asked the representatives of market players if their companies' sales performance had increased, decreased or remained unchanged in the past six months. As shown in Fig. 8.12, in the first half of 2019, thirty-eight percent of Guangdong market players reported increased performance, forty percent

Fig. 8.11 In 2019, 28% of Guangdong market players upsized

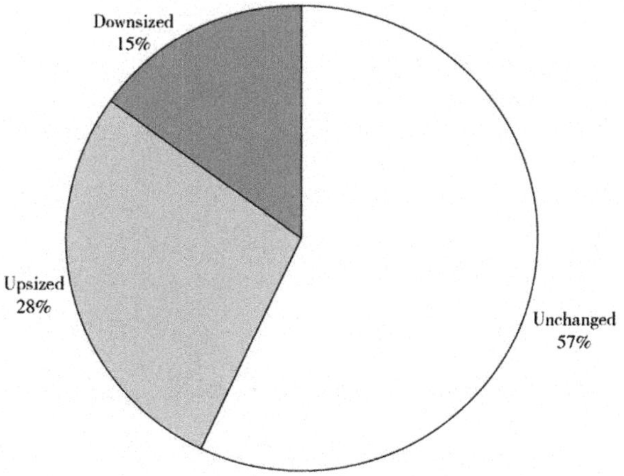

had unchanged performance, and twenty-three percent had decreased performance. This shows that in the first half of 2019, nearly forty percent of market players performed better.

(5) **Forty-three percent of Guangdong market players innovated**

During the field survey, our research team asked the representatives of market players if their companies had launched new products or services in the past six months. As Fig. 8.13 shows, in the first half of 2019, forty-three percent of market players launched new products or services, that is, forty-three percent of Guangdong market players innovated in the past six months.

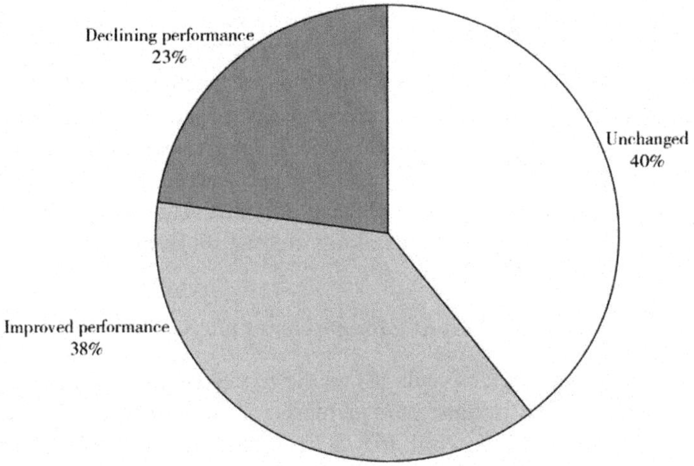

Fig. 8.12 In 2019, 38% of Guangdong market players performed better

Fig. 8.13 In 2019, 43% of Guangdong market players launched new products or services

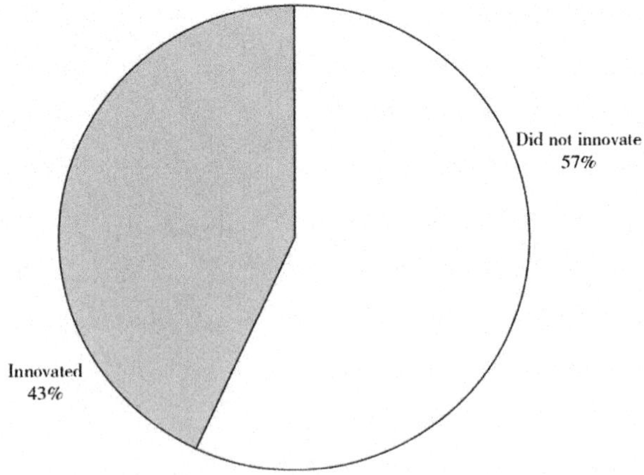

(6) **Summary**

The survey results show that Guangdong's business system reform has strongly supported high-quality economic development, by promoting entrepreneurship, assuring employment, stabilizing growth, restructuring the market, promoting innovation, and improving the business environment. The details are as follows:

The business environment construction promotes mass entrepreneurship: after the reform, the proportion of registered market players accounted for fifty percent, for a dramatic increase in the total number.

It creates more employment opportunities: twenty-eight percent of market players upsized in the first half of 2019.

It promotes growth: thirty-eight percent of market players had increased performance in the first half of 2019.

It promotes innovation among the people: forty-three percent of market players innovated in the first half of 2019.

8.4 Problems in Guangdong Province's Business Environment Construction

(1) **Guangdong has low online service hall awareness, usage and single-network access rates**

Internet + government services is an inevitable trend in the information age. In early 2018, Guangdong pioneered the construction of digital government. However, judging from the responses from market players, the Internet + government services of Guangdong market players exhibited three major "lows":

First, a low online service hall awareness rate. As Fig. 8.14 shows, Guangdong's online service hall awareness rate was fifty-two percent, fourteen percentage points below the national average of sixty-six percent.

Second, a low online service system usage rate. As Fig. 8.15 shows, Guangdong's online service hall usage rate was thirty-seven percent, eleven percentage points below the national average of forty-eight percent.

Third, a low single-network access rate. rate. As Fig. 8.16 shows, this rate was forty-one percent 2018, and dropped to nine percent in 2019, a reduction of thirty-two percentage points.

(2) **Guangdong's work efficiency remains below the national average**

The proportion of market players in Guangdong who completed all tasks in one visit was lower than the national average. As Fig. 8.17 shows, the proportion of market players in Guangdong who only needed one trip to complete a task was forty-one percent. Compared with its 2018 value of twenty-seven percent, the province has made progress in this stage, and is now slightly below the national average of forty-two percent.

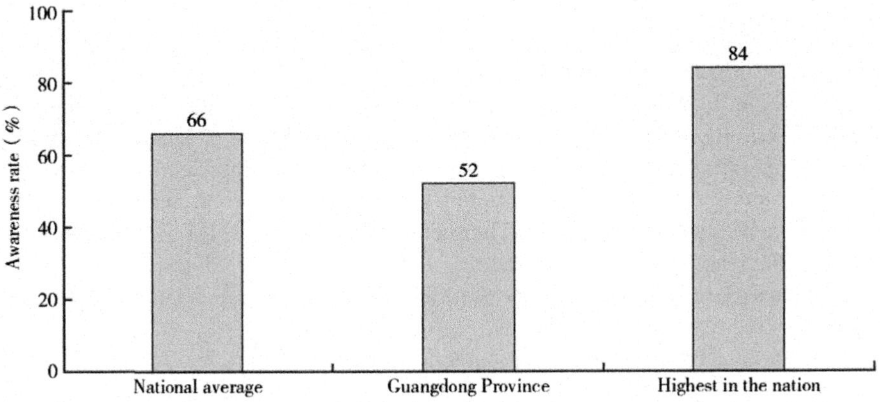

Fig. 8.14 Guangdong's online service hall awareness rate was 52%

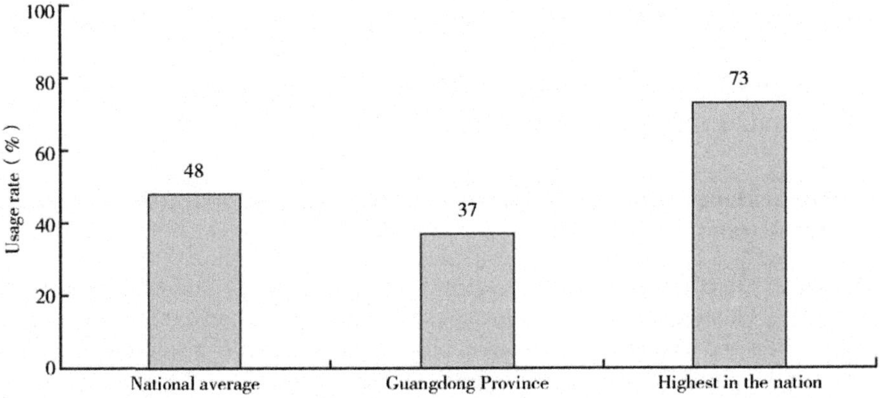

Fig. 8.15 Guangdong's online service hall usage rate was 37%

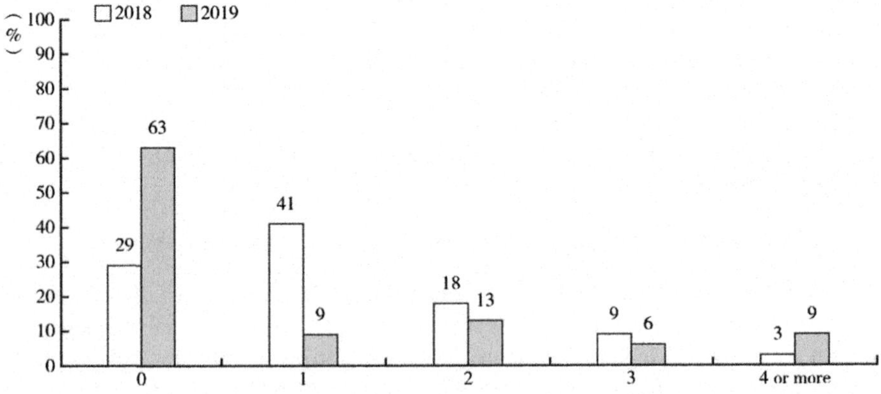

Fig. 8.16 Guangdong's single-network access rate decreased from 41% in 2018 to 9% in 2019

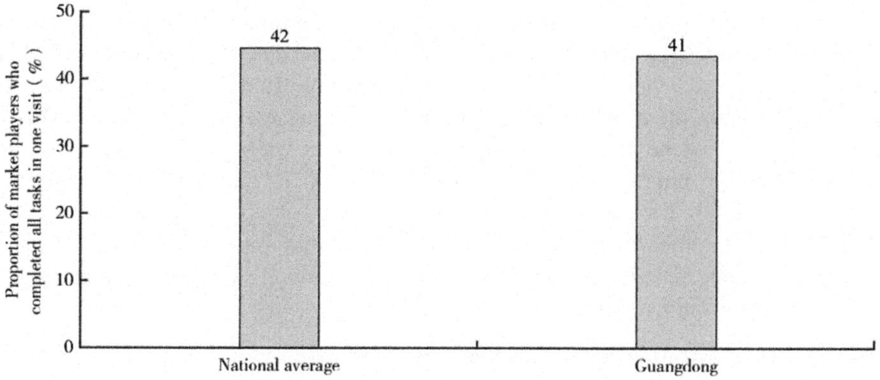

Fig. 8.17 In 2019, the proportion of Guangdong market players who completed all tasks in one visit in 2019 was lower than the national average

Guangdong's thirty-minute completion rate was lower than the national average. As Fig. 8.18 shows, in the first half of 2019, the nationwide proportion of market players who completed all their tasks in thirty minutes was thirty-three percent, while that in Guangdong was only twenty-three percent, ten percentage points lower than the national average. This shows that there remains a large gap between Guangdong's thirty-minute completion rate and the national average, thus there is still much room for improvement in the efficiency of government services there.

According to the market player responses, an intermediary representing a Hong Kong company in one city reported that, although the Guangdong–Hong Kong–Macao Greater Bay Area has stimulated the enthusiasm of investors, the process of starting a business there is still quite complex for investors. For example, since their ID cards differ from those of mainland China, a corporate legal player must

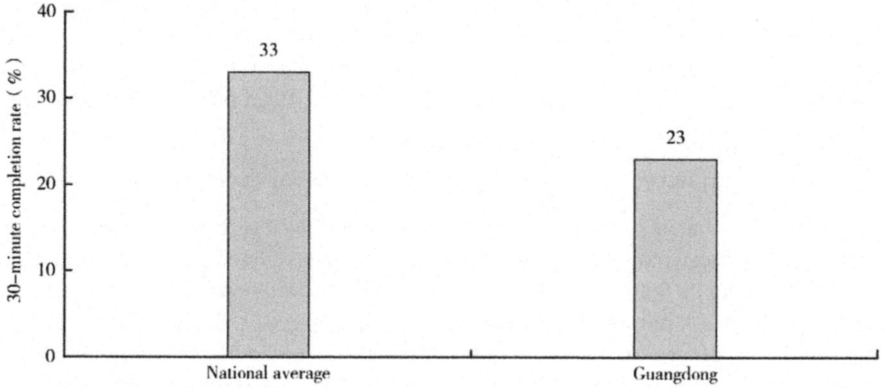

Fig. 8.18 In 2019, the proportion of Guangdong market players who completed their tasks in 30 min was lower than the national average

be present to complete the process. How to further optimize this process to attract more investment is an important issue worth the government's consideration. At a government service hall in another city, many people told us that it took two or three days to complete one task, with each visit taking two or three hours. This is excessively high. One woman complained, "I've been waiting since two-thirty and now it's after five, but they still haven't called my number." She also said that the staff are not completely focused on processing tasks for businesspeople, and often leave their posts to do other things. Therefore, we can see that there is still much progress to make to compensate for the shortcomings of Guangdong's business system reform and to deepen its construction.

(3) **Development of cities in Guangdong varies widely**

As one of China's first provinces to carry out the business system reform, Guangdong's business environment is continually being optimized, yet the problem of imbalanced and inadequate development between cities there remains prominent.

Business standards and procedures are not uniform across the province, with large differences between them. In Guangzhou City, the business process and required materials are relatively standardized, but in another city the government service hall is less efficient. One woman said, "How many trips you have to make depends on which clerk you get. Some of the window clerks are easygoing in reviewing your materials, and you'll probably pass the first time. But some are more strict, and if they don't approve your materials, then you'll have to change them, meaning more trips."

The ease of market access in Guangdong varies greatly from place to place. In terms of the proportion of market players who completed their company registration in one day, sixty-seven percent of market players in the best-performing city (Yangjiang) did so, while in the worst-performing city the proportion was only eleven percent. As for single-window completion, ninety percent of market players in Chaozhou did so, while the worst-performing city's rate was only fourteen percent.

The efficiency of government services throughout Guangdong Province varies greatly. For completing all tasks in one visit, the proportion of market players who achieved this in the best-performing city (Shenzhen) was sixty-three percent, while the proportion in the worst-performing city was only fifteen percent, less than one-quarter of the former.

(4) **Challenges: fierce market competition, high labor costs, recruitment**

The difficulties faced by market players in Guangdong are basically the same as those faced by those nationwide. Previously, the business system reform has centered around resolving difficulties such as acquiring licenses and permits, and dissolving a company. However, judging from the market player responses, these are no longer the main challenges faced by market players. As shown in Fig. 8.19, Guangdong market players reported that their main difficulties in 2019 were fierce market competition, high labor costs, and difficulty in recruitment, respectively mentioned by twenty-seven percent, eighteen percent and seventeen percent. These three challenges are also the main ones commonly faced by market players nationwide.

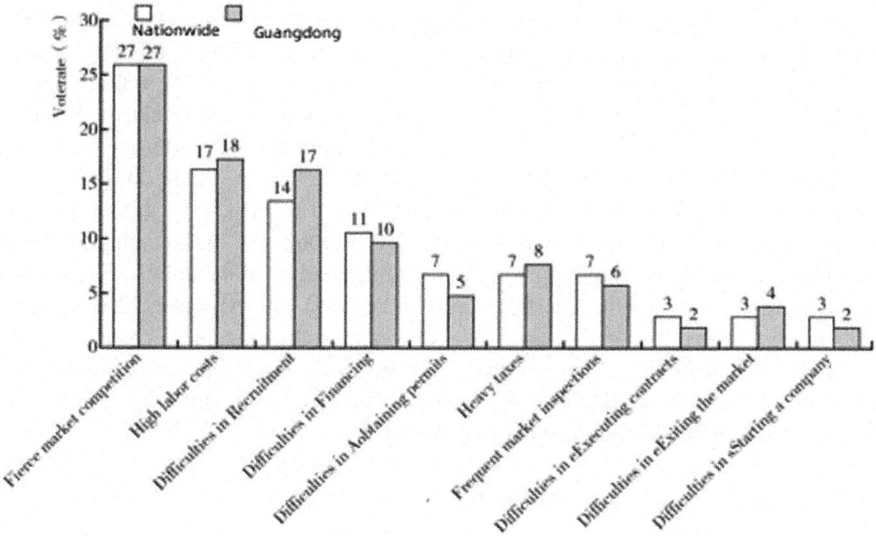

Fig. 8.19 Fierce market competition, high labor costs, and recruitment difficulties are the main challenges faced by Guangdong market players

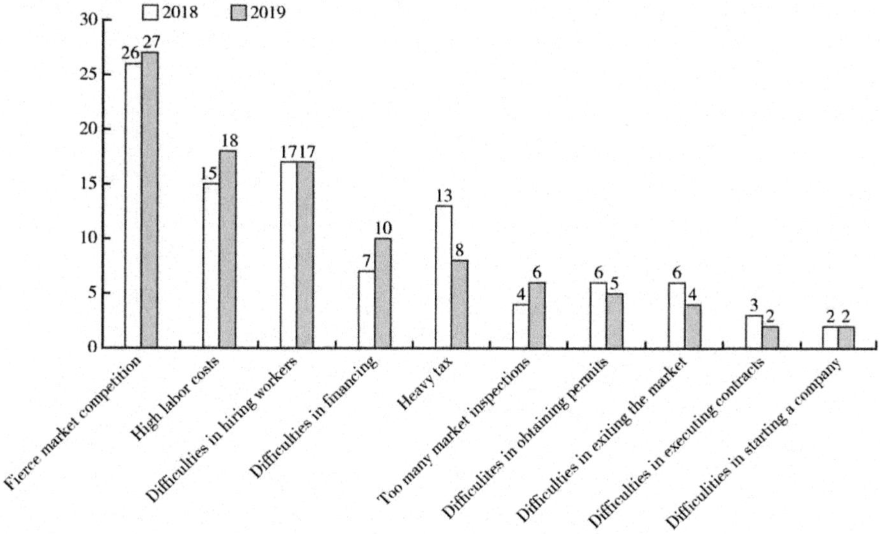

Fig. 8.20 Comparison of the main challenges faced by market players in 2018 and 2019

Compared to 2018, the problem of high labor costs was further exacerbated in 2019. As shown in Fig. 8.20, compared to 2018, the challenges faced by market players in 2019, including rising labor costs, financing difficulties, and frequent market inspections of various types, have intensified. It must be clarified that, to a certain extent, it was inevitable that such new challenges would arise during the business system reform. The increase of market players in Guangdong is a great achievement in the business system construction and reform, yet it also poses new challenges to the business system reform. The doubling of market players means that the increase in market supply will inevitably lead to more intense competition in the product market, while increased market demand will inevitably lead to greater difficulties in recruitment, rising factor prices, and rising enterprise costs.

Therefore, the new challenges currently faced by Guangdong market players stem from the increase of market players brought about by the business system reform, and at present this is difficult to resolve directly.

Methods and Data

Theoretical Framework

1. **Theoretical Basis**

The CPC Central Committee and State Council attach great importance to China's business environment construction. Since the 18th National Congress, the CPC Central Committee and State Council have attached great importance to China's business environment construction, and have carried out a series of reforms, represented by that of the business system. These have become the "first move" in the "streamlining, delegating and strengthening" reform and comprehensive deepening reform, and the main handhold for moving toward high-quality development. On July 17, 2017, General Secretary Jinping Xi announced China's goal of creating a "stable, fair, transparent and predictable business environment." On several other occasions since that time, General Secretary Jinping Xi has reiterated the importance of business environment reform. On December 8, 2017, while presiding over the second collective study of the Politburo of the Chinese Communist Party, the General Secretary proposed implementing a national big data strategy to accelerate the construction of a digital China, thus beginning a new era of "digital government" governance in China. The Fourth Plenary Session of the 19th CPC Central Committee clearly proposed optimizing the business environment, establishing system rules for sound use of the Internet, big data, artificial intelligence and other technical means for government services management, and promoting the construction of a digital government.

Jinping Xi's ideology of socialism with Chinese characteristics in the new era is the fundamental guideline for China's reform and development in the new era. The progress and results in China's business environment construction are major achievements under the comprehensive leadership of the Party. The report of the 19th National Congress of the Party pointed out that adhering to the Party's leadership of all work, the Fourth Plenary Session of the 19th CPC Central Committee chose the various systems of firm maintenance of the Party's authority

X. Xu et al. (eds.), *Report on the Chinese Business Environment Survey 2020*, Research Series on the Chinese Dream and China's Development Path,
https://doi.org/10.1007/978-981-99-6112-2

and centralized unified leadership to be important components of the Party's leadership system. General Secretary Jinping Xi stressed that Party leadership is the fundamental guarantee of effectively performing all work involving the Party and the state, and that it is the "guiding principle" for overcoming all difficulties and risks. The successful implementation of the reform and opening up over **the past four decades has thoroughly proven that, regardless what changes are made and in what stage they are made, we must adhere to the Party's leadership.** To comprehensively deepen the reforms, we must be guided by Jinping Xi's ideology of socialism with Chinese characteristics in the new era. The business environment construction, as one of the most important matters today, has always adhered to the Party's comprehensive leadership of reform. **The results achieved in the business environment construction are inseparable from the top-down policy promotion of the CPC Central Committee and State Council.** General Secretary Jinping Xi has repeatedly emphasized the importance of the business environment, pointing out that "the business environment will never be perfect, but it can always be better." In recent years, the Party and State Council have issued a series of important documents, including the *Regulations on Optimizing the Business Environment* and *Notice of the General Office of the State Council on Typical Practices for Optimizing the Business Environment in Select Regions.* These have become important driving forces in the process of building a business environment.

"Reform for whom" is the core issue in reform and development. The construction of China's business environment has always adhered to the people-centered concept of development. At the First Plenary Session of the 18th Central Committee, General Secretary Jinping Xi clearly stated that the people-centered concept of development must be reflected in all aspects of economic and social development, so that the reform may grasp and promote the matters which will fulfill the hopes and desires of the people, and that, through the reform, the market players among the people may acquire a greater sense of fulfillment. The 19th National Congress Report emphasized adhering to the people-centered approach, carrying out the fundamental purpose of serving the people wholeheartedly, implementing the Party's mass line in all activities of governing the country, and making the goal of their efforts the people's yearning for improved quality of life. At the conference celebrating the fortieth anniversary of China's reform and opening up, General Secretary Jinping Xi pointed out that one of the important experiences gained over the past four decades of reform and opening up is that "we must adhere to the people-centered approach and continuously fulfill the people's yearning for a better life." Adhering to the people-centered approach is the basic strategy for upholding and developing socialism with Chinese characteristics in the new era. The business environment construction has always adhered to the people-centered concept of development, and is established with a people-centered work orientation. Starting with the issues that are most pressing and of greatest concern to market players, such as difficulty in entering the market and doing business, the business reform has been continuously deepened, thus helping to solve the challenges faced by market players, and to achieve the goals of improving market players' sense of fulfillment and promoting high-quality development. Therefore, guided by the people-centered concept of development, the starting point for the business environment construction is the needs of the people; its success or failure depends on the people's evaluation, and its results are shared by the people.

In this report China's business environment construction is evaluated. **This evaluation is guided by Jinping Xi's ideology of socialism with Chinese characteristics in the new era, carried out according to the people-centered idea of development, and based on responses from market players.** The people-centered concept of development signifies that the evaluation of the business environment construction extends beyond the traditional limitations of the government's own judgment and reform, by handing over the power of judgment to market players. This report implements the people-centered concept of development to evaluate the business environment construction based on the responses of market players. Also based on these responses, the report identifies the issues and shortcomings in the business environment construction, and finally proposes countermeasures and directions for further optimizing the business environment.

The theoretical framework of the report is shown in Fig. A.1.

This report is both problem-oriented and goal-oriented, and performs a three-dimensional analysis based on responses from market players. China's business environment construction is clearly problem-oriented. The main problems that enterprises face are difficulties in market entry, operations and growth. The focus of the reform is to reduce the institutional costs of market players throughout their life cycle. China's business environment construction also has clear long-term goals, so as to serve both market players' growth and high-quality economic development. Therefore, this report, being both problem- and goal-oriented, systematically evaluates China's business environment construction from the three progressive dimensions of "problem–mechanism–effectiveness."

First, the report examines the progress and problems in China's business environment construction. The report examines the progress of the business environment construction from multiple dimensions, such as market entry, market regulation, Internet + government services, and service efficiency. The business environment construction is both problem- and goal-orientated. Through the transformation of the government's function in the reforms to "streamline government services, delegate power and strengthen regulation," the business environment construction enhances market players' sense of fulfillment and serves high-quality development. Starting from the perspective of market players, this report examines the progress of the business environment construction, so as to examine if market players' pain points and difficulties have been effectively solved and if the goals of the reform have been achieved. Specific metrics are whether market entry has been facilitated, whether market regulation has been optimized, and whether government services have been improved, all of which contribute to enhancing market players' sense of fulfillment. In line with these problems and goals, the report examines the accomplishments, shortcomings and potential directions for improvement in the business environment construction, from the perspective of advancing the "streamlining government services, delegating power and strengthening regulation" reform.

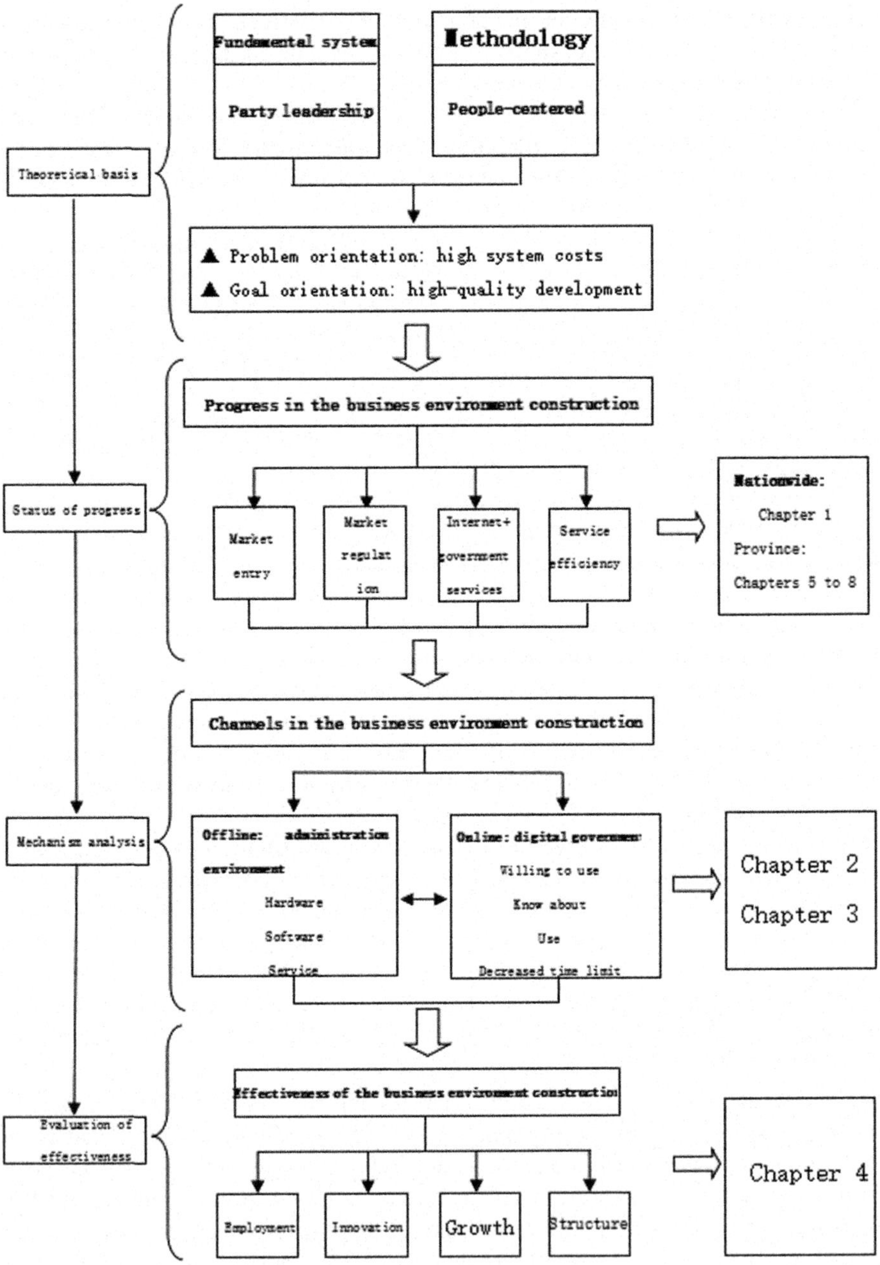

Fig. A.1 Theoretical framework of this report

Second, this report examines the mechanisms and channels of China's business environment construction. At present, there are two main ways for market players to deal with the government: the service halls at physical government service centers, and "digital government," represented by online service halls and various mobile apps. These online and offline methods act as the main channels for optimizing the business environment. This report examines how these two channels respectively promote the optimization of the business environment. The first aspect covered is **the construction of the offline government service environment**. Viewing this from the perspective of market players, we examine the hardware, software, and service levels of physical government service halls. The second aspect covered is **the construction of the online "digital government."** This is evaluated from the three stages of market players' desire to use, awareness of, and use of digital government.

Third, this report examines the performance of China's business environment construction. The business environment construction serves China's overall situation of high-quality economic development. How the business environment construction is matched with and provides support for China's high-quality development is broken down into four aspects: **(1) Employment.** Employment is the greatest livelihood of the people. The number of people employed reflects market players' ability to absorb employment, and is an important foothold for maintaining stability and promoting development. **(2) Growth.** Macroeconomic growth depends not only on the number of market players, but also on their growth. The business environment construction promotes market players' performance improvement and growth at the micro level, and reflects the macro effects of the reform in terms of steady growth. **(3) Structure.** The business environment construction has promoted enthusiasm in entrepreneurship. Many new market players have registered companies, thus providing an opportunity for industrial transformation, and laying the foundation for the market players to transform the Chinese economy into a service-dominated one. **(4) Innovation.** Innovation is an urgent requirement and an important means of support for promoting high-quality development and conversion of momentum.

2. Indicator System

Based on the above theoretical analysis framework, this report's indicator system is detailed in Table A.1.

(1) Indicator system for the progress of the business environment

1. **Convenience of market entry. This includes three level 3 indicators: time required, windows visited, and permits needed to register a company.** From the perspective of building a service-oriented government, facilitating market access is the first step in the reform of "streamlining government services, delegating power and strengthening regulation." From the market players' perspective, registering a company and entering the market are the first steps in their life cycle. Starting with business licenses and permits, the report includes three levels of indicators: the time required to register a company, the number of service windows visited, and the number of permits needed to be processed. Through these indicators, the report then examines

Table A.1 Indicator system of the report on doing business in China

Level 1 indicators	Level 2 indicators	Level 3 indicators
Main progress	Market entry	Number of days needed to register a company
		Number of service windows needed to visit
		Number of permits needed
	Market regulation	National Enterprise Credit Information Publicity System usage rate (%)
	Internet + government services	Online service hall awareness rate (%)
		Online service hall usage rate (%)
	Service efficiency	Number of trips taken to complete a task in the past six months
		Number of service windows visited to complete a task in the past six months
		Votes received from out-of-province market players in evaluating the province's business environment
Government service environment	Hardware	Convenience of public transportation
		Availability of performance facilities
		Availability of convenience facilities
		Availability of feedback facilities
	Software	Clarity of processing instructions
		Rate of open service windows
	Service	Number of services provided
		Quality of services provided
Digital government	Potential usage rate	Proportion of market players willing to use digital government
	Actual awareness rate	Proportion of market players who know about digital government
	Actual usage rate	Proportion of market players who use digital government
Macro performance	Employment	Proportion of market players who upsized in the past six months (%)
	Growth	Proportion of market players with increased performance in the past six months (%)

(continued)

Table A.1 (continued)

Level 1 indicators	Level 2 indicators	Level 3 indicators
	Innovation	Proportion of market players who innovated in the past six months (%)
	Structure	Proportion of newly registered market players who are in the service sector (%)

the convenience of market entry. The less time and fewer windows and permits required to register a company, the more convenient market entry is.[1]

2. **Popularization of credit regulation.** "Delegating power" is the second step in the "streamlining, delegating and strengthening" reform. With so many new market players, the regulation required after the reform is twice that required before it, thus credit regulation has become a new type of regulation model. To this end, the state has created a new type of regulation system with unified credit as its core. The higher the usage rate of the National Enterprise Credit Information Publicity System, the greater the popularization of credit regulation.
3. **Popularization of completing business-related tasks online. This includes both the awareness and usage rates.** The online service hall awareness rate is defined as the proportion of market players surveyed who knew about the online service hall, while the usage rate is defined as the proportion of those who used it. The higher the proportion, the greater the popularization of completing tasks online.
4. **Degree of improvement in service efficiency, including the number of trips taken, service windows visited, and evaluations by market players.** Whether the efficiency of government services has improved, from the perspective of market players, is whether the numbers of trips and service windows and the amount time required to complete business-related tasks have been reduced. Specifically, the report starts from the demand side of market players, and calculates the average numbers of trips and service windows required to complete a single task. The lower the value, the higher the service efficiency. Attention is also given to the evaluation of the

[1] It must be clarified that, when calculating the market entry convenience indicators at the national level, only samples of market players who registered in the year of the survey were used. For example, when calculating the time required for market players to register a company in 2019, only market players who registered in 2019 were included, while those who were interviewed in 2019 but had registered in previous years were not. However, when calculating the ease of market entry in the 110 cities covered in the survey, in general, fewer than thirty market players surveyed in each city had registered in 2019. Therefore, the time frame for this metric was extended to the 2014 business system reform period, and calculated using a sample of market players registered between 2014 and 2019.

province's business environment by market players outside the province. The higher the vote rate, the higher the score.

(2) **Government service environment indicator system**

1. **The hardware level consists of four dimensions: convenience of public transportation, and availability of performance facilities, convenience facilities and feedback facilities.** Among these, the convenience of public transportation is measured by roughly how long it takes to walk from the nearest bus stop to the government service hall: a shorter time means greater convenience. The availability of performance facilities is measured by whether the government affairs hall has a waiting number machine, an LED display, self-serve computers, photocopiers and printers, and photography equipment. The availability of convenience facilities includes if there is a waiting area, if there are seats there and if they are adequate, if there are seats near the service windows and if they are adequate, and if there is air conditioning, a café, washrooms, and so on. The availability of feedback facilities is measured whether or not there is a feedback box. The more complete the facilities, the higher the score.
2. **The software level consists of two dimensions: the clarity of processing instructions and how many service windows are open.** The clarity of the process instructions refers to whether there are inquiry staff, whether basic procedure outlines are provided, whether there are templates for filling in forms, and whether there is a commitment to completion time. Clearer process instructions yield a higher score. The open service window rate is the ratio of open services windows. The greater the rate of open windows, the higher the score.
3. **The service level consists of two dimensions: quantity and quality of the services provided.** The number of services provided was measured by how many people a given window served within twenty minutes; the more people served, the higher the score. The quality of service provided was measured by the numbers of trips and service windows and the amount of time it took to complete tasks over the past six months. The higher these values were, the lower the quality of service, and thus the lower the score.

(3) **Digital government construction indicator system**

1. **Potential usage rate.** This report collectively refers to all Internet-based channels for completing business-related tasks, including online service halls and mobile service platforms, as "digital government." Potential usage rate refers to the proportion of market players willing to use digital government if they are able to complete the tasks they need through it. The potential usage rate represents the development foundation of digital government and its room for future development. The higher the potential usage rate, the more market players are willing to use it, and thus the more solid its development foundation and broader its developmental potential.

2. **Actual awareness rate.** The actual awareness rate refers to the proportion of market players who are aware of digital government platforms such as online service halls and mobile service platforms. Knowledge is the basis for use, and the actual awareness rate reflects the popularity of digital government among market players, as well as the publicity and promotion efforts of digital government, and is an important foundation for it to enter the usage stage. The higher the actual awareness rate, the more solid the promotion and publicity work of the digital government, and this is a prerequisite for increasing the usage rate.
3. **Actual usage rate.** The actual usage rate refers to the proportion of market players who complete business-related tasks using digital government. A high digital government actual usage rate means that it is used on a large scale. Among market players who know about digital government, a higher actual usage rate proves that it is easy to use, and appealing to market players.

(4) **Indicator system for the macro performance of the business environment construction**

1. **Employment, measured by the proportion of market players who create new jobs.** The 19th National Congress Report stated that employment is the greatest livelihood of the people. It is necessary to encourage entrepreneurship to drive employment, and achieve higher quality and more abundant employment, so as to provide livelihood assurance for high-quality development. The more jobs created, the greater the support for high-quality development.
2. **Growth, measured by the proportion of market players with increased performance.** Maintaining and increasing market players' activity is the key to promoting stable economic growth. The increase in performance reflects the growth of market players, and provides qualitative support for high-quality development.
3. **Structure, measured by the proportion of market players in the service industry.** To promote high-quality economic development, it is necessary to focus on promoting the transformation and upgrading of the industrial structure. The more market players who entered the service industry after the reform, the firmer the foundation for the industrial transformation in high-quality development.
4. **Innovation, measured by the proportion of market players who innovated.** Innovation is an urgent requirement and an important means of support for promoting high-quality development and conversion of momentum. The more market players there are who innovate, the more new momentum there will be for high-quality development.

All four of the above indicators—market players who create new jobs, who have increased performance, who are in the service industry, and who innovate—contribute support for high-quality development.

Field Survey

1. **Field Survey Samples**

In the first round of the survey, held in 2018, 182 districts across 84 cities in 16 provinces were sampled using stratified random sampling.

The survey used stratified random sampling. First, the samples were sampled at the provincial government services division level, following three rules. First, considering factors such as the number of municipal and district and county government service halls under its jurisdiction and traffic within the province, five provincial government services units (Xinjiang, Tibet, Inner Mongolia, Qinghai and Hainan) were excluded. Then, 16 out of 26 provincial-level units were selected. Second, to distinguish between regular cities and municipalities directly under the Central Government, we ensured that we drew at least half of the latter. Third, between the 16 provincial units drawn and the 15 not drawn, there was no significant difference in nominal GDP or regulated gross industrial output in 2015.

Based on the above three criteria, we selected 16 provincial government services division units for the survey. Two of these were municipalities directly under the Central Government, namely Beijing and Tianjin. The twelve provinces included were Jilin, Zhejiang, Anhui, Fujian, Shandong, Henan, Hunan, Guangdong, Guizhou, Yunnan, Shaanxi and Gansu. Finally, two autonomous regions were included, namely Guangxi Zhuang Autonomous Region and Ningxia Hui Autonomous Region. The eastern region was considered to include Beijing, Tianjin, Zhejiang, Fujian, Shandong and Guangdong; Anhui, Henan and Hunan formed the central region; Guizhou, Yunnan, Shaanxi, Gansu, Guangxi and Ningxia the western region; and Jilin the northeast region.

Next, from among the selected provincial government services units, the cities at the prefectural and sub-provincial levels were selected, and the following four rules were followed. First, if the number of cities at the district and sub-provincial levels under the jurisdiction of a provincial government services unit did not exceed twelve, then half the cities were drawn; if it exceeded twelve then six were drawn. Second, we ensured that all of the provincial capitals were drawn. Third, between the cities

X. Xu et al. (eds.), *Report on the Chinese Business Environment Survey 2020*, Research Series on the Chinese Dream and China's Development Path,
https://doi.org/10.1007/978-981-99-6112-2

drawn and those not drawn, within the provincial government services units there was no significant difference in nominal GDP or regulated gross industrial output value in 2015. Fourth, nationwide, there was no significant difference in nominal GDP or regulated gross industrial output in 2015 between the cities drawn and those not drawn. Based on the above four criteria, a total of 72 prefecture-level cities were selected for the survey.

Finally, from among the 72 prefecture-level cities, numerous districts were randomly selected following three rules. First, only municipal districts were selected as the survey areas. Second, if the number of municipal districts did not exceed eight, then half were drawn; if it did exceed eight, then four were drawn. Third, among the surveyed cities, there was no significant difference in nominal GDP and total population in 2015 between the districts that were drawn and those that were not.

Based on the above hierarchical sampling method, the survey covered a total of 16 provinces (including twelve provinces, two municipalities and two autonomous regions), 72 prefecture-level cities, twelve municipalities directly under the Central Government, and 182 districts and counties.

In the 2019 survey, in addition to the provinces covered the previous year, eight new provinces were added. First, two municipalities directly under the Central Government—Shanghai and Chongqing—were added, so that the survey covered all four of China's municipalities directly under the Central Government. Second, six provinces were added: Shanxi, Jiangsu, Hebei, Hubei, Hainan and Qinghai.

Therefore, in 2019, there were 24 provinces surveyed: (1) Four municipalities directly under the Central Government: Beijing, Tianjin, **Shanghai and Chongqing**. (2) Eighteen provinces: Jilin, Zhejiang, Anhui, Fujian, Shandong, Henan, Hunan, Guangdong, Guizhou, Yunnan, Shaanxi, Gansu, **Shanxi, Jiangsu, Hebei, Hubei, Hainan and Qinghai**. (3) Two Autonomous Regions: Guangxi and Ningxia.

In addition, in 2019, **34 new prefectures were added**. **First, stratified random sampling was carried out in the four provinces of Shanxi, Jiangsu, Hebei and Hubei, and samples from prefecture-level cities were collected.** The sampling followed three rules: (1) If the number of cities at the district and sub-provincial levels under the jurisdiction of the provincial government services unit did not exceed twelve, then half were sampled; if it did exceed twelve, then six were sampled. (2) It was ensured that all provincial capitals were selected. (3) Within the provincial government services units, there was no significant difference in nominal GDP or gross industrial output value above scale in 2015. **Second, two new prefecture-level cities were added: Haikou, Hainan, and Xining, Qinghai. Third, based on the random sampling, samples of the second-largest cities in 20 provinces and autonomous regions were added.** In addition to the capitals of each province, the city with the highest nominal GDP in 2015 is defined as the second largest city, such as Shenzhen in Guangdong Province, Qingdao in Shandong Province, and Tangshan in Hebei Province. If the sample did not include the second-largest city, it was supplemented.

As a result, a total of 106 prefecture-level cities were covered in 2019. In addition, municipal districts were selected from the two new municipalities directly under the Central Government and 34 new prefectural municipalities. In the cities surveyed, if the number of municipal districts did not exceed eight, then half were taken; if it exceeded eight, then four were taken to ensure that there was no significant difference in nominal GDP and total population in 2015 between the districts drawn and those not drawn.

Based on this rule, the 2019 survey covered a total of 24 provinces (including four municipalities directly under the Central Government, 18 provinces, and two autonomous regions), 106 prefecture-level cities, and 281 municipal districts. In this report, the scores and rankings of 110 municipalities (including four municipalities and 106 prefectures) were calculated.

2. **Field Survey Process**

(1) **2018 survey**

1. Personnel recruitment and plan establishment

   From May to June 2018, after resume screening, interview, training assessment and pre-research screening, the project team recruited a final total of 29 researchers. In June 2018, following thorough discussion, the research plan was determined, and the survey rules and methods were formulated.
2. Questionnaire system and electronic questionnaire system adjustment

   In June 2018, work such as questionnaire design and electronic questionnaire system adjustment was completed. The entire survey process was performed electronically. The electronic questionnaire system allowed the researchers to position and upload the questionnaire information in real time.
3. Personnel training

   From June to July 2018, four investigator training sessions were conducted so that the researchers could learn about the survey process, familiarize themselves with the survey questionnaire, and learn how to operate the electronic questionnaire system. In addition, supervisors and inspectors underwent three training sessions to establish their work standards.
4. Pre-survey

   From June 28 to 29, 2018, the project team organized all members of the research team to conduct pre-research in Guangzhou's Haizhu, Yuexiu, Huangpu and Baiyun Districts. At these sessions, the personnel were trained, the questionnaire design was checked for reasonability, the electronic questionnaire system was checked to ensure it worked properly, and preparations for the official nationwide investigation were made.
5. Official nationwide survey

   From July 19 to August 20, 2018, the research team visited 182 districts across 16 provinces (municipalities) throughout China to conduct the field survey. A group of two to three researchers was responsible for all survey work within a given province (municipality). The survey targeted market regulation bureau windows at service halls throughout the country, and representatives of market players who were there to complete business-related tasks were interviewed. According to the content of the questionnaire, the interviews were conducted from the dimensions of market entry, market regulation, Internet + government services, and service efficiency. The interviewees then truthfully filled out the electronic questionnaire system, and uploaded it to the back-end staff.

(2) **2019 survey**

1. Personnel recruitment and plan establishment

   From May to June 2019, after resume screening, interviews, training assessment and pre-research screening, the project team recruited a total of 40 researchers. In June 2019, based on the 2018 research plan, after thorough discussion, the research plan was determined, and research rules and methods were formulated.
2. Questionnaire system and electronic questionnaire system adjustment

   In June 2019, on the basis of the 2018 electronic questionnaire system, the questionnaire design and electronic questionnaire system were adjusted. The entire research process was performed electronically. The electronic questionnaire system allowed the researchers to orient and upload the questionnaire information in real time.
3. Personnel training

   From June to July 2019, four investigator training sessions were conducted so that the researchers could learn about the survey process, familiarize themselves with the survey questionnaire, and learn how to operate the electronic questionnaire system. In addition, supervisors and inspectors underwent three training sessions to establish their work standards.
4. Pre-survey

   On June 3, 11 and 12, 2019, all members of the research team underwent pre-survey training in Guangzhou's Haizhu, Yuexiu, Huangpu, Baiyun and Panyu Districts. At the training sessions, the questionnaire design was checked for reasonability, the electronic questionnaire system was checked to see if it worked properly, and preparations for the official nationwide survey were made.
5. Official nationwide survey

   From July 15 to August 10, 2019, researchers at Sun Yat-sen University conducted further research on the business environment construction. The summer 2019 nationwide survey team visited 281 districts across 24 provinces (municipalities) throughout China to conduct the field survey. Each group consisted of two researchers, who were responsible for all research work within one to two provinces (municipalities).

(3) **Survey methods**

1. Survey subjects
   (1) The market regulation bureau windows at the service halls in the sampled areas;
   (2) Representatives of market players who were completing business-related tasks at the market regulation bureau windows.
2. Survey content
   (1) Hardware, software and other facilities at local service halls;
   (2) The business environment as perceived by market players throughout the country.
3. Field study methods and processes
   (1) After arriving at a service hall to be surveyed, the researchers observed the hardware, software and services of the market regulation bureau window following the items on the questionnaire. Then they truthfully filled in the electronic questionnaire system and uploaded it to the back-end personnel.
   (2) The researchers randomly selected employees of market players who were visiting to complete business-related tasks. They then interviewed them following the items of the questionnaire from the dimensions of market entry, market regulation, Internet + government services, service efficiency, and so on. The researchers then truthfully filled in the electronic questionnaire system and uploaded it to the back-end personnel.
4. Alternative solution

   If a research team's normal research work was interrupted, resulting in their inability to complete the investigation, then a nearby non-research area was chosen as an alternative.

3. Quality Control

1. Precise positioning before and after the survey

   The investigation rules required the researchers to take a group photo at the entrance of the service hall before (after) the investigation, then upload the photos and GPS location for inspection, so as to ensure that there were no mistakes in the research sites and teams.
2. Real-time audio recording of the entire research process

   The research rules required the researchers to make an audio recording throughout the investigation, so that the entire investigation process were traceable.
3. Real-time upload of the survey data

   The entire research process was carried out electronically. The survey data were uploaded in real time, and the research data were traceable.
4. Survey process supervisors and inspectors

The investigation rules required the supervisor to check the photos and GPS location information uploaded by the research team before they began the investigation, so as to ensure there were no mistakes in the location and time of the investigation. The supervisors and inspectors reviewed the survey data and audio files uploaded by the researchers every day to ensure that the investigation process complied with the standards.

5. Accuracy testing of the survey data

   The first round was an overall inspection. According to the investigation rules, after receiving the investigators' research data, the inspector then automatically performed a technical inspection of the survey data according to the preparations and adjustment of the inspection procedure. During the technical inspection, both the inspector and the investigators checked for unqualified data. When unqualified research data were found, the researchers were required to conduct a new investigation, so to ensure the quality of the survey.

The second round consisted of "double random" spot checks. The first step of this was to automatically randomly select 10% from the questionnaires generated each day, then match them to the inspectors using a "double random" method. The inspectors could only see the questionnaire code and start and end times of each questionnaire, and could not see the answers to each question. In the second step, the inspector located the corresponding recording according to the questionnaire code and start and end times, then filled in all the questions in the questionnaire based on the content of the recording. The third step was to match the questionnaire filled out by the investigators with that filled out by the inspector. Only when the answers to all of the questions in the questionnaire were consistent could the quality inspection be passed. When questionnaires failed the quality inspection, the researchers were requested to re-investigate them.

Relevant Data

1. **Sample Distribution**

See Tables C.1, C.2, and C.3.

2. **Data for the China Doing Business Report**

See Tables C.4, C.5, and C.6.

3. **Report Data on China's Government Service Environment**

See Tables C.7, C.8, and C.9.

4. **Data for the China "Digital Government" Construction Report**

See Tables C.10 and C.11.

X. Xu et al. (eds.), *Report on the Chinese Business Environment Survey 2020*, Research Series on the Chinese Dream and China's Development Path,
https://doi.org/10.1007/978-981-99-6112-2

Table C.1 Regional distribution of market players surveyed in twenty-four provinces nationwide in 2019

Province	Number of questionnaires	Proportion of total (%)
Zhejiang	648	7.81
Hubei	544	6.56
Jiangsu	508	6.13
Guangdong	480	5.79
Guangxi	473	5.70
Yunnan	450	5.43
Shandong	435	5.25
Hebei	417	5.03
Anhui	415	5.00
Fujian	400	4.82
Henan	397	4.79
Hunan	391	4.71
Jilin	354	4.27
Gansu	329	3.97
Shaanxi	313	3.77
Guizhou	277	3.34
Shanghai	264	3.18
Ningxia	238	2.87
Chongqing	213	2.57
Beijing	207	2.50
Tianjin	197	2.38
Shanxi	158	1.91
Qinghai	114	1.37
Hainan	71	0.86

Table C.2 Basic situation of interviewees in 2019

		Number of questionnaires	Proportion of total (%)
Sex	Male	3858	46.52
	Female	4435	53.48
Age	Under 30	2964	35.74
	30–40	3844	46.35
	40–50	1252	15.10
	Over 50	233	2.81
Time at their position	1 year or less	2375	39.43
	2–5 years	2153	35.74
	6–10 years	907	15.06
	More than 10 years	589	9.77
Position	Regular employee	3122	51.59
	Mid-level manager	1263	20.87
	Senior manager	1504	24.85
	Other	163	2.69

Note The total number of questionnaires collected in 2019 was 8293, and the success rate was 75%. The interviewees' sex and age were directly observed and filled in by the researchers, thus the total number of questionnaires was 8293. First the interviewees were asked if they would like to be interviewed. If so, then their positions and the amount of time they had been in those positions were filled in

Table C.3 Basic characteristics of the interviewees in 2019

		Number of questionnaires	Proportion of total (%)
Ownership type	State-owned enterprise	360	7.67
	Private enterprise	2984	63.56
	Foreign-funded enterprise	61	1.30
	Joint venture	123	2.62
	Self-employed	965	20.55
	Other	202	4.30
Sector(s)	Agriculture, forestry, animal husbandry, fishery	158	3.38
	Industry and construction	891	19.08
	Service	2838	60.77
	Other	783	16.77
Number of employees	Fewer than 10	1866	31.94
	10–20	1320	22.59
	20–100	1442	24.68
	100–500	591	10.11
	More than 500	421	7.21
	Unsure	203	3.47

Note The total number of questionnaires was 8293, and the success rate was 75%. Intermediaries are not included in the statistics on ownership and industry types

Table C.4 Indicator system calculated by the distance to frontier method for business environment reporting

Level 1 indicator	Level 2 indicators	Level 3 indicators	Nationwide mean	Best frontier	Worst practice
Business environment	Market access	Number of days needed to register a company	6.9	1	22
		Number of service windows visited	1.8	1	9
		Number of permits processed	1.8	1	10
	Credit regulation	National Enterprise Credit Information Publicity System usage rate (%)	66%	100%	0
	Internet + government services	Online service hall awareness rate (%)	66%	100%	0
		Online service hall usage rate (%)	48%	100%	0
	Service efficiency	Number of trips taken to complete a task in the past six months	1.9	1	10
		Number of service windows visited to complete a task in the past six months	1.4	1	3
		Business environment vote rate		34%	0

Note The score was calculated using the World Bank's distance to frontier method when assessing the business environment of each country. Each city's score = 100 * (worst practice − own value)/(worst practice − best frontier). The definitions of best frontier and worst practice are the same as those for 2018, thus the scores for 2018 and 2019 are comparable. First, calculate the frontier distance score of each region's tertiary indicator. Then calculate the score of the secondary indicator, which is the average of each subordinate tertiary indicator. Finally, calculate the score of the primary indicator, which is the average of each subordinate secondary indicator. When calculating the scores for each region, the samples used for credit regulation, Internet + government services and service efficiency were the total samples of all market players surveyed, while for market entry only a sub-sample of market players registered between 2014 and 2019 was used

Table C.5 Distance to frontier law scores for each city in covered in the business environment report

City	Business environment									
	Total score	Market entry			Credit regulation	Internet + government services		Service efficiency		
		Average number of days taken to register	Average number of windows visited	Number of permits needed to process	Credit information system usage rate	Online service hall awareness rate (%)	Online service hall usage rate (%)	Number of trips taken to complete one task	Number of windows visited each trip	Business environment vote rate
Beijing	77	24	83	85	77	84	73	91	84	94
Tianjin	68	58	89	81	71	71	54	91	77	17
Shijiazhuang	66	79	85	74	81	58	37	86	86	6
Tangshan	61	72	81	74	61	55	40	89	76	6
Zhangjiakou	58	65	83	75	57	40	23	88	82	6
Chengde	58	73	90	74	40	38	23	93	82	6
Langfang	58	67	73	81	58	39	27	92	81	6
Hengshui	61	93	86	72	46	47	21	90	85	6
Taiyuan	–	–	–	–	–	–	–	–	–	–
Datong	–	–	–	–	–	–	–	–	–	–
Changzhi	–	–	–	–	–	–	–	–	–	–
Yuncheng	–	–	–	–	–	–	–	–	–	–
Lüliang	–	–	–	–	–	–	–	–	–	–
Changchun	66	67	84	87	57	80	57	90	67	1
Jilin	68	56	98	82	70	74	56	90	85	1
Siping	60	70	90	82	58	42	30	91	75	1
Baishan	68	79	82	87	46	86	60	91	81	1

(continued)

Table C.5 (continued)

City	Business environment									
	Total score	Market entry			Credit regulation	Internet + government services		Service efficiency		
		Average number of days taken to register	Average number of windows visited	Number of permits needed to process	Credit information system usage rate	Online service hall awareness rate (%)	Online service hall usage rate (%)	Number of trips taken to complete one task	Number of windows visited each trip	Business environment vote rate
Songyuan	59	81	93	89	39	66	24	84	58	1
Shanghai	76	24	81	98	73	59	40	85	81	142
Nanjing	72	59	91	81	79	62	45	89	88	55
Xuzhou	74	62	86	82	72	71	63	88	91	55
Changzhou	68	51	73	84	72	63	48	89	79	55
Suzhou	72	70	85	94	78	64	34	85	83	55
Yancheng	69	70	68	79	70	66	48	90	78	55
Taizhou	72	66	81	84	69	71	52	90	78	55
Suqian	76	82	86	75	78	78	63	91	73	55
Hangzhou	83	76	86	93	68	83	69	94	81	97
Ningbo	82	67	83	95	65	87	67	94	87	97
Huzhou	83	54	95	94	60	93	75	95	88	97
Jinhua	78	75	83	96	56	72	57	88	80	97
Quzhou	78	94	87	96	44	57	38	95	97	97
Zhoushan	77	86	96	90	47	59	40	91	84	97

(continued)

Table C.5 (continued)

City	Business environment									
	Total score	Market entry			Credit regulation	Internet + government services		Service efficiency		
		Average number of days taken to register	Average number of windows visited	Number of permits needed to process	Credit information system usage rate	Online service hall awareness rate (%)	Online service hall usage rate (%)	Number of trips taken to complete one task	Number of windows visited each trip	Business environment vote rate
Lishui	76	89	85	82	51	74	41	93	74	97
Hefei	70	72	72	96	75	78	64	91	74	5
Wuhu	69	75	88	80	76	72	56	92	79	5
Bengbu	65	76	74	88	60	64	54	92	74	5
Huaibei	68	75	88	86	71	74	52	89	68	5
Tongling	62	74	74	99	88	34	23	91	69	5
Fuyang	70	70	84	85	88	79	67	86	70	5
Fuzhou	72	83	96	77	82	61	43	93	91	25
Putian	69	60	90	72	75	66	53	88	92	25
Sanming	–	–	–	–	–	–	–	–	–	–
Quanzhou	63	36	88	91	79	46	31	88	80	25
Ningde	66	77	97	89	78	33	20	95	83	25
Jinan	66	61	78	84	74	63	48	92	80	9
Qingdao	73	68	90	96	67	81	74	94	79	9
Zibo	69	85	98	101	52	55	36	95	91	9

(continued)

Table C.5 (continued)

City	Business environment									
	Total score	Market entry			Credit regulation	Internet + government services		Service efficiency		
		Average number of days taken to register	Average number of windows visited	Number of permits needed to process	Credit information system usage rate	Online service hall awareness rate (%)	Online service hall usage rate (%)	Number of trips taken to complete one task	Number of windows visited each trip	Business environment vote rate
Zaozhuang	–	–	–	–	–	–	–	–	–	–
Dongying	67	75	83	96	70	59	29	93	93	9
Binzhou	–	–	–	–	–	–	–	–	–	–
Zhengzhou	70	60	89	85	70	83	65	90	81	4
Luoyang	69	63	88	80	68	77	63	91	84	4
Anyang	67	65	92	93	53	66	47	94	89	4
Xuchang	–	–	–	–	–	–	–	–	–	–
Luohe	67	57	89	91	62	73	52	91	84	4
Xinyang	69	70	94	79	68	74	56	93	88	4
Zhoukou	66	58	84	94	59	74	46	94	78	4
Wuhan	69	61	93	89	84	74	57	90	68	5
Yichang	68	76	98	87	61	68	47	96	74	5
Ezhou	67	52	96	89	60	72	50	91	90	5
Jingmen	64	73	90	85	50	56	42	89	87	5
Huanggang	64	39	86	87	61	67	56	92	81	5

(continued)

Table C.5 (continued)

City	Business environment									
	Total score	Market entry			Credit regulation	Internet + government services		Service efficiency		
		Average number of days taken to register	Average number of windows visited	Number of permits needed to process	Credit information system usage rate	Online service hall awareness rate (%)	Online service hall usage rate (%)	Number of trips taken to complete one task	Number of windows visited each trip	Business environment vote rate
Xianning	69	80	92	82	46	75	56	96	92	5
Suizhou	65	79	93	84	68	67	45	84	63	5
Changsha	71	56	93	106	70	77	65	90	77	7
Hengyang	68	72	92	92	68	64	45	91	78	7
Shaoyang	68	59	89	97	74	73	48	92	77	7
Yueyang	64	43	83	89	70	59	55	84	90	7
Changde	66	59	97	91	55	63	49	86	87	7
Huaihua	64	56	94	80	68	53	41	92	88	7
Guangdong	83	76	92	88	93	55	41	89	89	119
Shaoguan	76	63	94	89	57	43	33	92	91	119
Shenzhen	85	66	100	97	74	83	61	90	75	119
Jiangmen	79	87	92	95	63	56	41	90	66	119
Zhanjiang	–	–	–	–	–	–	–	–	–	–
Yangjiang	75	77	88	91	64	43	20	92	82	119
Chaozhou	–	–	–	–	–	–	–	–	–	–

(continued)

Table C.5 (continued)

City	Business environment									
	Total score	Market entry			Credit regulation	Internet + government services		Service efficiency		
		Average number of days taken to register	Average number of windows visited	Number of permits needed to process	Credit information system usage rate	Online service hall awareness rate (%)	Online service hall usage rate (%)	Number of trips taken to complete one task	Number of windows visited each trip	Business environment vote rate
Jieyang	–	–	–	–	–	–	–	–	–	–
Nanning	65	65	73	95	68	57	48	93	81	4
Liuzhou	65	73	85	85	68	58	38	89	86	4
Fangchenggang	–	–	–	–	–	–	–	–	–	–
Qinzhou	69	93	94	89	41	71	53	91	88	4
Guigang	64	73	71	95	57	54	37	92	89	4
Yulin	67	68	85	89	62	67	45	94	92	4
Chongzuo	–	–	–	–	–	–	–	–	–	–
Haikou	69	83	93	96	67	64	46	90	79	6
Chongqing	66	64	89	91	70	61	42	90	73	17
Guiyang	67	45	94	78	76	73	61	88	81	7
Zunyi	66	64	86	89	67	72	50	87	76	7
Bijie	66	90	91	85	61	61	39	94	67	7
Kunming	65	58	69	79	83	71	55	85	76	8
Qujing	66	64	80	80	72	70	60	84	78	8

(continued)

Table C.5 (continued)

City	Business environment									
	Total score	Market entry			Credit regulation	Internet + government services		Service efficiency		
		Average number of days taken to register	Average number of windows visited	Number of permits needed to process	Credit information system usage rate	Online service hall awareness rate (%)	Online service hall usage rate (%)	Number of trips taken to complete one task	Number of windows visited each trip	Business environment vote rate
Yuxi	67	52	88	85	75	72	59	85	81	8
Zhaotong	77	82	78	85	88	90	81	94	90	8
Pu'er	67	57	71	79	69	90	74	92	59	8
Xi'an	71	63	90	88	72	80	62	95	82	4
Tongchuan	61	74	96	71	34	65	23	94	83	4
Hanzhong	66	57	78	81	71	88	56	87	70	4
Yulin	63	82	84	93	44	60	31	88	75	4
Ankang	64	69	89	71	58	78	46	92	64	4
Lanzhou	62	47	89	88	56	56	48	85	88	2
Jiayuguan	–	–	–	–	–	–	–	–	–	–
Zhangye	63	74	84	88	39	71	42	85	78	2
Pingliang	–	–	–	–	–	–	–	–	–	–
Jiuquan	65	63	95	74	48	85	57	85	72	2
Longnan	–	–	–	–	–	–	–	–	–	–
Xining	51	63	70	73	60	47	27	82	38	3

(continued)

Table C.5 (continued)

City	Business environment									
	Total score	Market entry			Credit regulation	Internet + government services		Service efficiency		
		Average number of days taken to register	Average number of windows visited	Number of permits needed to process	Credit information system usage rate	Online service hall awareness rate (%)	Online service hall usage rate (%)	Number of trips taken to complete one task	Number of windows visited each trip	Business environment vote rate
Yinchuan	66	81	96	83	48	69	42	93	81	2
Wuzhong	57	90	85	85	45	47	18	84	52	2
Guyuan	58	63	94	83	49	56	21	90	67	2

Note The source of the data is the China Doing Business Enterprise Survey. When calculating the market entry indicators, only samples of market players registered between 2014 and 2019 were included. Several cities had fewer than thirty registered samples during this time, thus their scores for 2019 are absent. These cities are Sanming, Jiayuguan, Longnan, Pingliang, Chaozhou, Jieyang, Zhanjiang, Chongzuo, Xuchang, Binzhou, Zaozhuang, Fangchenggang, Datong, Lüliang, Taiyuan, Yuncheng and Changzhi

Table C.6 Raw data for each city in the business environment report

City	Business environment								
	Market entry			Credit regulation	Internet + government services		Service efficiency		
	Average number of days taken to register	Average number of windows visited	Number of permits needed to process	Credit information system usage rate (%)	Online service hall awareness rate (%)	Online service hall usage rate (%)	Number of trips taken to complete one task	Number of windows visited each trip	Business environment vote rate (%)
Beijing	16.9	2.4	2.3	77	84	73	1.9	1.3	32
Tianjin	9.8	1.8	2.7	71	71	54	1.8	1.5	6
Shijiazhuang	5.4	2.2	3.4	81	58	37	2.2	1.3	2
Tangshan	6.8	2.5	3.4	61	55	40	2.0	1.5	2
Zhangjiakou	8.3	2.3	3.2	57	40	23	2.1	1.4	2
Chengde	6.8	1.8	3.4	40	38	23	1.6	1.4	2
Langfang	8.0	3.2	2.7	58	39	27	1.7	1.4	2
Hengshui	2.5	2.1	3.5	46	47	21	1.9	1.3	2
Taiyuan	–	–	–	–	–	–	–	–	–
Datong	–	–	–	–	–	–	–	–	–
Changzhi	–	–	–	–	–	–	–	–	–
Yuncheng	–	–	–	–	–	–	–	–	–
Lüliang	–	–	–	–	–	–	–	–	–
Changchun	8.0	2.3	2.1	57	80	57	1.9	1.7	0
Jilin	10.1	1.2	2.6	70	74	56	1.9	1.3	0
Siping	7.4	1.8	2.6	58	42	30	1.9	1.5	0
Baishan	5.4	2.4	2.2	46	86	60	1.8	1.4	0

(continued)

Table C.6 (continued)

City	Business environment								
	Market entry			Credit regulation	Internet + government services		Service efficiency		
	Average number of days taken to register	Average number of windows visited	Number of permits needed to process	Credit information system usage rate (%)	Online service hall awareness rate (%)	Online service hall usage rate (%)	Number of trips taken to complete one task	Number of windows visited each trip	Business environment vote rate (%)
Songyuan	5.0	1.5	2.0	39	66	24	2.4	1.8	0
Shanghai	17.0	2.5	1.1	73	59	40	2.3	1.4	48
Nanjing	9.7	1.7	2.7	79	62	45	2.0	1.2	19
Xuzhou	9.0	2.1	2.6	72	71	63	2.0	1.2	19
Changzhou	11.3	3.2	2.5	72	63	48	2.0	1.4	19
Suzhou	7.3	2.2	1.6	78	64	34	2.3	1.3	19
Yancheng	7.3	3.5	2.9	70	66	48	1.9	1.4	19
Taizhou	8.1	2.5	2.4	69	71	52	1.9	1.4	19
Suqian	4.8	2.1	3.2	78	78	63	1.8	1.5	19
Hangzhou	6.0	2.1	1.7	68	83	69	1.5	1.4	33
Ningbo	8.0	2.3	1.5	65	87	67	1.5	1.3	33
Huzhou	10.6	1.4	1.6	60	93	75	1.5	1.2	33
Jinhua	6.2	2.3	1.4	56	72	57	2.0	1.4	33
Quzhou	2.2	2.1	1.4	44	57	38	1.5	1.1	33
Zhoushan	3.9	1.3	1.9	47	59	40	1.8	1.3	33

(continued)

Table C.6 (continued)

City	Business environment								
	Market entry			Credit regulation	Internet + government services		Service efficiency		
	Average number of days taken to register	Average number of windows visited	Number of permits needed to process	Credit information system usage rate (%)	Online service hall awareness rate (%)	Online service hall usage rate (%)	Number of trips taken to complete one task	Number of windows visited each trip	Business environment vote rate (%)
Lishui	3.4	2.2	2.6	51	74	41	1.6	1.5	33
Hefei	6.9	3.3	1.4	75	78	64	1.8	1.5	2
Wuhu	6.2	2.0	2.8	76	72	56	1.7	1.4	2
Bengbu	6.0	3.1	2.1	60	64	54	1.7	1.5	2
Huaibei	6.3	2.0	2.3	71	74	52	2.0	1.6	2
Tongling	6.4	3.1	1.1	88	34	23	1.8	1.6	2
Fuyang	7.3	2.3	2.4	88	79	67	2.2	1.6	2
Fuzhou	4.7	1.3	3.1	82	61	43	1.7	1.2	8
Putian	9.4	1.8	3.5	75	66	53	2.0	1.2	8
Sanming	–	–	–	–	–	–	–	–	–
Quanzhou	14.3	2.0	1.8	79	46	31	2.1	1.4	8
Ningde	5.8	1.3	2.0	78	33	20	1.4	1.3	8
Jinan	9.1	2.7	2.4	74	63	48	1.7	1.4	3
Qingdao	7.7	1.8	1.3	67	81	74	1.5	1.4	3
Zibo	4.2	1.2	0.9	52	55	36	1.5	1.2	3

(continued)

Table C.6 (continued)

City	Business environment								
	Market entry			Credit regulation	Internet + government services		Service efficiency		
	Average number of days taken to register	Average number of windows visited	Number of permits needed to process	Credit information system usage rate (%)	Online service hall awareness rate (%)	Online service hall usage rate (%)	Number of trips taken to complete one task	Number of windows visited each trip	Business environment vote rate (%)
Zaozhuang	–	–	–	–	–	–	–	–	–
Dongying	6.2	2.4	1.4	70	59	29	1.7	1.1	3
Binzhou	–	–	–	–	–	–	–	–	–
Zhengzhou	9.3	1.9	2.3	70	83	65	1.9	1.4	1
Luoyang	8.8	2.0	2.8	68	77	63	1.8	1.3	1
Anyang	8.3	1.6	1.6	53	66	47	1.5	1.2	1
Xuchang	–	–	–	–	–	–	–	–	–
Luohe	10.0	1.9	1.8	62	73	52	1.8	1.3	1
Xinyang	7.3	1.5	2.9	68	74	56	1.6	1.3	1
Zhoukou	9.7	2.3	1.5	59	74	46	1.5	1.4	1
Wuhan	9.2	1.6	2.0	84	74	57	1.9	1.6	2
Yichang	6.0	1.2	2.2	61	68	47	1.4	1.5	2
Ezhou	11.1	1.3	2.0	60	72	50	1.8	1.2	2
Jingmen	6.7	1.8	2.3	50	56	42	2.0	1.3	2
Huanggang	13.7	2.2	2.2	61	67	56	1.8	1.4	2

(continued)

Table C.6 (continued)

City	Business environment								
	Market entry			Credit regulation	Internet + government services		Service efficiency		
	Average number of days taken to register	Average number of windows visited	Number of permits needed to process	Credit information system usage rate (%)	Online service hall awareness rate (%)	Online service hall usage rate (%)	Number of trips taken to complete one task	Number of windows visited each trip	Business environment vote rate (%)
Xianning	5.2	1.7	2.6	46	75	56	1.4	1.2	2
Suizhou	5.5	1.6	2.4	68	67	45	2.5	1.7	2
Changsha	10.2	1.6	0.5	70	77	65	1.9	1.5	2
Hengyang	6.9	1.7	1.7	68	64	45	1.8	1.4	2
Shaoyang	9.7	1.9	1.3	74	73	48	1.8	1.5	2
Yueyang	13.0	2.3	2.0	70	59	55	2.4	1.2	2
Changde	9.6	1.2	1.8	55	63	49	2.3	1.3	2
Huaihua	10.3	1.5	2.8	68	53	41	1.7	1.2	2
Guangdong	6.0	1.7	2.1	93	55	41	2.0	1.2	41
Shaoguan	8.8	1.5	2.0	57	43	33	1.7	1.2	41
Shenzhen	8.1	1.0	1.3	74	83	61	1.9	1.5	41
Jiangmen	3.8	1.7	1.5	63	56	41	1.9	1.7	41
Zhanjiang	–	–	–	–	–	–	–	–	–
Yangjiang	5.7	2.0	1.8	64	43	20	1.7	1.4	41
Chaozhou	–	–	–	–	–	–	–	–	–

(continued)

Table C.6 (continued)

City	Business environment								
	Market entry			Credit regulation	Internet + government services		Service efficiency		
	Average number of days taken to register	Average number of windows visited	Number of permits needed to process	Credit information system usage rate (%)	Online service hall awareness rate (%)	Online service hall usage rate (%)	Number of trips taken to complete one task	Number of windows visited each trip	Business environment vote rate (%)
Jieyang	–	–	–	–	–	–	–	–	–
Nanning	8.4	3.2	1.5	68	57	48	1.7	1.4	1
Liuzhou	6.8	2.2	2.3	68	58	38	2.0	1.3	1
Fangchenggang	–	–	–	–	–	–	–	–	–
Qinzhou	2.5	1.5	2.0	41	71	53	1.8	1.3	1
Guigang	6.7	3.3	1.5	57	54	37	1.7	1.2	1
Yulin	7.7	2.2	2.0	62	67	45	1.6	1.2	1
Chongzuo	–	–	–	–	–	–	–	–	–
Haikou	4.6	1.5	1.3	67	64	46	1.9	1.4	2
Chongqing	8.5	1.9	1.8	70	61	42	1.9	1.5	6
Guiyang	12.5	1.5	3.0	76	73	61	2.0	1.4	2
Zunyi	8.6	2.1	2.0	67	72	50	2.2	1.5	2
Bijie	3.1	1.7	2.3	61	61	39	1.6	1.7	2
Kunming	9.9	3.5	2.9	83	71	55	2.3	1.5	3
Qujing	8.6	2.6	2.8	72	70	60	2.4	1.4	3

(continued)

Table C.6 (continued)

City	Business environment								
	Market entry			Credit regulation	Internet + government services		Service efficiency		
	Average number of days taken to register	Average number of windows visited	Number of permits needed to process	Credit information system usage rate (%)	Online service hall awareness rate (%)	Online service hall usage rate (%)	Number of trips taken to complete one task	Number of windows visited each trip	Business environment vote rate (%)
Yuxi	11.0	2.0	2.3	75	72	59	2.4	1.4	3
Zhaotong	4.9	2.8	2.4	88	90	81	1.5	1.2	3
Pu'er	9.9	3.3	2.9	69	90	74	1.7	1.8	3
Xi'an	8.9	1.8	2.1	72	80	62	1.5	1.4	2
Tongchuan	6.4	1.3	3.6	34	65	23	1.5	1.3	2
Hanzhong	10.0	2.8	2.7	71	88	56	2.2	1.6	2
Yulin	4.9	2.3	1.6	44	60	31	2.1	1.5	2
Ankang	7.4	1.9	3.6	58	78	46	1.7	1.7	2
Lanzhou	12.0	1.9	2.0	56	56	48	2.4	1.3	1
Jiayuguan	–	–	–	–	–	–	–	–	–
Zhangye	6.5	2.3	2.1	39	71	42	2.3	1.4	1
Pingliang	–	–	–	–	–	–	–	–	–
Jiuquan	8.8	1.4	3.3	48	85	57	2.3	1.6	1
Longnan	–	–	–	–	–	–	–	–	–
Xining	8.7	3.4	3.5	60	47	27	2.6	2.2	1

(continued)

Table C.6 (continued)

City	Business environment								
	Market entry			Credit regulation	Internet + government services		Service efficiency		
	Average number of days taken to register	Average number of windows visited	Number of permits needed to process	Credit information system usage rate (%)	Online service hall awareness rate (%)	Online service hall usage rate (%)	Number of trips taken to complete one task	Number of windows visited each trip	Business environment vote rate (%)
Yinchuan	5.0	1.3	2.6	48	69	42	1.6	1.4	1
Wuzhong	3.1	2.2	2.4	45	47	18	2.4	2.0	1
Guyuan	8.7	1.5	2.5	49	56	21	1.9	1.7	1

Note The data are from the China Doing Business Enterprise Survey. When calculating the market entry indicators, only samples of market players registered between 2014 and 2019 were included. Several cities had fewer than thirty registered samples during this time, thus their scores for 2019 are absent. These cities are Sanming, Jiayuguan, Longnan, Pingliang, Chaozhou, Jieyang, Zhanjiang, Chongzuo, Xuchang, Binzhou, Zaozhuang, Fangchenggang, Datong, Lüliang, Taiyuan, Yuncheng and Changzhi

Table C.7 Indicator system used to calculate the distance to frontier in the government service environment

Level 1 indicator	Level 2 indicators	Level 3 indicators	Level 4 indicators	Nationwide average	Best frontier	Worst practice
Administration environment	Hardware	Convenience of public transportation	How many minutes it takes to walk from the nearest bus stop to the government service hall	3.83	1	10
		Availability of performance facilities	Availability of waiting number machine	0.80	1	0
			Availability of LED display	0.75	1	0
			Availability of self-serve computer	0.78	1	0
			Availability of photocopying and printing service	0.91	1	0
			Availability of photography equipment	0.48	1	0
		Availability of convenience facilities	Availability of waiting area	0.96	1	0
			Availability of seats in the waiting area	1	1	0
			Sufficient number of seats	0.82	1	0
			Seats or stools at the service windows	0.99	1	0
			Comfort level of the seats at the service windows	0.74	1	0
			Availability of air conditioning or heating (radiators)	0.95	1	0
			Availability of café	0.74	1	0
			Availability of washrooms	0.99	1	0

(continued)

Table C.7 (continued)

Level 1 indicator	Level 2 indicators	Level 3 indicators	Level 4 indicators	Nationwide average	Best frontier	Worst practice
		Availability of feedback facilities	Availability of a comment box	0.93	1	0
	Software	Clarity of procedure instructions	Availability of inquiry staff	0.89	1	0
			Availability of basic procedures for completing tasks	0.92	1	0
			Availability of form filling templates	0.72	1	0
			Commitment to completion time	0.54	1	0
		Service window open rate	All service windows open	0.92	1	0
	Service	Number of services provided	Number of people served at one window within 20 min	1.93	6	0
		Quality of services provided	Completion in one visit rate over the past six months	0.35	1	0
			Estimated time required each visit (hours)	1.36	0.64	3.45
			Single-window service rate	0.49	1	0

Source The Sun Yat-sen University Research Group on "Deepening the Reform of the Business System" used the World Bank's distance to frontier method for calculating the score when assessing the business environment of each country. Each city's score = 100 * (worst practice − own value)/(worst practice − best frontier). First, calculate the distance to frontier score for each level 4 indicator. The score for the level 3 indicator is the average for each of the subordinate level 4 indicators. The score for the level 2 indicator is the average of each subordinate level 3 indicator. Finally, the score for the level 1 indicator is calculated as the average value for each subordinate level 2 indicator

Table C.8 Scores of each province and city in the government service environment report

City	Total score	Government service environment					
		Hardware					
		Convenience of public transportation	Availability of performance facilities				
		How many minutes it takes to walk from the nearest bus stop to the government service hall	Availability of waiting number machine	Availability of LED display	Availability of self-serve computer	Availability of photocopying or printing service	Availability of photography equipment
Beijing	83	44	100	100	100	100	45
Tianjin	80	67	100	100	100	80	0
Changchun	67	24	100	100	100	100	0
Siping	72	83	100	45	100	100	0
Baishan	60	91	0	0	0	100	0
Songyuan	71	78	100	100	100	100	0
Hangzhou	78	61	100	100	100	100	37
Huzhou	75	44	100	100	100	41	41
Jinhua	67	71	29	29	100	71	29
Quzhou	79	78	100	100	100	100	42
Zhoushan	77	78	100	100	0	100	100
Lishui	82	78	100	100	100	100	100
Hefei	81	32	100	100	57	100	100
Wuhu	86	58	100	100	100	100	100
Bengbu	66	58	42	0	42	100	42
Huaibei	86	67	100	100	100	100	100

(continued)

Table C.8 (continued)

City	Total score	Government service environment					
		Hardware					
		Convenience of public transportation	Availability of performance facilities				
		How many minutes it takes to walk from the nearest bus stop to the government service hall	Availability of waiting number machine	Availability of LED display	Availability of self-serve computer	Availability of photocopying or printing service	Availability of photography equipment
Tongling	68	94	0	0	46	100	46
Fuyang	74	76	71	71	61	71	32
Fuzhou	108	92	100	100	100	100	100
Putian	85	94	100	100	100	100	100
Sanming	91	100	100	100	100	100	100
Quanzhou	76	92	83	83	100	100	17
Ningde	86	89	100	100	100	100	100
Jinan	81	57	100	100	100	100	29
Zibo	82	81	68	44	100	100	25
Zaozhuang	71	80	74	39	39	100	35
Dongying	84	53	61	61	100	100	61
Laiwu	74	79	0	0	100	100	0
Binzhou	73	92	66	66	100	100	0

(continued)

Table C.8 (continued)

City	Total score	Government service environment					
		Hardware					
		Convenience of public transportation	Availability of performance facilities				
		How many minutes it takes to walk from the nearest bus stop to the government service hall	Availability of waiting number machine	Availability of LED display	Availability of self-serve computer	Availability of photocopying or printing service	Availability of photography equipment
Zhengzhou	65	91	50	50	15	100	15
Anyang	73	86	100	76	100	100	76
Xuchang	79	89	0	100	100	100	100
Luohe	66	76	62	62	37	100	63
Xinyang	50	100	0	0	0	100	0
Zhoukou	66	78	100	100	0	100	0
Changsha	91	59	100	100	100	100	71
Hengyang	91	89	100	100	100	100	100
Shaoyang	65	62	0	0	53	100	0
Yueyang	76	60	82	82	100	82	100
Changde	83	70	43	43	43	100	100
Huaihua	92	67	100	100	100	100	100
Guangdong	88	59	100	100	100	64	64

(continued)

Table C.8 (continued)

City	Total score	Government service environment					
		Hardware					
		Convenience of public transportation	Availability of performance facilities				
		How many minutes it takes to walk from the nearest bus stop to the government service hall	Availability of waiting number machine	Availability of LED display	Availability of self-serve computer	Availability of photocopying or printing service	Availability of photography equipment
Jiangmen	81	64	100	100	100	61	0
Yangjiang	84	100	100	100	100	100	0
Chaozhou	76	6	100	100	100	25	0
Jieyang	67	5	39	39	39	100	0
Nanning	62	84	76	76	25	24	24
Fangchenggang	58	86	30	30	30	100	0
Qinzhou	68	62	51	0	0	100	0
Guigang	70	78	100	100	100	100	0
Yulin	79	56	100	100	100	100	100
Chongzuo	83	89	100	100	100	100	100
Guiyang	79	74	100	100	100	83	83
Zunyi	87	77	100	100	100	100	100
Bijie	89	78	100	100	100	100	100

(continued)

Table C.8 (continued)

City	Total score	Government service environment					
		Hardware					
		Convenience of public transportation	Availability of performance facilities				
		How many minutes it takes to walk from the nearest bus stop to the government service hall	Availability of waiting number machine	Availability of LED display	Availability of self-serve computer	Availability of photocopying or printing service	Availability of photography equipment
Kunming	85	72	100	100	100	100	100
Yuxi	77	64	64	64	64	64	64
Zhaotong	67	100	0	0	0	100	100
Pu'er	88	100	100	100	100	100	100
Xi'an	80	51	100	100	100	100	71
Tongchuan	73	84	52	52	52	100	0
Hanzhong	77	78	100	100	100	100	0
Yulin	80	0	100	100	69	100	69
Ankang	83	78	100	0	100	100	100
Lanzhou	78	81	100	74	74	60	60
Zhangye	69	78	100	0	0	100	0
Jiuquan	84	67	100	0	100	100	100
Longnan	85	89	100	0	100	100	100
Yinchuan	82	75	100	100	100	100	100
Wuzhong	82	78	100	100	30	100	30
Guyuan	61	56	0	0	0	0	0

(continued)

Table C.8 (continued)

City	Total score	Government service environment								
		Hardware								
		Availability of convenience facilities								Availability of feedback facilities
		Availability of waiting area	Availability of seats in the waiting area	Sufficient number of seats	Seats or stools at the service windows	Comfort level of the seats at the service windows	Availability of air conditioning or heating (radiators)	Availability of café	Availability of washrooms	Availability of a comment box
Beijing	83	100	100	100	100	85	100	0	100	71
Tianjin	80	100	100	100	100	90	100	34	100	55
Changchun	67	100	100	60	100	100	100	0	100	31
Siping	72	100	100	100	100	55	100	0	100	0
Baishan	60	100	100	59	41	21	100	41	100	0
Songyuan	71	100	100	100	100	100	100	0	100	0
Hangzhou	78	100	100	63	100	50	100	100	100	100
Huzhou	75	100	100	100	100	50	100	100	100	100
Jinhua	67	71	71	71	100	85	100	71	100	100
Quzhou	79	100	100	58	100	50	100	100	100	100
Zhoushan	77	100	100	100	100	50	100	100	100	100
Lishui	82	100	100	100	100	100	100	100	100	100
Hefei	81	100	100	100	100	71	100	100	100	100
Wuhu	86	100	100	37	100	100	100	100	100	100

(continued)

Table C.8 (continued)

City	Total score	Government service environment								
		Hardware								
		Availability of convenience facilities								Availability of feedback facilities
		Availability of waiting area	Availability of seats in the waiting area	Sufficient number of seats	Seats or stools at the service windows	Comfort level of the seats at the service windows	Availability of air conditioning or heating (radiators)	Availability of café	Availability of washrooms	Availability of a comment box
Bengbu	66	100	100	42	100	100	100	100	100	100
Huaibei	86	100	100	100	100	100	100	100	100	100
Tongling	68	100	100	100	100	100	100	100	100	46
Fuyang	74	100	100	32	100	100	100	100	100	100
Fuzhou	108	100	100	100	100	71	100	100	100	77
Putian	85	100	100	100	100	50	100	100	100	100
Sanming	91	100	100	100	100	100	100	100	100	100
Quanzhou	76	100	100	53	100	74	100	36	100	100
Ningde	86	100	100	100	100	100	100	100	100	100
Jinan	81	100	100	100	100	100	100	100	100	100
Zibo	82	100	100	100	100	68	100	100	100	100
Zaozhuang	71	100	100	100	74	56	100	74	100	100
Dongying	84	100	100	100	100	100	100	100	100	100
Laiwu	74	100	100	100	100	50	100	100	100	100

(continued)

Table C.8 (continued)

City	Total score	Government service environment								
		Hardware								
		Availability of convenience facilities								Availability of feedback facilities
		Availability of waiting area	Availability of seats in the waiting area	Sufficient number of seats	Seats or stools at the service windows	Comfort level of the seats at the service windows	Availability of air conditioning or heating (radiators)	Availability of café	Availability of washrooms	Availability of a comment box
Binzhou	73	100	100	100	100	67	100	100	100	100
Zhengzhou	65	100	100	0	85	25	100	50	100	100
Anyang	73	100	100	100	100	64	100	27	100	73
Xuchang	79	100	100	0	100	50	100	100	100	100
Luohe	66	100	100	75	100	50	100	62	100	100
Xinyang	50	0	100	100	100	50	100	0	100	100
Zhoukou	66	100	100	0	100	0	100	100	100	100
Changsha	91	100	100	100	100	100	100	100	100	100
Hengyang	91	100	100	100	100	100	100	100	100	100
Shaoyang	65	53	100	53	100	50	100	100	100	100
Yueyang	76	100	100	18	100	59	100	100	100	100
Changde	83	100	100	100	100	71	100	100	100	100
Huaihua	92	100	100	100	100	100	100	100	100	100
Guangdong	88	100	100	100	100	100	100	100	100	100

(continued)

Table C.8 (continued)

City	Total score	Government service environment								
		Hardware								
		Availability of convenience facilities								Availability of feedback facilities
		Availability of waiting area	Availability of seats in the waiting area	Sufficient number of seats	Seats or stools at the service windows	Comfort level of the seats at the service windows	Availability of air conditioning or heating (radiators)	Availability of café	Availability of washrooms	Availability of a comment box
Jiangmen	81	100	100	100	100	100	100	47	100	100
Yangjiang	84	100	100	100	100	100	100	0	100	100
Chaozhou	76	100	100	100	100	50	100	25	100	100
Jieyang	67	100	100	100	100	50	100	39	100	100
Nanning	62	100	100	49	100	50	100	0	75	76
Fangchenggang	58	30	100	0	100	50	100	0	100	70
Qinzhou	68	100	100	100	100	50	100	0	100	100
Guigang	70	100	100	100	100	50	100	0	100	100
Yulin	79	100	100	100	100	100	100	0	100	100
Chongzuo	83	100	100	100	100	50	100	0	100	100
Guiyang	79	100	100	62	100	81	100	100	100	100
Zunyi	87	100	100	100	100	100	100	100	100	100
Bijie	89	100	100	100	100	100	100	100	100	100
Kunming	85	100	100	100	100	76	49	100	100	100
Yuxi	77	100	100	100	100	82	0	100	100	100

(continued)

Table C.8 (continued)

City	Total score	Government service environment								
		Hardware								
		Availability of convenience facilities								Availability of feedback facilities
		Availability of waiting area	Availability of seats in the waiting area	Sufficient number of seats	Seats or stools at the service windows	Comfort level of the seats at the service windows	Availability of air conditioning or heating (radiators)	Availability of café	Availability of washrooms	Availability of a comment box
Zhaotong	67	100	100	100	100	50	0	100	100	100
Pu'er	88	100	100	100	100	100	0	100	100	100
Xi'an	80	100	100	100	100	100	100	71	100	100
Tongchuan	73	100	100	100	100	100	100	100	100	52
Hanzhong	77	100	100	100	100	100	100	100	100	0
Yulin	80	100	100	100	100	100	100	100	100	69
Ankang	83	100	100	100	100	100	100	100	100	100
Lanzhou	78	100	100	100	100	87	100	100	74	60
Zhangye	69	100	100	100	100	50	100	100	100	100
Jiuquan	84	100	100	100	100	50	100	100	100	100
Longnan	85	100	100	100	100	50	100	100	100	100
Yinchuan	82	100	100	47	100	50	100	100	100	100
Wuzhong	82	100	100	100	100	50	100	100	100	100
Guyuan	61	100	100	0	100	50	100	100	100	100

(continued)

Table C.8 (continued)

City	Total score	Government service environment								
		Software					Service			
		Clarity of procedure instructions				Service window open rate	Number of services provided	Quality of services provided		
		Availability of inquiry staff	Availability of basic procedures for completing tasks	Availability of form filling templates	Commitment to completion time	All service windows open	Number of people served at one window within 20 min	Completion in one visit rate over the past six months	Estimated time required each visit (hours)	Single-window service rate
Beijing	83	100	100	100	100	100	62	27	75	71
Tianjin	80	100	100	100	100	96	33	27	75	70
Changchun	67	100	31	31	31	96	32	43	72	68
Siping	72	100	100	45	45	100	17	52	86	96
Baishan	60	100	100	100	0	90	26	75	87	100
Songyuan	71	100	100	0	0	100	17	52	82	71
Hangzhou	78	100	80	80	0	92	31	36	70	71
Huzhou	75	100	100	41	0	78	17	38	77	70
Jinhua	67	100	100	0	0	100	17	55	75	62
Quzhou	79	100	100	58	0	96	20	41	77	78
Zhoushan	77	100	100	0	0	90	33	45	85	76
Lishui	82	100	100	0	0	100	25	52	73	35

(continued)

Table C.8 (continued)

City	Total score	Government service environment								
		Software					Service			
		Clarity of procedure instructions				Service window open rate	Number of services provided	Quality of services provided		
		Availability of inquiry staff	Availability of basic procedures for completing tasks	Availability of form filling templates	Commitment to completion time	All service windows open	Number of people served at one window within 20 min	Completion in one visit rate over the past six months	Estimated time required each visit (hours)	Single-window service rate
Hefei	81	100	57	100	57	100	44	17	46	62
Wuhu	86	100	100	100	100	96	9	25	86	58
Bengbu	66	42	100	42	0	100	17	22	57	81
Huaibei	86	100	100	100	0	90	58	19	63	76
Tongling	68	100	46	0	46	95	17	15	85	88
Fuyang	74	100	61	100	0	97	22	37	85	66
Fuzhou	108	77	100	100	590	98	44	15	65	71
Putian	85	100	100	42	58	90	35	25	86	64
Sanming	91	100	100	100	100	90	33	7	83	80
Quanzhou	76	100	100	100	17	95	29	10	77	62
Ningde	86	100	100	0	100	90	25	7	86	68
Jinan	81	100	100	29	29	90	26	49	76	61
Zibo	82	100	100	25	100	100	24	53	100	72

(continued)

Table C.8 (continued)

City	Total score	Government service environment								
		Software					Service			
		Clarity of procedure instructions				Service window open rate	Number of services provided	Quality of services provided		
		Availability of inquiry staff	Availability of basic procedures for completing tasks	Availability of form filling templates	Commitment to completion time	All service windows open	Number of people served at one window within 20 min	Completion in one visit rate over the past six months	Estimated time required each visit (hours)	Single-window service rate
Zaozhuang	71	39	74	0	35	100	31	57	98	87
Dongying	84	100	100	81	80	94	35	53	73	73
Laiwu	74	100	100	100	0	92	12	72	100	59
Binzhou	73	100	66	0	0	90	22	52	79	56
Zhengzhou	65	100	100	100	0	90	68	17	63	31
Anyang	73	100	49	49	0	100	12	29	78	44
Xuchang	79	100	100	100	100	70	83	8	27	64
Luohe	66	38	63	25	62	81	12	18	75	33
Xinyang	50	0	100	0	0	100	25	16	76	42
Zhoukou	66	0	100	100	100	70	8	9	56	v
Changsha	91	100	100	100	100	97	39	44	84	78
Hengyang	91	100	100	100	100	100	25	22	75	80

(continued)

Table C.8 (continued)

City	Total score	Government service environment								
		Software					Service			
		Clarity of procedure instructions				Service window open rate	Number of services provided	Quality of services provided		
		Availability of inquiry staff	Availability of basic procedures for completing tasks	Availability of form filling templates	Commitment to completion time	All service windows open	Number of people served at one window within 20 min	Completion in one visit rate over the past six months	Estimated time required each visit (hours)	Single-window service rate
Shaoyang	65	100	53	53	47	100	25	42	87	82
Yueyang	76	100	82	82	18	90	26	22	83	45
Changde	83	100	100	100	100	100	23	31	96	78
Huaihua	92	100	100	100	100	90	33	45	94	68
Guangdong	88	100	100	100	100	91	33	40	96	72
Jiangmen	81	100	100	100	100	90	28	24	82	59
Yangjiang	84	100	100	100	100	90	33	32	84	79
Chaozhou	76	100	100	100	100	97	25	21	94	79
Jieyang	67	100	100	0	100	78	37	24	88	61
Nanning	62	100	76	76	0	95	37	39	51	49
Fangchenggang	58	100	100	70	30	93	22	23	77	39
Qinzhou	68	100	100	100	100	95	29	12	73	67
Guigang	70	100	100	0	0	100	17	16	65	52

(continued)

Table C.8 (continued)

City	Total score	Government service environment								
		Software					Service			
		Clarity of procedure instructions				Service window open rate	Number of services provided	Quality of services provided		
		Availability of inquiry staff	Availability of basic procedures for completing tasks	Availability of form filling templates	Commitment to completion time	All service windows open	Number of people served at one window within 20 min	Completion in one visit rate over the past six months	Estimated time required each visit (hours)	Single-window service rate
Yulin	79	100	100	100	100	70	17	3	0	41
Chongzuo	83	100	100	100	100	90	17	15	76	57
Guiyang	79	100	100	100	0	78	49	13	21	58
Zunyi	87	68	100	100	78	81	29	8	63	78
Bijie	89	100	100	100	100	70	42	24	49	73
Kunming	85	100	100	100	100	95	37	24	57	34
Yuxi	77	100	100	100	100	83	39	32	74	64
Zhaotong	67	0	100	100	100	90	25	39	72	40
Pu'er	88	100	100	100	100	90	8	26	87	100
Xi'an	80	100	71	33	0	97	61	31	79	60
Tongchuan	73	100	100	52	0	80	54	37	80	59
Hanzhong	77	100	100	100	0	90	25	31	82	45

(continued)

Table C.8 (continued)

City	Total score	Government service environment								
		Software					Service			
		Clarity of procedure instructions				Service window open rate	Number of services provided	Quality of services provided		
		Availability of inquiry staff	Availability of basic procedures for completing tasks	Availability of form filling templates	Commitment to completion time	All service windows open	Number of people served at one window within 20 min	Completion in one visit rate over the past six months	Estimated time required each visit (hours)	Single-window service rate
Yulin	80	100	100	100	0	93	53	46	65	57
Ankang	83	100	100	100	0	100	42	19	81	64
Lanzhou	78	100	100	100	0	100	41	17	81	67
Zhangye	69	0	100	100	0	100	25	42	78	82
Jiuquan	84	100	100	100	100	100	17	12	85	79
Longnan	85	100	100	100	100	100	8	33	90	67
Yinchuan	82	100	100	100	0	95	100	38	0	69
Wuzhong	82	100	100	70	70	84	61	13	79	92
Guyuan	61	100	100	100	0	90	67	50	55	100

Source The Sun Yat-sen University Research Group on "Deepening the Reform of the Business System" used the World Bank's distance to frontier method for calculating the score when assessing the business environment of each country. Each city's score = 100 * (worst practice − own value)/(worst practice − best frontier). First, calculate the distance to frontier score for each level 4 indicator. The score for the level 3 indicator is the average for each of the subordinate level 4 indicators. The score for the level 2 indicator is the average of each subordinate level 3 indicator. Finally, the score for the level 1 indicator is calculated as the average value for each subordinate level 2 indicator

Table C.9 Raw data for each province and city in the government service environment report

City	Government service environment					
	Hardware					
	Convenience of public transportation	Availability of performance facilities				
	How many minutes it takes to walk from the nearest bus stop to the government service hall	Availability of waiting number machine	Availability of LED display	Availability of self-serve computer	Availability of photocopying or printing service	Availability of photography equipment
Beijing	6.02	1.00	1.00	1.00	1.00	0.45
Tianjin	3.97	1.00	1.00	1.00	0.80	0.00
Changchun	7.85	1.00	1.00	1.00	1.00	0.00
Siping	2.55	1.00	0.45	1.00	1.00	0.00
Baishan	1.77	0.00	0.00	0.00	1.00	0.00
Songyuan	3.00	1.00	1.00	1.00	1.00	0.00
Hangzhou	4.47	1.00	1.00	1.00	1.00	0.37
Huzhou	6.07	1.00	1.00	1.00	0.41	0.41
Jinhua	3.64	0.29	0.29	1.00	0.71	0.29
Quzhou	3.00	1.00	1.00	1.00	1.00	0.42
Zhoushan	3.00	1.00	1.00	0.00	1.00	1.00
Lishui	3.00	1.00	1.00	1.00	1.00	1.00
Hefei	7.13	1.00	1.00	0.57	1.00	1.00
Wuhu	4.75	1.00	1.00	1.00	1.00	1.00
Bengbu	4.79	0.42	0.00	0.42	1.00	0.42
Huaibei	4.00	1.00	1.00	1.00	1.00	1.00

(continued)

Table C.9 (continued)

City	Government service environment					
	Hardware					
	Convenience of public transportation	Availability of performance facilities				
	How many minutes it takes to walk from the nearest bus stop to the government service hall	Availability of waiting number machine	Availability of LED display	Availability of self-serve computer	Availability of photocopying or printing service	Availability of photography equipment
Tongling	1.54	0.00	0.00	0.46	1.00	0.46
Fuyang	3.19	0.71	0.71	0.61	0.71	0.32
Fuzhou	1.71	1.00	1.00	1.00	1.00	1.00
Putian	1.58	1.00	1.00	1.00	1.00	1.00
Sanming	1.00	1.00	1.00	1.00	1.00	1.00
Quanzhou	1.69	0.83	0.83	1.00	1.00	0.17
Ningde	2.00	1.00	1.00	1.00	1.00	1.00
Jinan	4.87	1.00	1.00	1.00	1.00	0.29
Zibo	2.75	0.68	0.44	1.00	1.00	0.25
Zaozhuang	2.78	0.74	0.39	0.39	1.00	0.35
Dongying	5.21	0.61	0.61	1.00	1.00	0.61
Laiwu	2.90	0.00	0.00	1.00	1.00	0.00
Binzhou	1.68	0.66	0.66	1.00	1.00	0.00
Zhengzhou	1.85	0.50	0.50	0.15	1.00	0.15
Anyang	2.27	1.00	0.76	1.00	1.00	0.76
Xuchang	2.00	0.00	1.00	1.00	1.00	1.00

(continued)

Table C.9 (continued)

City	Government service environment					
	Hardware					
	Convenience of public transportation	Availability of performance facilities				
	How many minutes it takes to walk from the nearest bus stop to the government service hall	Availability of waiting number machine	Availability of LED display	Availability of self-serve computer	Availability of photocopying or printing service	Availability of photography equipment
Luohe	3.14	0.62	0.62	0.37	1.00	0.63
Xinyang	1.00	0.00	0.00	0.00	1.00	0.00
Zhoukou	3.00	1.00	1.00	0.00	1.00	0.00
Changsha	4.73	1.00	1.00	1.00	1.00	0.71
Hengyang	2.00	1.00	1.00	1.00	1.00	1.00
Shaoyang	4.42	0.00	0.00	0.53	1.00	0.00
Yueyang	4.64	0.82	0.82	1.00	0.82	1.00
Changde	3.72	0.43	0.43	0.43	1.00	1.00
Huaihua	4.00	1.00	1.00	1.00	1.00	1.00
Guangdong	4.71	1.00	1.00	1.00	0.64	0.64

(continued)

Table C.9 (continued)

City	Government service environment					
	Hardware					
	Convenience of public transportation	Availability of performance facilities				
	How many minutes it takes to walk from the nearest bus stop to the government service hall	Availability of waiting number machine	Availability of LED display	Availability of self-serve computer	Availability of photocopying or printing service	Availability of photography equipment
Jiangmen	4.21	1.00	1.00	1.00	0.61	0.00
Yangjiang	1.00	1.00	1.00	1.00	1.00	0.00
Chaozhou	9.49	1.00	1.00	1.00	0.25	0.00
Jieyang	9.52	0.39	0.39	0.39	1.00	0.00
Nanning	2.46	0.76	0.76	0.25	0.24	0.24
Fangchenggang	2.30	0.30	0.30	0.30	1.00	0.00
Qinzhou	4.43	0.51	0.00	0.00	1.00	0.00
Guigang	3.00	1.00	1.00	1.00	1.00	0.00
Yulin	5.00	1.00	1.00	1.00	1.00	1.00
Chongzuo	2.00	1.00	1.00	1.00	1.00	1.00
Guiyang	3.35	1.00	1.00	1.00	0.83	0.83
Zunyi	3.08	1.00	1.00	1.00	1.00	1.00
Bijie	3.00	1.00	1.00	1.00	1.00	1.00

(continued)

Table C.9 (continued)

City	Government service environment					
	Hardware					
	Convenience of public transportation	Availability of performance facilities				
	How many minutes it takes to walk from the nearest bus stop to the government service hall	Availability of waiting number machine	Availability of LED display	Availability of self-serve computer	Availability of photocopying or printing service	Availability of photography equipment
Kunming	3.54	1.00	1.00	1.00	1.00	1.00
Yuxi	4.28	0.64	0.64	0.64	0.64	0.64
Zhaotong	1.00	0.00	0.00	0.00	1.00	1.00
Pu’er	1.00	1.00	1.00	1.00	1.00	1.00
Xi’an	5.41	1.00	1.00	1.00	1.00	0.71
Tongchuan	2.40	0.52	0.52	0.52	1.00	0.00
Hanzhong	3.00	1.00	1.00	1.00	1.00	0.00
Yulin	10.00	1.00	1.00	0.69	1.00	0.69
Ankang	3.00	1.00	0.00	1.00	1.00	1.00
Lanzhou	2.74	1.00	0.74	0.74	0.60	0.60
Zhangye	3.00	1.00	0.00	0.00	1.00	0.00
Jiuquan	4.00	1.00	0.00	1.00	1.00	1.00
Longnan	2.00	1.00	0.00	1.00	1.00	1.00
Yinchuan	3.22	1.00	1.00	1.00	1.00	1.00
Wuzhong	3.00	1.00	1.00	0.30	1.00	0.30
Guyuan	5.00	0.00	0.00	0.00	0.00	0.00

(continued)

Table C.9 (continued)

City	Government service environment								
	Hardware								
	Availability of convenience facilities								Availability of feedback facilities
	Availability of waiting area	Availability of seats in the waiting area	Sufficient number of seats	Seats or stools at the service windows	Comfort level of the seats at the service windows	Availability of air conditioning or heating (radiators)	Availability of café	Availability of washrooms	Availability of a comment box
Beijing	1.00	1.00	1.00	1.00	0.85	1.00	0.00	1.00	0.71
Tianjin	1.00	1.00	1.00	1.00	0.90	1.00	0.34	1.00	0.55
Changchun	1.00	1.00	0.60	1.00	1.00	1.00	0.00	1.00	0.31
Siping	1.00	1.00	1.00	1.00	0.55	1.00	0.00	1.00	0.00
Baishan	1.00	1.00	0.59	0.41	0.21	1.00	0.41	1.00	0.00
Songyuan	1.00	1.00	1.00	1.00	1.00	1.00	0.00	1.00	0.00
Hangzhou	1.00	1.00	0.63	1.00	0.50	1.00	1.00	1.00	1.00
Huzhou	1.00	1.00	1.00	1.00	0.50	1.00	1.00	1.00	1.00
Jinhua	0.71	0.71	0.71	1.00	0.85	1.00	0.71	1.00	1.00
Quzhou	1.00	1.00	0.58	1.00	0.50	1.00	1.00	1.00	1.00
Zhoushan	1.00	1.00	1.00	1.00	0.50	1.00	1.00	1.00	1.00
Lishui	1.00	1.00	1.00	1.00	1.00	1.00	1.00	1.00	1.00
Hefei	1.00	1.00	1.00	1.00	0.71	1.00	1.00	1.00	1.00
Wuhu	1.00	1.00	0.37	1.00	1.00	1.00	1.00	1.00	1.00

(continued)

Table C.9 (continued)

City	Government service environment								
	Hardware								
	Availability of convenience facilities								Availability of feedback facilities
	Availability of waiting area	Availability of seats in the waiting area	Sufficient number of seats	Seats or stools at the service windows	Comfort level of the seats at the service windows	Availability of air conditioning or heating (radiators)	Availability of café	Availability of washrooms	Availability of a comment box
Bengbu	1.00	1.00	0.42	1.00	1.00	1.00	1.00	1.00	1.00
Huaibei	1.00	1.00	1.00	1.00	1.00	1.00	1.00	1.00	1.00
Tongling	1.00	1.00	1.00	1.00	1.00	1.00	1.00	1.00	0.46
Fuyang	1.00	1.00	0.32	1.00	1.00	1.00	1.00	1.00	1.00
Fuzhou	1.00	1.00	1.00	1.00	0.71	1.00	1.00	1.00	1.00
Putian	1.00	1.00	1.00	1.00	0.50	1.00	1.00	1.00	1.00
Sanming	1.00	1.00	1.00	1.00	1.00	1.00	1.00	1.00	1.00
Quanzhou	1.00	1.00	0.53	1.00	0.74	1.00	0.36	1.00	1.00
Ningde	1.00	1.00	1.00	1.00	1.00	1.00	1.00	1.00	1.00
Jinan	1.00	1.00	1.00	1.00	1.00	1.00	1.00	1.00	1.00
Zibo	1.00	1.00	1.00	1.00	0.68	1.00	1.00	1.00	1.00
Zaozhuang	1.00	1.00	1.00	0.74	0.56	1.00	0.74	1.00	1.00
Dongying	1.00	1.00	1.00	1.00	1.00	1.00	1.00	1.00	1.00
Laiwu	1.00	1.00	1.00	1.00	0.50	1.00	1.00	1.00	1.00

(continued)

Table C.9 (continued)

City	Government service environment								
	Hardware								
	Availability of convenience facilities								Availability of feedback facilities
	Availability of waiting area	Availability of seats in the waiting area	Sufficient number of seats	Seats or stools at the service windows	Comfort level of the seats at the service windows	Availability of air conditioning or heating (radiators)	Availability of café	Availability of washrooms	Availability of a comment box
Binzhou	1.00	1.00	1.00	1.00	0.67	1.00	1.00	1.00	1.00
Zhengzhou	1.00	1.00	0.00	0.85	0.25	1.00	0.50	1.00	1.00
Anyang	1.00	1.00	1.00	1.00	0.64	1.00	0.27	1.00	0.73
Xuchang	1.00	1.00	0.00	1.00	0.50	1.00	1.00	1.00	1.00
Luohe	1.00	1.00	0.75	1.00	0.50	1.00	0.62	1.00	1.00
Xinyang	0.00	1.00	1.00	1.00	0.50	1.00	0.00	1.00	1.00
Zhoukou	1.00	1.00	0.00	1.00	0.00	1.00	1.00	1.00	1.00
Changsha	1.00	1.00	1.00	1.00	1.00	1.00	1.00	1.00	1.00
Hengyang	1.00	1.00	1.00	1.00	1.00	1.00	1.00	1.00	1.00
Shaoyang	0.53	1.00	0.53	1.00	0.50	1.00	1.00	1.00	1.00
Yueyang	1.00	1.00	0.18	1.00	0.59	1.00	1.00	1.00	1.00
Changde	1.00	1.00	1.00	1.00	0.71	1.00	1.00	1.00	1.00
Huaihua	1.00	1.00	1.00	1.00	1.00	1.00	1.00	1.00	1.00
Guangdong	1.00	1.00	1.00	1.00	1.00	1.00	1.00	1.00	1.00

(continued)

Table C.9 (continued)

City	Government service environment								
	Hardware								
	Availability of convenience facilities								Availability of feedback facilities
	Availability of waiting area	Availability of seats in the waiting area	Sufficient number of seats	Seats or stools at the service windows	Comfort level of the seats at the service windows	Availability of air conditioning or heating (radiators)	Availability of café	Availability of washrooms	Availability of a comment box
Jiangmen	1.00	1.00	1.00	1.00	1.00	1.00	0.47	1.00	1.00
Yangjiang	1.00	1.00	1.00	1.00	1.00	1.00	0.00	1.00	1.00
Chaozhou	1.00	1.00	1.00	1.00	0.50	1.00	0.25	1.00	1.00
Jieyang	1.00	1.00	1.00	1.00	0.50	1.00	0.39	1.00	1.00
Nanning	1.00	1.00	0.49	1.00	0.50	1.00	0.00	0.75	0.76
Fangchenggang	0.30	1.00	0.00	1.00	0.50	1.00	0.00	1.00	0.70
Qinzhou	1.00	1.00	1.00	1.00	0.50	1.00	0.00	1.00	1.00
Guigang	1.00	1.00	1.00	1.00	0.50	1.00	0.00	1.00	1.00
Yulin	1.00	1.00	1.00	1.00	1.00	1.00	0.00	1.00	1.00
Chongzuo	1.00	1.00	1.00	1.00	0.50	1.00	0.00	1.00	1.00
Guiyang	1.00	1.00	0.62	1.00	0.81	1.00	1.00	1.00	1.00
Zunyi	1.00	1.00	1.00	1.00	1.00	1.00	1.00	1.00	1.00
Bijie	1.00	1.00	1.00	1.00	1.00	1.00	1.00	1.00	1.00
Kunming	1.00	1.00	1.00	1.00	0.76	0.49	1.00	1.00	1.00
Yuxi	1.00	1.00	1.00	1.00	0.82	0.00	1.00	1.00	1.00

(continued)

Table C.9 (continued)

City	Government service environment								
	Hardware								
	Availability of convenience facilities								Availability of feedback facilities
	Availability of waiting area	Availability of seats in the waiting area	Sufficient number of seats	Seats or stools at the service windows	Comfort level of the seats at the service windows	Availability of air conditioning or heating (radiators)	Availability of café	Availability of washrooms	Availability of a comment box
Zhaotong	1.00	1.00	1.00	1.00	0.50	0.00	1.00	1.00	1.00
Pu'er	1.00	1.00	1.00	1.00	1.00	0.00	1.00	1.00	1.00
Xi'an	1.00	1.00	1.00	1.00	1.00	1.00	0.71	1.00	1.00
Tongchuan	1.00	1.00	1.00	1.00	1.00	1.00	1.00	1.00	0.52
Hanzhong	1.00	1.00	1.00	1.00	1.00	1.00	1.00	1.00	0.00
Yulin	1.00	1.00	1.00	1.00	1.00	1.00	1.00	1.00	0.69
Ankang	1.00	1.00	1.00	1.00	1.00	1.00	1.00	1.00	1.00
Lanzhou	1.00	1.00	1.00	1.00	0.87	1.00	1.00	0.74	0.60
Zhangye	1.00	1.00	1.00	1.00	0.50	1.00	1.00	1.00	1.00
Jiuquan	1.00	1.00	1.00	1.00	0.50	1.00	1.00	1.00	1.00
Longnan	1.00	1.00	1.00	1.00	0.50	1.00	1.00	1.00	1.00
Yinchuan	1.00	1.00	0.47	1.00	0.50	1.00	1.00	1.00	1.00
Wuzhong	1.00	1.00	1.00	1.00	0.50	1.00	1.00	1.00	1.00
Guyuan	1.00	1.00	0.00	1.00	0.50	1.00	1.00	1.00	1.00

(continued)

Table C.9 (continued)

City	Government service environment								
	Software					Service			
	Clarity of procedure instructions				Service window open rate	Number of services provided	Quality of services provided		
	Availability of inquiry staff	Availability of basic procedures for completing tasks	Availability of form filling templates	Commitment to completion time	All service windows open	Number of people served at one window within 20 min	Completion in one visit rate over the past six months	Estimated time required each visit (hours)	Single-window service rate
Beijing	1.00	1.00	1.00	1.00	1.00	3.75	0.33	1.34	0.73
Tianjin	1.00	1.00	1.00	1.00	0.96	2.01	0.28	1.33	0.70
Changchun	1.00	0.31	0.31	0.31	0.96	1.92	0.43	1.42	0.68
Siping	1.00	1.00	0.45	0.45	1.00	1.05	0.52	1.03	0.96
Baishan	1.00	1.00	1.00	0.00	0.90	1.59	0.75	1.00	1.00
Songyuan	1.00	1.00	0.00	0.00	1.00	1.00	0.52	1.14	0.71
Hangzhou	1.00	0.80	0.80	0.00	0.92	1.89	0.36	1.50	0.71
Huzhou	1.00	1.00	0.41	0.00	0.78	1.00	0.38	1.29	0.70
Jinhua	1.00	1.00	0.00	0.00	1.00	1.00	0.55	1.35	0.62
Quzhou	1.00	1.00	0.58	0.00	0.96	1.21	0.41	1.28	0.78
Zhoushan	1.00	1.00	0.00	0.00	0.90	2.00	0.45	1.06	0.76
Lishui	1.00	1.00	0.00	0.00	1.00	1.50	0.52	1.39	0.35

(continued)

Table C.9 (continued)

City	Government service environment								
	Software					Service			
	Clarity of procedure instructions				Service window open rate	Number of services provided	Quality of services provided		
	Availability of inquiry staff	Availability of basic procedures for completing tasks	Availability of form filling templates	Commitment to completion time	All service windows open	Number of people served at one window within 20 min	Completion in one visit rate over the past six months	Estimated time required each visit (hours)	Single-window service rate
Hefei	1.00	0.57	1.00	0.57	1.00	2.64	0.17	2.15	0.62
Wuhu	1.00	1.00	1.00	1.00	0.96	0.56	0.25	1.05	0.58
Bengbu	0.42	1.00	0.42	0.00	1.00	1.00	0.22	1.85	0.81
Huaibei	1.00	1.00	1.00	0.00	0.90	3.50	0.19	1.68	0.76
Tongling	1.00	0.46	0.00	0.46	0.95	1.04	0.15	1.07	0.88
Fuyang	1.00	0.61	1.00	0.00	0.97	1.34	0.37	1.07	0.66
Fuzhou	0.77	1.00	1.00	0.59	0.98	2.64	0.15	1.63	0.71
Putian	1.00	1.00	0.42	0.58	0.90	2.08	0.25	1.03	0.64
Sanming	1.00	1.00	1.00	1.00	0.90	2.00	0.07	1.11	0.80
Quanzhou	1.00	1.00	1.00	0.17	0.95	1.74	0.10	1.29	0.62
Ningde	1.00	1.00	0.00	1.00	0.90	1.50	0.07	1.04	0.68
Jinan	1.00	1.00	0.29	0.29	0.90	1.56	0.49	1.32	0.61
Zibo	1.00	1.00	0.25	1.00	1.00	1.47	0.53	0.64	0.72

(continued)

Table C.9 (continued)

City	Government service environment								
	Software					Service			
	Clarity of procedure instructions				Service window open rate	Number of services provided	Quality of services provided		
	Availability of inquiry staff	Availability of basic procedures for completing tasks	Availability of form filling templates	Commitment to completion time	All service windows open	Number of people served at one window within 20 min	Completion in one visit rate over the past six months	Estimated time required each visit (hours)	Single-window service rate
Zaozhuang	0.39	0.74	0.00	0.35	1.00	1.87	0.57	0.69	0.87
Dongying	1.00	1.00	0.81	0.80	0.94	2.11	0.52	1.39	0.73
Laiwu	1.00	1.00	1.00	0.00	0.92	0.74	0.72	0.64	0.59
Binzhou	1.00	0.66	0.00	0.00	0.90	1.33	0.52	1.23	0.56
Zhengzhou	1.00	1.00	1.00	0.00	0.90	4.07	0.17	1.69	0.31
Anyang	1.00	0.49	0.49	0.00	1.00	0.74	0.29	1.26	0.44
Xuchang	1.00	1.00	1.00	1.00	0.70	5.00	0.08	2.69	0.64
Luohe	0.38	0.63	0.25	0.62	0.81	0.75	0.18	1.36	0.33
Xinyang	0.00	1.00	0.00	0.00	1.00	1.50	0.16	1.31	0.42
Zhoukou	0.00	1.00	1.00	1.00	0.70	0.50	0.09	1.89	0.37
Changsha	1.00	1.00	1.00	1.00	0.97	2.35	0.44	1.10	0.78
Hengyang	1.00	1.00	1.00	1.00	1.00	1.50	0.22	1.34	0.80

(continued)

Table C.9 (continued)

City	Government service environment								
	Software					Service			
	Clarity of procedure instructions				Service window open rate	Number of services provided	Quality of services provided		
	Availability of inquiry staff	Availability of basic procedures for completing tasks	Availability of form filling templates	Commitment to completion time	All service windows open	Number of people served at one window within 20 min	Completion in one visit rate over the past six months	Estimated time required each visit (hours)	Single-window service rate
Shaoyang	1.00	0.53	0.53	0.47	1.00	1.50	0.42	1.01	0.82
Yueyang	1.00	0.82	0.82	0.18	0.90	1.59	0.22	1.12	0.45
Changde	1.00	1.00	1.00	1.00	1.00	1.35	0.31	0.76	0.78
Huaihua	1.00	1.00	1.00	1.00	0.90	2.00	0.45	0.83	0.68
Guangdong	1.00	1.00	1.00	1.00	0.91	2.00	0.40	0.75	0.72
Jiangmen	1.00	1.00	1.00	1.00	0.90	1.70	0.24	1.14	0.59
Yangjiang	1.00	1.00	1.00	1.00	0.90	2.00	0.32	1.10	0.79
Chaozhou	1.00	1.00	1.00	1.00	0.97	1.50	0.21	0.81	0.79
Jieyang	1.00	1.00	0.00	1.00	0.78	2.20	0.24	0.98	0.61
Nanning	1.00	0.76	0.76	0.00	0.95	2.24	0.33	2.02	0.65
Fangchenggang	1.00	1.00	0.70	0.30	0.93	1.30	0.23	1.29	0.58
Qinzhou	1.00	1.00	1.00	1.00	0.95	1.76	0.15	1.40	0.77
Guigang	1.00	1.00	0.00	0.00	1.00	1.00	0.18	1.63	0.67

(continued)

Table C.9 (continued)

City	Government service environment								
	Software					Service			
	Clarity of procedure instructions				Service window open rate	Number of services provided	Quality of services provided		
	Availability of inquiry staff	Availability of basic procedures for completing tasks	Availability of form filling templates	Commitment to completion time	All service windows open	Number of people served at one window within 20 min	Completion in one visit rate over the past six months	Estimated time required each visit (hours)	Single-window service rate
Yulin	1.00	1.00	1.00	1.00	0.70	1.00	0.09	3.45	0.59
Chongzuo	1.00	1.00	1.00	1.00	0.90	1.00	0.18	1.31	0.71
Guiyang	1.00	1.00	1.00	0.00	0.78	2.92	0.13	2.86	0.58
Zunyi	0.68	1.00	1.00	0.78	0.81	1.77	0.08	1.68	0.78
Bijie	1.00	1.00	1.00	1.00	0.70	2.50	0.24	2.06	0.73
Kunming	1.00	1.00	1.00	1.00	0.95	2.24	0.24	1.85	0.55
Yuxi	1.00	1.00	1.00	1.00	0.83	2.32	0.29	1.37	0.75
Zhaotong	0.00	1.00	1.00	1.00	0.90	1.50	0.33	1.44	0.58
Pu'er	1.00	1.00	1.00	1.00	0.90	0.50	0.25	1.00	1.00
Xi'an	1.00	0.71	0.33	0.00	0.97	3.66	0.31	1.23	0.60
Tongchuan	1.00	1.00	0.52	0.00	0.80	3.26	0.37	1.21	0.59
Hanzhong	1.00	1.00	1.00	0.00	0.90	1.50	0.31	1.16	0.45

(continued)

Table C.9 (continued)

City	Government service environment								
	Software					Service			
	Clarity of procedure instructions				Service window open rate	Number of services provided	Quality of services provided		
	Availability of inquiry staff	Availability of basic procedures for completing tasks	Availability of form filling templates	Commitment to completion time	All service windows open	Number of people served at one window within 20 min	Completion in one visit rate over the past six months	Estimated time required each visit (hours)	Single-window service rate
Yulin	1.00	1.00	1.00	0.00	0.93	3.19	0.46	1.63	0.57
Ankang	1.00	1.00	1.00	0.00	1.00	2.50	0.19	1.17	0.64
Lanzhou	1.00	1.00	1.00	0.00	1.00	2.43	0.17	1.18	0.67
Zhangye	0.00	1.00	1.00	0.00	1.00	1.50	0.42	1.25	0.82
Jiuquan	1.00	1.00	1.00	1.00	1.00	1.00	0.12	1.05	0.79
Longnan	1.00	1.00	1.00	1.00	1.00	0.50	0.33	0.92	0.67
Yinchuan	1.00	1.00	1.00	0.00	0.95	6.00	0.38	3.45	0.69
Wuzhong	1.00	1.00	0.70	0.70	0.84	3.64	0.13	1.22	0.92
Guyuan	1.00	1.00	1.00	0.00	0.90	4.00	0.50	1.91	1.00

Source The Sun Yat-sen University Research Group on "Deepening the Reform of the Business System" used the World Bank's distance to frontier method for calculating the score when assessing the business environment of each country. Each city's score = 100 * (worst practice – own value)/(worst practice – best frontier). First, calculate the distance to frontier score for each level 4 indicator. The score for the level 3 indicator is the average for each of the subordinate level 4 indicators. The score for the level 2 indicator is the average of each subordinate level 3 indicator. Finally, the score for the level 1 indicator is calculated as the average value for each subordinate level 2 indicator

Table C.10 Distance to frontier method calculation indicator system

Level 1 indicator	Level 2 indicators	Nationwide average (%)	Best frontier	Worst practice
Total score of digital government construction	Potential usage rate	92	1	0
	Actual awareness rate	69	1	0
	Actual usage rate	53	1	0

Note The business environment scores for each city were calculated by the distance to frontier method used by the World Bank. Each city's score = (worst practice − own value)/(worst practice − best frontier)

Table C.11 Distance to frontier method scores for each city

City	Digital government construction			
	Total score	Potential usage rate	Actual awareness rate	Actual usage rate
Beijing	89	98	90	80
Tianjin	75	94	74	57
Shijiazhuang	70	97	66	46
Tangshan	59	78	57	43
Zhangjiakou	55	94	44	27
Chengde	52	87	39	29
Langfang	55	88	45	30
Hengshui	53	82	50	26
Taiyuan	66	91	60	48
Datong	60	88	54	38
Changzhi	–	–	–	–
Yuncheng	71	88	69	57
Lüliang	–	–	–	–
Changchun	80	96	81	63
Jilin	76	96	74	58
Siping	57	91	45	33
Baishan	84	97	89	66
Songyuan	61	94	66	24
Shanghai	66	98	61	41
Nanjing	66	85	64	49
Xuzhou	76	90	73	65
Changzhou	68	93	63	48
Suzhou	69	95	67	45
Yancheng	70	85	71	56

(continued)

Table C.11 (continued)

City	Digital government construction			
	Total score	Potential usage rate	Actual awareness rate	Actual usage rate
Taizhou	74	95	71	55
Suqian	76	85	78	63
Hangzhou	85	100	83	72
Ningbo	84	96	87	68
Huzhou	87	89	95	77
Jinhua	74	86	74	62
Quzhou	65	92	63	40
Zhoushan	67	91	65	46
Lishui	71	91	77	46
Hefei	82	96	82	69
Wuhu	75	96	74	56
Bengbu	70	88	66	56
Huaibei	73	92	74	52
Tongling	53	97	38	25
Fuyang	81	94	82	67
Fuzhou	76	93	76	59
Putian	79	97	78	62
Sanming	47	86	39	17
Quanzhou	66	92	60	46
Ningde	58	93	51	29
Jinan	70	94	66	49
Qingdao	83	93	81	76
Zibo	60	88	55	36
Zaozhuang	–	–	–	–
Dongying	59	87	59	32
Binzhou	77	90	80	60
Zhengzhou	78	81	83	68
Luoyang	80	95	79	66
Anyang	72	92	68	56
Xuchang	83	91	85	73
Luohe	73	83	75	60
Xinyang	76	97	74	59
Zhoukou	74	95	77	50
Wuhan	78	90	79	65

(continued)

Table C.11 (continued)

City	Digital government construction			
	Total score	Potential usage rate	Actual awareness rate	Actual usage rate
Yichang	69	85	73	50
Ezhou	71	88	74	52
Jingmen	65	94	58	42
Huanggang	77	100	71	60
Xianning	73	80	78	61
Suizhou	70	97	67	48
Changsha	84	93	87	73
Hengyang	71	90	71	52
Shaoyang	74	86	78	59
Yueyang	73	95	64	59
Changde	67	82	66	54
Huaihua	69	97	59	50
Guangdong	64	84	61	46
Shaoguan	59	88	52	38
Shenzhen	85	99	86	70
Jiangmen	72	97	67	53
Zhanjiang	65	93	63	41
Yangjiang	57	85	52	32
Chaozhou	57	95	39	37
Jieyang	42	95	18	13
Nanning	71	96	63	55
Liuzhou	66	96	63	38
Fangchenggang	76	86	81	62
Qinzhou	78	100	76	59
Guigang	61	91	54	37
Yulin	73	100	70	48
Chongzuo	–	–	–	–
Haikou	71	93	67	52
Chongqing	67	92	63	45
Guiyang	77	96	73	61
Zunyi	76	96	74	58
Bijie	69	94	70	42
Kunming	77	92	77	61
Qujing	81	93	79	69

(continued)

Table C.11 (continued)

City	Digital government construction			
	Total score	Potential usage rate	Actual awareness rate	Actual usage rate
Yuxi	79	100	75	63
Zhaotong	95	100	94	90
Pu'er	87	92	90	79
Xi'an	79	95	80	64
Tongchuan	56	69	65	35
Hanzhong	82	94	91	61
Yulin	62	83	60	42
Ankang	74	94	78	49
Lanzhou	67	94	57	49
Jiayuguan	74	82	72	69
Zhangye	71	92	71	49
Pingliang	84	93	90	70
Jiuquan	83	94	91	64
Longnan	72	83	73	60
Xining	59	93	51	32
Yinchuan	71	90	73	48
Wuzhong	52	74	55	26
Guyuan	56	88	56	25

Data source China Doing Business Enterprise Survey. The total score is the average of the three secondary indicators. The sample used in the calculation was a total sample of all market players interviewed. The valid sample sizes of Changzhi, Lüliang, Zaozhuang and Chongzuo were all less than thirty, thus no score was calculated for these cities

SPRINGER NATURE

GPSR Compliance

The European Union's (EU) General Product Safety Regulation (GPSR) is a set of rules that requires consumer products to be safe and our obligations to ensure this.

If you have any concerns about our products, you can contact us on ProductSafety@springernature.com

In case Publisher is established outside the EU, the EU authorized representative is:

Springer Nature Customer Service Center GmbH
Europaplatz 3
69115 Heidelberg, Germany

The manufacturer's authorised representative in the EU is Springer Nature Customer Service Centre GmbH, Europaplatz 3, 69115 Heidelberg, Germany. If you have any concerns regarding our products, please contact ProductSafety@springernature.com

Printed and bound by CPI Group (UK) Ltd, Croydon, CR0 4YY
01/10/2026
02225867-0007